THE ATLANTIC WALL

Also published by Enigma Books

Hitler's Table Talk 1941–1944
Hugh Trevor-Roper, ed.

In Stalin's Secret Service
W. G. Krivitsky

Hitler and Mussolini:
The Secret Meetings
Santi Corvaja

The Jews in Fascist Italy: A History
Renzo De Felice

The Man Behind the Rosenbergs
Alexander Feklisov and
Sergei Kostin

Roosevelt and Hopkins:
An Intimate History
Robert E. Sherwood

Diary 1937–1943
Galeazzo Ciano

The Battle of the Casbah:
Terrorism and Counter-Terrorism in
Algeria 1955–1957
General Paul Aussaresses

Secret Affairs:
FDR, Cordell Hull, and Sumner
Welles
Irwin F. Gellman

Hitler and His Generals:
Military Conferences 1942–1945
Helmut Heiber & David M.
Glantz, eds.

Stalin and the Jews: The Red Book
Arno Lustiger

The Secret Front:
Nazi Political Espionage 1938–
1945
Wilhelm Höttl

Fighting the Nazis:
French Military Intelligence and
Counterintelligence 1935–1945
Colonel Paul Paillole

A Death in Washington:
Walter G. Krivitsky and the Stalin
Terror
Gary Kern

Hitler's Second Book
The Unpublished Sequel to Mein
Kampf
Gerhard L. Weinberg, ed.

Alan F. Wilt

THE ATLANTIC WALL

1941-1944

HITLER'S DEFENSES FOR D-DAY

Introduction by Carlo D'Este

enigma books

Enigma Books
580 Eighth Avenue, New York, NY 10018
www.enigmabooks.com

First Enigma Printing

ISBN 1-929631-19-7

Copyright © 2004 Alan F. Wilt

Printed in the United States of America

Library of Congress Cataloging-in-Publication Data

Publisher's Cataloging-in-Publication Data
(Prepared by The Donohue Group, Inc.)

Wilt, Alan F.
   The Atlantic Wall, 1941-1944 : Hitler's defenses for D-Day / Alan F.
Wilt ; introduction by Carlo D'Este.— [1st ed.].
   p. cm.
   Includes bibliographical references and index.
   ISBN: 1-929631-19-7
1. World War, 1939-1945—Germany. 2. World War, 1939-1945—Cam-
paigns—France—Normandy. 3. Germany—History—1933-1945. 4.
Normandy (France)—History. 5. Atlantic Wall (France and Belgium)
I. D'Este, Carlo. II. Title.

D757 .W55 2004
940.54'21—dc21

Contents

List of Maps

Figure

Page

Acknowledgments

A number of individuals and institutions have been helpful in completing this study of Hitler's Atlantic Wall. Special thanks are in order to Gerhard L. Weinberg of the University of North Carolina for his extremely incisive criticisms and suggestions. His vast knowledge of the period has never ceased to be a source of amazement to me. Thanks are also due to John Bowditch, of the University of Michigan and Walter Rundell, Jr., of the University of Maryland, who read portions of the manuscript and offered their comments and advice. Dean Allard and H.E. Rilley of the Naval History Division in Washington, D.C.; Robert Wolfe and George Wagner of the Captured Branch, U.S. National Archives; William Cunliffe and Edward Reese of the Modern Military Records Branch, also at the National Archives; and Joseph Avery of the Washington National Records Center, Suitland, Maryland, also aided me a great deal in my research endeavors.

I further acknowledge my appreciation to the Horace H., Rackman School of Graduate Studies, University of Michigan; the Department of History, University of Michigan; and especially the Sciences and Humanities Research Institute, Iowa State University, for research grants that allowed me to purchase microfilm and to pursue this investigation of the Atlantic Wall concept at various critical stages.

Susan Ulrickson typed and retyped the manuscript without complaint. Finally, I express my gratitude to my wife, Maureen, whose help and encouragement have sustained me from the inception of this project more than eight years ago.

Introduction by Carlo D'Este

After the successful German invasion of France in May 1940, with the exception of neutral Switzerland, which posed no threat, Hitler's armies occupied practically the entire continent of Europe. In the wake of the virtual destruction of the French Army and the disastrous defeat and withdrawal of the British Expeditionary Force from Dunkirk, Britain was suddenly vulnerable to a German invasion.

Unless the British sued for peace, which Hitler fervently hoped would be the result, a major component of the German master plan for the occupation and domination of Europe was an invasion of England before the end of 1940.

Codenamed Operation Sea Lion, it was contingent upon the attainment of air supremacy by Hermann Goering's Luftwaffe over the Royal Air Force during the summer of 1940. Convinced that Britain had every incentive to avoid war on its home soil, Hitler believed that the pressure of the blitz and the crushing defeat of the BEF would bring the British government to the peace table. However, the new British prime minister, Winston Churchill, spurned Germany's peace feelers and vowed that Britain would resist to the death.

Although preparations for the invasion were complete by September, the Luftwaffe had failed to destroy the RAF during the Battle of Britain, and by the end of 1940 Hitler's enthusiasm for Sea Lion had waned to the point where the plan was virtually scrapped. Instead, Hitler issued War Directive 21 that directed the Wehrmacht to begin planning an operation, codenamed Barbarossa, an invasion "to crush Soviet Russia in a rapid campaign" in 1941.

With Sea Lion now little more than an afterthought, Hitler turned his attention to the establishment of a defense of his newly conquered empire. In the aftermath of Hitler's strategic decision to open an Eastern Front, the defense of the West became a Catch-22. Of necessity the logistical and manpower priority went to Barbarossa, while, at the same time, defensive measures were necessary to protect the western flank of the expanded Third Reich. Moreover, the entry of the United States into the war in December 1941 raised the bar of probability of an eventual Allied invasion of the continent of Europe somewhere in the West.

Hitler ordered the construction of what has became known as the Atlantic Wall. From 1942, when it first began taking shape, it was far more than a series of fortifications constructed along likely invasion sites from the Netherlands to Spain. Hitler's Atlantic Wall was to be the very foundation of the German defense of Festung Europa*. Popular mythology holds that the Wall was merely a series of fortifications, situated largely in France. Professor Alan F. Wilt's important new study of the origins and development of the Atlantic Wall between 1941 and 1944 reveals the full extent of not only its physical aspects as the guardian of the West, but also its importance to the Germans after they unleashed Barbarossa.

Within the German armed forces there were conflicting divisions over control of the Western defenses. Wilt thoroughly documents the problems of command and control. When the tide of the war turned against the Germans in the Mediterranean in 1943 a

---

* "Fortress Europe"

major Allied invasion of Western Europe went from a probability to a certainly. The issue became not one of "if" but of "when."

Wilt's account also reinforces my longstanding conviction that the success of the Allied invasion of Normandy was never inevitable, as some have viewed it in hindsight. To the contrary, Operation Overlord was fraught with risk and the potential for its failure loomed large. Both Eisenhower and Churchill understood the risks. Eisenhower had even prepared for this eventuality by writing a note (found crumpled in one of his shirt pocket's long after D-Day by his naval aide) accepting full responsibility for Overlord's failure had the Allies been compelled to withdraw from Normandy. The defenses of the Atlantic Wall, combined with Hitler's refusal to allow Rommel the freedom to station the powerful German armored reserve forces closer to the Normandy coast instead of far inland, were compelling factors in the successful Allied invasion.

What also emerges from this landmark book are clear answers to the longstanding unresolved questions of exactly how effective the Atlantic Wall was, and the important role it played in the development of Allied thinking and planning for the cross-Channel invasion of June 6, 1944.

The 60th anniversary of the D-Day landings is an appropriate moment for the publication of this book. Alan Wilt has combined meticulous scholarship with an extensive historical knowledge to resolve one of the last missing chapters in the history of World War II in the European Theater of Operations. *The Atlantic Wall* not only enhances our understanding of the historic events that began on D-Day, but also the historiography of the most devastating war in human history.

Carlo D'Este
Cape Cod, Massachusetts

Author's Introduction

Hitler often discussed the ongoing war during mealtime. In many instances the conversation was rambling and pointless, but occasionally his table talk gives us insights into the man and his views toward the war. One spring evening in 1942 the Führer was describing a recent inspection trip in the western theater:

> I was accosted by one of the workmen. "Mein Führer," he said, "I hope we're never going away from here. After all this tremendous work, that would be a pity." There is a wealth of wisdom in the man's remark, for it shows that a man hates to abandon such safe positions as those on the Channel coast, captured during the campaign in France and consolidated by the Organization Todt, and retire into the narrow confines of the North Sea.[1]

What Hitler was discussing was the Atlantic Wall. It was not a new idea in May of 1942, for the Führer had formally decreed an Atlantic Wall to be built late in 1941 and with this Wall he hoped to defeat any attempt by the Western Allies to invade Western Europe.[2]

The overwhelming success of British and American forces on D-Day in piercing the Wall led German officers and writers soon after the war to characterize it as a mere propaganda term or an enormous bluff or an illusion designed "to deceive the German people as well as the Allies."[3] But other writers soon began to recognize that Germany's western defenses were much more than a series of deceptions, and that they actually constituted a fairly formidable defensive barrier.[4] Still little formal work has been done to assess the relative effectiveness of what Hitler called "the greatest line of fortifications in history."[5] How effective actually was the Atlantic Wall? Was it merely a propaganda device, or was it truly a defensive system of considerable proportions? What factors determined its strengths as well as its weaknesses? The answers to these questions should help us to derive a better understanding of Germany's western defensive system.

One of the problems in dealing with the Atlantic Wall is the term itself. It is most often thought of as a number of fortifications, which were quite extensive in some places along the coast, and almost nonexistent in other places. While this is true, to think of the Atlantic Wall solely in terms of fortifications is misleading. A more realistic appraisal has to take into account manpower and firepower as well as fortifications, for these three factors, and not fortifications alone, formed the essential components of the Atlantic Wall concept.

The term "Atlantic Wall" is also imprecise when it comes to defining the area which it actually encompassed. It might be thought of within the narrow context of the Atlantic coast of France and in this case it would extend only from the Brittany Peninsula to the Spanish border. Or it might be discussed within a much broader context so as to include the Norwegian and Danish coasts and even possibly the Iberian Peninsula within its framework. But the Germans themselves came to think of the Wall primarily as encompassing the Dutch, Belgian, and French coasts, and after 1942 the Mediterranean beaches of southeastern France as well. This area, which became a separate entity under its own theater commander, Commander-in-Chief West (*Oberbefehlshaber West*), will form the geographic focus of our study.

Another consideration is the chronological focus of the Atlantic Wall concept. The period between the middle of 1940, when the Wehrmacht appeared to be invincible, and the Normandy and Provence invasion of 1944, when German military fortunes were in definite decline, seems most appropriate. For during these four years National Socialist Germany and her Axis partners and collaborators shifted primarily from an offensive to a defensive orientation and at the same time instituted the Atlantic Wall concept as an integral part of that reorientation.

Although other approaches could be taken, we will stress primarily the military side of the Atlantic Wall concept, for it is above all a military problem determined by the flow of military events. The emphasis will be to examine Germany's defensive buildup for the western theater as it developed from 1940 to 1944, how it changed, if any, during this time, and the numerous problems the Germans faced and never completely overcame. Thus the main theme will be to analyze the Atlantic Wall on a year-by-year basis.

But a number of supporting themes must also be kept in mind if one is to evaluate the relative effectiveness of the Wall. Particularly important in this regard is the realization that other fronts, especially the Russian front, often relegated the less critical western theater to a secondary status. Germany, as productive as its society might be, did not possess infinite resources and, especially after 1941, manpower and goods had to be allocated to those areas considered most endangered. Germany's defensive system in the West suffered as a result.

In addition, the German military took on the almost insoluble problem of trying to adjust its defensive priorities in relation to the probable intentions of the Western Allies, while attempting to meet at the same time the constantly changing internal situation on the continent, whether it was in Spain or southern France or Italy or even Hungary. At times the Wehrmacht managed to readjust its defensive posture in the West, and to have these changes correlate with the changes that were occurring inside each of the countries of occupied and neutral Europe. But most of the time there was no correlation, and the German military found itself taking on more and more tasks with fewer and fewer resources.

The building up of the Atlantic Wall also exemplifies several perennial military problems. One of these issues, which hinders every large military establishment, was that of interservice frictions. Just how well did the German army, the navy, and the air force cooperate, and to what degree did the different priorities of the three services affect the western defensive system? In the parlance of an old cliché, what is best for one of the services may not be best for the overall war effort. This was especially the case in the West, where the Wehrmacht shifted from an offensive to a defensive orientation between 1940 and 1944.

Another military problem, that of conflict in command, also existed in the western theater. It has become best known as a controversy between Field Marshals Erwin Rommel and Gerd von Rundstedt early in 1944, but it took other forms as well. The lack of clear lines of command authority fits in well with Hitler's dictum of "divide and rule," by which the Führer himself ultimately settled all of the major disputes whether they related to the military or the civilian sphere of German society.

An assessment of the Atlantic Wall is therefore incomplete unless we take into account the relationship of the western theater to probable enemy intentions, the alterations within each of the European nations, the pressing conditions on Germany's other combat fronts, and the interservice and command conflicts. In this way a clearer understanding of German military thinking in the West from 1940 to the summer of 1944 will emerge. General Günther Blumentritt, Chief of Staff to von Rundstedt when the latter was Commander-in-Chief West, contends that "the reader would find it wearisome to read long descriptions of the day-to-day happenings during this period [in the West]."[6] One might get the impression from Blumentritt's statement that Western Europe was a static and dull place at the time. Actually it was far from static. It was a period of preparation, of movement, of privation and heroism on both sides, a time during which the making of the Atlantic Wall came to assume a significant role in Germany's wartime thinking. In a sense its role shows how military factors tend to overshadow ultimately more important nonmilitary factors during wartime. In another sense, however, the Atlantic Wall concept demonstrates again that military history is much more than battlefield history.[7]

THE ATLANTIC WALL

Chapter 1

The East Solution

The Atlantic Wall concept did not figure into Germany's early war plans, for Hitler was not thinking defensively in 1939 and 1940. To all appearances the Wehrmacht seemed invincible. The German military had disposed of Poland and then Norway and Denmark before rapidly and convincingly defeating Dutch, Belgian, French, and British forces in the Battle of France. England was held out to be the next victim. The Führer hoped initially to come to a "compromise peace" with Great Britain rather than having to subdue the *Engländer* by force, and he considered his terms to be quite generous.[1] If Britain would acknowledge Germany's preeminent position on the continent and return her former African colonies, then the Reich, for its part, would recognize England's right to maintain its Empire and to participate in the division of France's colonial possessions. When Britain refused, Hitler moved, albeit reluctantly at first, to the position that an invasion of England was necessary.[2]

By the time Hitler issued Directive No. 16, "Preparations for a Landing Operation Against England," on July 16, 1940, plans for

Operation "Sea Lion" were already underway.[3] Eventually the Germans considered two plans, a "broad plan" at the end of July, and, upon the insistence of the navy because of a lack of suitable ships, a revised or "narrow plan" in September. The revised "Sea Lion" scheme differed from its hastily conceived predecessor in that Wehrmacht forces were to land along a smaller, narrower front, fewer divisions were to take part in the initial assault, and the rate of reinforcement was to be slower than in the original plan. In both proposals German troops were to attack the coast in several places, thrust inland after reinforcements had come ashore, and then connect the beachheads as a basis for future operations.

The navy, or *Kriegsmarine*, for its part, was to secure the sea-lanes for the invasion and then to insure that German supply lines could be protected at all times from British naval attacks. The key to the entire operation was the Luftwaffe, which was to gain air superiority over the Channel and portions of Britain before the cross-Channel landing attempt could proceed. As we know, the German air force never achieved its goals. The British navy and air force remained supreme, and the Führer postponed the proposed invasion in October. He left open the possibility that he might consider a resurrected "Sea Lion" in 1941, but the operation, for the time being, was not to be executed.[4] Hitler did not expect that its temporary abandonment in the fall of 1940 would be final.

Germany's failure to subdue Great Britain obviously necessitated a major alteration in Hitler's strategy, and he began casting about for other alternatives to perpetuate Germany's drive for world power status. He had no difficulty finding alternatives which he deemed appropriate. Actually even before the Luftwaffe had engaged the Royal Air Force in August, the German dictator had started to consider other possibilities. The operations which Hitler felt to be most promising were ones directed either against Gibraltar in the Western Mediterranean, or against one of his supposed allies, the Soviet Union, in the East.

His reasoning is not difficult to ascertain. In the West, Hitler eventually wanted to establish an "Atlantic empire" which would rival the combined strength of the United States and Great Britain. (It was a foregone conclusion to the Führer that if the United States came into the war, it would be on the side of the British. Hitler also envisioned a war with the United States as unavoidable sooner or later.)[5] To erect such an "empire," the Führer greatly desired the help of Spain, Vichy France, and possibly even Portugal.

But their help was not forthcoming. The areas which the Germans wanted conflicted with large Spanish and Vichy French territories in sections of Northwest Africa and several island groups in the Atlantic. And even if the conflicting claims could be reconciled, both Francisco Franco, the Spanish dictator, and Marshal Pétain, the octogenarian French military hero and head of the Vichy regime, were disinclined to help. Their equivocation no doubt irked Hitler, and he could have sent Wehrmacht troops to take over Spain if he had wished to do so. But an operation of this nature would have tied down a great deal of German striking power (*deutschen Streitkraefte*) in Southwestern Europe, and by this time a further complication had come to the fore. Italy was in trouble in the Balkans and in Africa, and the Führer decided to begin preparations to bail out Mussolini's forces. Such a move opened up the danger of a two-front war, and the Wehrmacht did not have sufficient resources, especially air craft, to pursue operations in both Southwestern and Southeastern Europe at the same time. And there was also the overriding factor that by now Hitler had decided on the invasion of Russia, which he had long considered to be his main foe. At least for the time being Hitler therefore pushed aside the possibility of bringing Southwest Europe into the Nazi orbit.[6]

Hitler had resolved to strike at his Soviet partner mainly because, having failed to bring the war against Britain to a speedy conclusion, he decided to defeat the Russians first before disposing of England.[7] In this way he felt that the British would be cut off from the possibility of eventually being able to secure an alliance with the Russians.

Although both the Germans and the Soviets had considered their agreement in 1939 to be one of convenience, in the end the pact was more beneficial to Germany. The Soviets, to be sure, did gain time to reorganize the army on a more modern basis, and also gained additional territory in Eastern Europe, but they lost those areas within a few days in 1941. They also lost, as a result of the agreement, the "second front" they were to clamor for later. National Socialist Germany, on the other hand, benefited by receiving vital raw materials from the USSR, and by being allowed to use the Murmansk-Archangel area as a sanctuary for its shipping away from the British fleet. And the pact also secured Germany's "back door" so that she could concentrate her forces in the western theater. Now Hitler decided to open the door himself.

This decision was not reached on the "spur of the moment." The winning of "living space" (*Lebensraum*) had been a cardinal feature of National Socialist ideology almost from its inception, and the vast lands of Soviet Russia had long been considered a prime target. More recently, while the Battle of Britain was still raging, Hitler offered the additional reason, as noted earlier, that the British held out only in the expectation of gaining Soviet support. In other words, the Wehrmacht should go east as a prelude to securing ultimate victory in the West. On July 31, 1940, the Führer told his generals to prepare for a possible invasion of the USSR in the spring of 1941. The German dictator never deviated from this course during the remainder of 1940 and on into 1941. As historian Andreas Hillgruber asserts:

> There remained then for Hitler only the last great possibility: a military solution in the East [*militärische Ostlösung*] in 1940 as the decisive prerequisite for maintaining its [Germany's] power position in Europe and for erecting a "world power" position in opposition to united Anglo-Saxon sea power.[8]

In this euphoric future vision of new conquests and an expanding empire, Hitler and his close associates devoted little attention to Western Europe. In fact, even while the Führer had been preoccupied with the invasion of Great Britain, France and the rest of the western countries had faded into the background. The Wehrmacht wanted a minimum of trouble during the initial period of adjustment. For this reason, although the Germans had placed the Netherlands and Belgium under occupation governments, numerous Dutch and Belgian officials continued to function in an administrative capacity.[9] The Germans also treated France with deference, for the French, though beaten, still retained a considerable naval fleet as well as extensive unconquered colonies.[10] And its civil servants, as in the Low Countries, could administer the country with only nominal German control, thus freeing the Wehrmacht to dispose of Britain. It is little wonder then that Germany was content to occupy only a portion of metropolitan France, or that part which lay closest to England and the Atlantic coast. The coastal region was, to be sure, vulnerable to British attack, but it had also the attraction of containing a number of harbors capable of supporting expanded U-boat operations in the Atlantic.[11] The southeastern two-fifths of the country was placed under the control of a new French government, established at the resort spa of Vichy. The Germans even allowed the Vichy government to retain an armed force of 100,000 men to help maintain order in its zone. French historian Robert Aron relates that there was little brutality at first on the part of the German occupiers. "On the contrary numerous anecdotes gave witness to Nazi 'courtesies.'"[12]

Germany treated the defeated West European nations with moderation for another reason: the nature of the German wartime economy.[13] The Nazi war machine had been able initially to fight a series of short, one-front wars. These short wars (or campaigns) did not place an inordinate strain on the German economy while its war machine was being pulled together. The Battle of France fit in well with German economic thinking. Why prolong the campaign by imposing harsh terms on the French? The French can be exploited, the Germans reasoned, to bolster the German war effort, for the French economy, though damaged, could well prove to be a tremendous asset.

Several approaches that the Germans might have used to exploit the situation in France are brought out in a letter sent by General Carl-Heinrich von Stülpnagel, chairman of the German Armistice Commission, to General Alfred Jodl, head of the Armed Forces operations staff, and a person who enjoyed close liaison with Hitler as his main briefing officer.[14] Von Stülpnagel, whose commission was to work out relations between Germany and the new Vichy government, warned in September 1940 that the French economy was "weakened to the core" (*bis ins Mark geschwächt*). With two million French skilled workers serving as German prisoners, with millions more displaced refugees wandering far from their places of work, with the losses in production from the destruction during the war and from the demobilization after the war, and with the British blockage, "the French have already had enough."[15] Von Stülpnagel then recommended that the German government stop removing machines and foodstuffs from France and concentrate instead on repairing the French economy so that it could be integrated more closely and more rationally into German military planning. In short, he recommended that Germany should take advantage of France's economic potential rather than reducing her to a subsistence level.

Von Stülpnagel's view, of course, did not prevail. As Alan Milward put it:

> Failure to exploit these territories systematically drove her [Germany] into the administratively simpler habit of merely living off the country. Consequently, the German occupation came to resemble gigantic looting operations. There was little that was new and less that was orderly in the New Order.[16]

But at the end of 1940 the "New Order" was barely in its planning stages, and an Atlantic Wall was far from the minds of German military planners. Instead, they were envisioning victories of vast proportions in the East, and Hitler's decision to dispose of the Soviet Union also dictated German military thinking for Western Europe. These measures included the movement of German troops from west to east, plans for a takeover of Vichy France or the Iberian Peninsula if that proved necessary, and the prevention of any British incursion against the continent. In effect, Germany wanted its western door secure so that it could focus its attention toward the East.

To mask the eastern troop movements, the Wehrmacht devised several bogus operations for the West as a "cover" for actual German intentions. Even though the cover operations relate more directly to Operation "Barbarossa" than they do to the evolution of a defensive strategy for Western Europe, they do help illustrate the problems which Germany encountered because of its ever-increasing commitments. As one might expect, the projected invasion of the Soviet Union necessitated transferring the bulk of the Wehrmacht from the western theater to the East. The eastern movement began in the fall of 1940 and continued even after "Barbarossa" had started on June 22, 1941. Army Group C (*Heeresgruppe C*), which had kept part of the French forces occupied in their Maginot Line defenses during the Battle of France, was removed to Germany as early as July 1940. Field Marshal von Bock's Army Group B followed several months later in September. The other army group instrumental in defeating the French, Army Group A, stayed in the West until March 1941, just in case Hitler revived the idea of an invasion attempt against England and also not to "tip off" the eastern offensive.[17]

After March only one army group, *Heeresgruppe D*, remained for operations in Western Europe. Formed in October 1940, it consisted at that time of three armies—the First, Seventh, and Sixth (later replaced by the Fifteenth)—and at first it exercised operational control over the interior of occupied France and France's Atlantic coast south of St. Malo. When almost all of the twenty-five divisions which composed Army Group A moved out of the Channel sector by March 15, 1941, Army Group D extended its command authority in military matters over all of Occupied France, Belgium, and also, if threatened, the Netherlands. At the same time Army Group D assumed the additional title of Commander-in-Chief West (*Oberbefehlshaber West*).

One should not presume that Army Group D was made up of battle-hardened troops. Of the thirty-nine divisions listed on January 10, 1941, only four remained on duty in the West by the middle of May, and even these formations had no combat experience.[18] Although Army Group D added three more divisions left behind by Army Group A, this meant, in effect, that the Germans retained only seven of their former divisions in Western Europe, while the others were shuttled east.[19] The rest of the forces under Theater Command West were drawn from inexperienced, if not totally new, formations that were being assembled within the Reich.

The air force also moved most of its units to the eastern front, but the navy had little to do in a direct way with the invasion of Russia and continued to concentrate its efforts in the West. As pointed out in a naval directive of March 6, "The main target for the Navy, even during the eastern campaign, remains Britain."[20]

Like the Navy, the rest of the German military forces that remained in the West continued to fulfill important tasks. One of their most important duties was to cover the movement east.

The cover operations took the form of two interrelated deceptions directed against England during the spring and summer of 1941. These two elaborate schemes, codenamed "Shark" (*Haifisch*) and "Harpoon" (*Harpune*), were designed to mislead both the British and the Soviets into thinking that a major assault was to be launched against British, rather than Russian, soil.[21] The main deception, "Shark," was to be an assault against the English coast between Folkestone and Worthing, while "Harpoon" was to augment the "Shark" operation in the form of two flanking actions, "Harpoon North" and "Harpoon South," directed against the east and southwest British coasts. Wehrmacht staff officers were to make use of the previous "Sea Lion" plans to the fullest extent possible.

The Wehrmacht divided the preparations for "Haifisch" and "Harpune" into three time periods with appropriate deception measures for each.[22] During the first phase in May, German planners were to work out the tactical details for "Shark" and "Harpoon," but at the same time a few local Belgian and French inhabitants were to "find out" that an operation of some type was being prepared. During the second phase in June, the Germans hoped to deceive the actual and prospective enemies still further by assembling ships and barges in the harbor areas and by conducting loading and landing exercises along the coast. The Armed Forces High Command acknowledged that by this time it could no longer mask the movement from west to east.[23] Therefore, the deployment to the east was to appear, so far as possible, as a deception, while preparations in the west were to resemble an actual attack against England. The third phase of the operations was to be worked out later, depending on the military and political situation. Nevertheless, "Shark" and "Harpoon" were to appear ready for implementation by the first of August.

To lend an atmosphere of authenticity, division commanders were instructed that "troops are to be led to believe that at present all preparations and measures are being conducted in connection with 'Sea Lion.'"[24] In addition, the Germans did transfer troops and supplies to the coast, collected landing craft in major ports, and conducted onloading and offloading exercises during the summer months.[25]

A memorandum from the Chief of Staff of Army Group D as early as May 20 indicated that, in general, he felt the Germans were "confusing the English as to our future intentions."[26] But the British were not deceived.[27] Even before any of the coastal maneuvers had been carried out, they had begun to receive information that the Germans were shifting large numbers of divisions eastward, and the British had warned the Soviet Union to this effect as early as April 1941. At first British officials felt that Hitler was merely involved in a "war of nerves" to gain concessions from his Russian ally, but by the middle of June, British intelligence had amassed enough evidence to become convinced that a war in the East was a definite possibility unless Soviet leaders gave in completely to German demands. The British, as well as the Americans (and even Soviet intelligence), continued to send warnings to the Russians until the very day of the invasion, warnings which Stalin chose to ignore.

The Wehrmacht actually continued to engage in deception measures in the West even after "Barbarossa" had begun, but on August 7, 1941, the Army High Command ordered that the simulated measures for "Haifisch" and "Harpune" cease since they had completely fulfilled their purposes.[28] Even though "Shark" and "Harpoon" were bogus operations in support of the Russian campaign, they are significant in underscoring the offensive nature of German thinking during the first half of 1941. It is doubtful if the Wehrmacht would have used the exact plans for these deceptions as the basis for any future undertaking, but the experiences gained from them had been catalogued and no doubt would have proved helpful if an invasion attempt of Britain were ever revived.

The German military's second major task in the West during 1941—possible operations into Vichy-controlled France or Spain and Portugal—had both an offensive and a defensive orientation. The takeover of additional territory obviously gave the operation an offensive cast, but they were also designed, especially in the case of the Iberian Peninsula, to stave off a British landing on the continent.

Spain and Portugal were neutral countries, and Hitler preferred to deal with them diplomatically rather than militarily.[29] He realized that Portugal's neutrality would be difficult to break because of its isolated position and because of British sea power. But the Germans considered Spain's neutrality to be something different. In

June of 1940, when German military power seemed irresistible, Spain's Franco showed interest in joining the Axis cause. But when relations between Franco and Hitler cooled noticeably by the end of the year, and when the Führer became preoccupied with the projected invasion of the Soviet Union, military planning as related to Spain and Portugal underwent considerable alterations.

During the course of 1940 and 1941, German staff officers proposed two different operations for the Iberian Peninsula. The 1940 operation, codenamed "Felix," was an ambitious plan designed during the last months of 1940 to occupy with Spanish assistance Gibraltar, Spanish Morocco, and possibly the Canary Islands, as well as parts of Spain and Portugal.[30] However, "Felix" encountered several complications from the start. One was that Franco remained obdurate, and by the winter months, time for the Germans was running out, for the operations had to take place before the bulk of German military power was shifted East. This problem eventually led the Führer on December 10 to request Field Marshal Wilhelm Keitel, head of the Armed Forces High Command, to issue a brief order stating that "Operation 'Felix' would not now be carried out as the necessary political situation no longer exists." One month later, on the exact day when "Felix" had originally been scheduled to begin, the Germans called it off officially.[31]

There is little doubt that the Wehrmacht could have taken over Spain at this time with or without Franco's consent. And it is understandable if Hitler considered Spain, and Franco in particular, as being ungrateful for German aid rendered during the Spanish Civil War. But Franco in the end refused to join the Axis cause. The obvious question is why? Certainly Franco felt no ideological affinity for the West. And by associating with Germany, the Spanish leader might ultimately expect to gain Gibraltar and some additional territory in Africa, although in the latter case he probably would not have been allowed to take over as much land as he wanted.[32]

But for a number of reasons Franco stalled for time and eventually succeeded in keeping Spain neutral. Probably foremost in his mind was his desire to consolidate his hold over that war-torn country rather than sending Spanish troops into battle again. Moreover, he desperately needed credit with which to pay back debts contracted to Germany and Italy during the Civil War and goods, particularly oil, from the Western nations.[33] Finally, by the end of 1940, the *Caudillo* did not want German troops on Spanish soil. Even though Nazi units had served in Franco's army during the Civil War, the possibility of Spain's becoming part of a vast German empire had seemed remote at the time. Now the situation had altered. German presence in southwestern Europe could easily become permanent. To receive assistance from the Nazis was one thing; to risk becoming one of Hitler's satellite states was quite another.

Hitler, of course, did not write off Spain completely. But during the course of 1941 his plans for the Iberian Peninsula took on a defensive orientation. If Gibraltar could be taken, so much the better, but German staff officials began placing more emphasis on defending Spain and Portugal from possible British encroachments. The Nazi dictator still issued directives, such as Führer Directive No. 32 on June 11, 1941, which asserted that "preparations for 'Undertaking Felix': already planned, will be resumed to the fullest extent even during the course of operations in the East."[34] But during this period he was more concerned with protecting German interests in the West than in controlling southwestern Europe.

Hitler considered a British attack against Spain and Portugal as possible at the end of April, and he directed the army to prepare appropriate countermeasures. He felt that eight to ten divisions would be sufficient to repel any British landing attempt.[35] Accordingly, the army produced Operation "Isabella" early in May.[36] The entire undertaking was to be compared and executed under the guidance of Commander-in-Chief West. It is hardly surprising that the plans which *Ob West* had drawn up allotted two army corps, seven infantry divisions, one panzer brigade, and one motorized battalion to carry out "Isabella," for it accorded closely with the April 30 estimate of Hitler's staff. The personnel were to come from forty-six divisions stationed in the western theater.[37]

One might legitimately question if "Isabella," which was to include a number of motorized divisions penetrating rapidly into the heart of Spain, could have been carried out with the types of units at hand. But there is no doubt that the Armed Forces High Command expected it to be ready if necessary for implementation, for an entry in the OKW War Diary early in June asserted that "Isabella" could possibly take place any time after June 20.[38] As is well known, this plan, as well as later ones directed toward the Iberian Peninsula, were never put into effect. Still, they might have been put into operation, and Hitler continued to keep the Spanish option open.

The possibility of taking over Unoccupied France was related to another aspect of Germany's wartime situation, the control and disposition of its newly conquered territories. German distrust of Vichy French intentions was manifest from the start, and plans for occupying southeastern France were formulated toward the end of 1940. Führer Directive No. 19, dated December 10, christened the undertaking Operation "Attila."[39] The reasoning behind "Attila" was set forth in the first paragraph:

> In case those parts of the French Colonial Empire now controlled by General Weygand (at that time the Vichy representative in North Africa) should show signs of revolt, preparations will be made for the rapid occupation of the still unoccupied portion of continental France (Operation Attila). At the same time it will be necessary to capture the French home fleet and those parts of the Air Force in home bases, or at least to prevent their going over to the enemy.
>
> For military as well as political reasons, preparations for the operation will be camouflaged so as to avoid alarming the French.

The directive went on to indicate that the occupation would be handled by Commander-in-Chief West and executed in two stages. The first stage was to consist of strong motorized columns supported by air cover moving rapidly through the valleys of the Garonne and the Rhône rivers to the Mediterranean, taking over the ports as quickly as possible (especially the important naval base at Toulon), and sealing off southeastern France from the sea. During the second, or followup, phase German formations stationed near the demarcation line were to move forward to occupy the key installations in the zone itself.

German planners did not expect any organized resistance on the part of Vichy French forces, but if it appeared, it was to be suppressed ruthlessly. Luftwaffe bomber groups and naval units were to be made available to help against any possible disturbances and to keep the French fleet and French aircraft from leaving their home bases. Finally, Hitler directed that the Italians were to be given no information about the plan.

By early 1941, the western theater commander named fifteen divisions from the First and Seventh Armies to participate in the operation.[40] But on February 3 the OKW War Diary indicated that "Attila" could be undertaken only with great difficulty after the exodus of troops to the East.[41] For this same reason preparations for "Felix" and "Sea Lion" had already been discontinued a month earlier. In the case of "Attila," however, higher headquarters ordered that it must be carried through, even though this would mean that a smaller force would take part.

By June 10, "Attila" had been pared to ten divisions. Of the fifteen army and SS formations originally involved, only one division was listed to take part in "Attila" both on February 3 and June 10.[42] Of more consequence was the conspicuous absence of armored and motorized divisions from the new "Attila" plan. Whereas four panzer and two motorized formations were to be involved in February, by late spring, with the invasion of Russia less than a month away, only one panzer brigade located near Paris could be called upon to participate.

Further orders from Commander-in-Chief West made it clear that "Attila" and "Isabella," the thrust into Spain, could not take place at the same time. There were simply not enough troops for both operations.[43] A frank discussion between First Army Quartermaster officers and staff members under Theater Command West pointed up that "many factors remain uncertain" in implementing the "Attila" operation.[44]

Despite the uncertainties, German distrust of French officials did not abate, and "Attila" continued in existence throughout 1941 and into 1942, even in its weakened form. Toward the end of 1942, when the Allies powers invaded North Africa, it was implemented, though under the code name "Anton."

The other major task performed by the Wehrmacht in the West during 1941 was the protection of its newly won territory against a British landing. During the course of the year this duty assumed a defensive orientation, and within this framework a defensive system for Western Europe began to evolve.

At first the German military viewed any defensive measures purely as precautionary. This fact is made clear in a directive from Army Group A on November 10, 1940. "Even though attacks by England can scarcely be expected to any great extent, still partial attacks against the Belgian-French coast must be reckoned with. Even a temporary success against a single important strong-point can cause difficulties..."[45] In short, German planners did not expect a major assault, but its forces must prevent any English success no matter how limited. This attitude prevailed for several months into 1941.

The main focus during this initial period of the occupation was on offensive rather than defensive thinking. In practical terms this meant concentrating on the construction of submarine bases at Brest, Lorient, St. Nazaire, Bordeaux, and later on at La Pallice to pursue the U-boat war against Britain. It meant further the erection of coastal batteries by Organization Todt workers between Calais

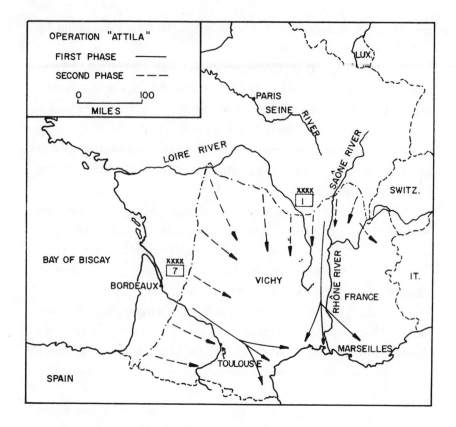

Fig. 1.1. Operation "Attila"

and Boulogne to assist in the invasion of England.[46] The Germans positioned these long-range guns to hit targets as far away as the Kentish shore more than twenty miles away. Eventually, during the course of the war, they were responsible for killing or injuring scores of British civilians living near the Straits of Dover.[47]

The German outlook toward the West began to change, however, by the middle of February 1941. A memorandum from Field Marshal Walther von Brauchitsch, Army Commander-in-Chief, to Armed Forces High Command headquarters on February 15 still acknowledged the possibility of a British attack on the Dutch, Belgian, or French coasts, but this time he emphasized it might be either a *large* or *small* assault, especially since German strength in the area was being reduced and no longer posed an immediate threat to England.[48] Von Brauchitsch went on to say that German forces would have difficulty repelling a British attack with the meager strength at hand. While the memorandum might be construed as merely a "scare tactic" by von Brauchitsch to obtain more troops, it also points up an awareness on the part of the army leaders of its expanding defensive responsibilities and the additional problems that these responsibilities would entail.

One of the defensive problems was to make sure that any British attack, whether large or small, was met by a coordinated German effort, and such an effort required unified command in the West. In keeping with traditional German practice, the land commander, in this case Field Marshal Erwin von Witzleben as Commander-in-Chief West, was to exercise ultimate control. Directives during the first half of 1941 attest to the working out of this command relationship.[49]

Among the various armed services, the navy and the air force were to continue their own offensive missions, but if an enemy landing was imminent or being executed, von Witzleben was to take command. The directive defined a landing as imminent "if it can be observed by reconnaissance at sea or from the air, or can be ascertained from land."[50] In addition, *Ob West* was to direct all preparations and training for defense against a landing, and reconnaissance missions were to comply with the wishes of the army. Luftwaffe antiaircraft artillery was also to come under army jurisdiction in case of an invasion, insofar as the air situation permitted. The stress at this time was on cooperation among the services, and the navy, for example, foresaw no problems in coordinating naval artillery against landing attempts with army artillery units.[51]

Therefore, a representative of the army, Commander-in-Chief West, was in command. He became increasingly responsible not to the Army High Command (OKH), however, but to the Armed Forces High Command (OKW), which unofficially took over the western theater as one of its "theaters of war," while OKH directed the effort in the East. There was one exception to Commander-in-Chief West's control over the land forces in the West: the Armed Forces High Commander in the Netherlands (*Wehrmachtbefehlshaber in den Niederlanden*), who was responsible for the Dutch area, was a Luftwaffe officer. But even in this instance *Ob West* was to issue directives to the Netherlands commander in case of immediate danger. And as the war continued, the Netherlands became integrated more and more into the western defense complex.[52] Army control also extended to the lower echelons, and local army commanders were put in charge of their own sectors. Other German personnel in Western Europe, such as customs officials, police, labor service, and Organization Todt workers, were to take orders from Commander-in-Chief West during periods of possible external aggression. Additional directives in April and May elaborated further the army's preeminent position in the West, and the concept of unity of command seemed secure.[53] But the question continued to arise in 1942 and 1943, mainly because each of the armed forces would not accept the defensive thinking being advocated by other services. Although the army again eventually retained control, the issue was not settled without some misgivings among the three branches.

A second defensive problem was where and how to meet any invasion the British might attempt. Obviously, certain areas were more endangered than others, and the Germans set about deciding where a landing might take place. German staff officers in March 1941, determined that a large landing was probable in the area extending from the Dutch to the French coast south of Boulogne, but that such an operation would prove extremely difficult for British forces at this time.[54] Coastal raids by the British were much more likely to occur. The Wehrmacht felt that British commando teams could initiate this type of small operation anywhere along the coast, but they were expected only at night with the object of destroying installations, taking prisoners, or landing agents and then withdrawing quickly. German planners estimated further that an attack on the submarine bases for the purpose of blocking or putting them out of commission was inconceivable unless it were conducted as part of a large-scale attack.

Although the Germans did build some fortifications during the year, the basic defensive plan as it evolved during 1941 was to concentrate German troops and artillery in or near the most threatened sectors and then to back them up with a number of divisions in the rear. Wehrmacht officers considered the large harbors to be especially significant targets, since they felt that the British could sustain a large landing only by capturing a major port. Just as importantly the Germans had large portions of their fleet using the Atlantic and Channel harbors, and protection of them was essential if these naval craft were to continue to carry out their assigned missions. Wehrmacht commanders hoped to defend the less threatened coastal stretches with only small contingents of troops, but entire panzer and infantry (including artillery) divisions were to to be held in reserve to "destroy the enemy on land and throw him back into the sea if that proved necessary."[55]

The manpower and materiel situation, critical for the Germans during the buildup for the invasion of the USSR, eased to some degree during the summer months. They found they did have sufficient troops in the West as long as the situation remained quiet. To be sure, von Witzleben might not have the quantity or the quality of troops at his disposal that he would have liked, but on June 10, or less than two weeks before the attack on Russia, he still had forty-five divisions at his disposal. Nineteen of these formations were deployed along the coast, thirteen were held in reserve, and thirteen more occupied the French interior north of the Vichy zone.[56] Even though this number decreased to thirty-eight by June 27, *Ob West* listed the same divisions with one exception and the same exact number, thirty-eight, in his order of battle of September 3.[57] In fact, one might contend that the Germans had more than enough troops in the western theater at this time, troops which might have been used more productively on the eastern front.

Although the Germans could have utilized their manpower more effectively, they did make some progress in constructing artillery emplacements. By October 9 von Witzleben listed 1,215 pieces of artillery in his inventory, ranging from 75 mm. to 40.6 cm. (16 inch) guns.[58] Even though over one-third, or 455, of these guns were of French, Belgian, or Czech origin, a portion of the coastal artillery pieces—including those of German make—had been placed in positions. A report August 30 indicated that ninety-two batteries (with three or four guns per battery) were ready for use along the western coast.[59] Certainly the emplacements were not as elaborately built as the German offensive batteries that had been constructed the year before in support of "Sea Lion," but the Germans felt little need to protect their batteries so elaborately in 1941. To a military observer in 1944, German artillery in the West in 1941 might seem woefully inadequate, but at this time Wehrmacht leaders considered the measures they had taken to be sufficient to ward off any possible British landing attempt.

In terms of the overall military situation in 1941, this meant that German military power in Western Europe, other than the U-boat force, was no longer offensively oriented. It was probably insufficient to pursue a large-scale operation into Spain or possibly even against Unoccupied France, except as a reaction to internal or external provocations. But even though German forces had begun to assume a more defensive posture, they certainly possessed more than enough troops and firepower to meet any British threat from the West.

One other feature of German policy in Western Europe requires brief mention at this time—the relationship of the various German and local officials in France, Belgium, and the Netherlands to the operational German military forces stationed in the area. The complex German administration and its civilian counterpart in each of the countries were organized in 1940 and 1941, and the functions of these occupation governments no doubt did affect the Wehrmacht's defensive posture in the West throughout the period of German control.

The occupation of Western Europe reflected the nation-state structure which had existed there for a century or more, and the governing apparatus proved to be unique to each country. In the Netherlands, two offices—the High Commissioner for the Occupied Dutch Territories (*Reichskommissar für die besetzten niederlandischen Gebiete*) as well as the Commander of the Armed Forces in the Netherlands—exercised control.[60] The civil administration was turned over to the High Commissioner and his representatives, while the Commander of the Armed Forces coordinated the activities of the German military. In Belgium and two departments of Northern France, the Military Commander in Belgium and Northern France (*Militärbefehlshaber in Belgien und Nordfrankreich*) was in control of both the military and the civilian administration.[61]

France's situation was more complex.[62] Basically, the Military Commander in France (*Militärbefehlshaber in Frankreich*) ran Occupied France, and the Vichy government administered unoccupied France, but each government exercised at least some authority in the other's territory. In between, there was the German ambassador to France, Otto Abetz, a confirmed Francophile, who was responsible for all political matters in both zones.

In spite of the organizational differences, each country's administration exhibited marked similarities. First of all, one of the main functions of each government was to maintain internal security within its area of responsibility.[63] The problem of civilian resistance to Nazi control was to grow enormously during the next three years, but it was relatively slight in 1941. Cases of sabotage and arson were few in number, and incidents were confined mainly to scribbling "Vive de Gaulle!" in chalk on the side of a wall or hissing at the Führer's picture in a movie house.[64] Secondly, Dutch, Belgian, and French civil servants handled administration. In this way the Germans needed to use their own personnel only for supervisory duties, and knowledgeable local officials could be left relatively free to conduct their own local affairs. Thirdly, a number of German agencies in each country existed independent of the governments which supposedly exercised control. For example, the Reich Foreign Ministry and the Propaganda Ministry had their own representatives in Western Europe. Especially critical in this respect was the expanding role of the SS (*Schutzstaffeln*), the SD (*Sicherheitsdienst*), and the Gestapo in each nation. In the case of France, the SS toward the end of the war came to exert dominant executive power.[65] Fourthly, government officials were to exploit their regions and to support the Nazi war effort. In other words, these areas were to provide labor, goods, machinery, and money for the National Socialist cause.[66]

Finally, and more directly related to Germany's military strategy, the various administrations were subordinate to Commander-in-Chief West in tactical military questions and in cases of imminent danger. Thus *Ob West* was solely responsible for preparing the defensive system against an invasion, including direct control over the coastal area to a depth of thirty kilometers, and for preventing any enemy-landing attempt. His control over civilian and military governors in the area extended no further, but the notion of some German apologists after the war that this restriction severely handicapped his effectiveness is doubtful. The overall administrative structure described above was to prevail in Western Europe until the Normandy landing.

Chapter 2

The Atlantic Wall Takes Shape

W hen the "Eastern Solution" failed to materialize during the fall of 1941, Hitler felt he had little alternative but to continue the main German war effort against the Soviet Union in 1942. This policy meant, of course, the deployment of more and more combat units to the East, with the result that Commander-in-Chief West eventually sent large numbers of troops to the hard-pressed Russian front. As early as August 14, 1941, the German army, despite the great victories it was winning, began to consider sending additional forces from the western theater to assist in the effort against the Red Army. The Germans demurred at the time, but when the Soviets instituted a devastating winter counteroffensive in December, these troop movements became a common occurrence.[1] The eastern front finally stabilized in February–March 1942, but by this time fifteen of the best infantry divisions in the West had been moved out.[2] In total figures this meant that the number of divisions in Western Europe had dropped, despite some replacements, from thirty-eight in September 1941, to twenty-four the following April. This loss of nearly 40 percent of the German forces in the West was occurring at the same time that the possibility of a British landing against the continent was increasing. An operation of this nature would undoubtedly have benefited Britain's Soviet partner, and by the end of 1941 the Germans might well fear such an undertaking. With substantial numbers of their combat troops being siphoned off to the east, they could ill afford a British attack from the rear. This led the Wehrmacht to seek another solution to its western exposure, and within this context the Atlantic Wall began to evolve.[3]

The idea of an impregnable wall or fortress strategy was not new to Hitler, for he had had the West Wall built near Germany's western border in 1938 to serve as a screen while he concentrated on extending the Reich in an easterly direction. The West Wall consisted of several thousand small installations rather than large, elaborate structures, and it proved its worth during the Munich crisis when it contributed to the Führer's success in bluffing France and Britain.[4] Nor is there anything novel about the Atlantic Wall in the history of warfare. Walls from the Great Wall of China to Hadrian's Wall to the more recently conceived Maginot Line had generally been constructed with one purpose in mind: to keep out potential invaders, and the Atlantic Wall was to be no exception.

Although the Germans had not explicitly pursued a defensive strategy in the West in 1941, they had already started thinking in these terms before the end of the year. Now in 1942 the Wehrmacht began to intensify its efforts in this direction. First of all, since German military presence in Western Europe had become more than a temporary expedient, and since the bulk of the German forces was engaged on the Russian front, the Führer and his military planners decided to issue the necessary directives to put in motion a defensive orientation for the theater. *Ob West* then implemented these directives by standardizing procedures and by reorganizing the theater largely on a defensive basis. Secondly, the various components of the Atlantic Wall concept—fortifications, manpower, and firepower—began to reflect this thinking and to conform more to a defensive pattern. And thirdly, when the British and their allies undertook a number of coastal raids in 1942, the Wehrmacht's success in repulsing these attacks seemed to confirm in its mind the basic correctness of German strategy. The raids further convinced Hitler that the defensive posture in the West must be strengthened, and by the end of the year the Atlantic Wall concept had become an accepted component of Germany's overall war strategy.

The directives and orders which eventually put the Atlantic Wall on what the Germans conceived to be a permanent basis started with the issuance of a top-level directive on December 14, 1941. There is no indication why Hitler acted exactly when he did, but reverses on the eastern front and the sudden dismissal of Pierre Laval, Vichy's collaborationist premier, must have played a part. The directive which was signed by Field Marshal Keitel, set forth the "Wall" concept in its initial paragraph.[5]

> The coastal regions of the Arctic Ocean, North Sea and Atlantic Ocean controlled by us are ultimately to be built into a "new Westwall," in order that we can repel with certainty any landing attempts, even of the strongest enemy forces, with the smallest possible number of permanently assigned field troops.

The last clause was especially indicative of the German dilemma. They simply did not have enough resources to handle their increasing commitments. Even now they were beginning to feel the pinch in building materials and personnel. As the directive points out, "For the time being…, the strain on our troops compels us to restrict our construction"; and the coastal defense forces will "be reduced as far as possible, as the defenses are gradually strengthened."

Priorities were then assigned for construction by area. Norway was accorded top priority because it was difficult to utilize mobile reserves there, and because it was necessary to increase the number of harbors that could be used to protect coastal shipping. Belgium and France's western coasts were placed second in priority with the open coasts of the Netherlands and Jutland third.

Most of the planning and construction of coastal defenses was to be under army auspices, but the navy was to be responsible for the Norwegian coast and for all measures pertaining to sea warfare. Air defense, quite naturally, was placed in the hands of the Luftwaffe. Although the army was in charge of allocating materiel for construction purposes, the actual construction was to be handled by Organization Todt.

This directive and later ones dealing with the Atlantic Wall were posited on the basic assumption that the coastline was too long— 2,400 miles if one included Norway (later extending to 2,800 with the addition of the French Mediterranean coast)—to defend with the military personnel available. Thus fortifications were to serve as a substitute for manpower. This did not mean that the West was to be completely stripped of military units, for Hitler was well aware that building the Wall would of necessity be a long-term project, and that it would probably never be completely satisfactory—hence the need for an up-to-date mobile force in addition to the coastal divisions.[6] But it did mean that the primary focus was to be on the construction of fortifications in the West.

When reports persisted into 1942 that the British might attempt to establish a second front, and when they actually instituted a small raid on the French coast at the end of February, Hitler decided to act. The resulting directive, Führer Directive No. 40, dated March 23, 1942, established general guidelines for the defensive system to be adopted in Western Europe.[7] In effect, Führer Directive No. 40 ushered in the Atlantic Wall concept.

Although the directive dealt with the broad issue of coastal defense for all of Europe, it was especially pertinent when applied to the west. In many ways it mirrored the principles set forth in Keitel's directive the previous December. It warned that the British were now capable of launching every conceivable type of operation, from a large-scale landing to a small hit-and-run attack. It emphasized the construction of fortifications as the key factor in the defensive buildup, although mobile forces were to play a role. It stressed that the defenses should be built along the coast because an amphibious operation was weakest before it had established itself on land. And it noted that the supreme authority in the area was to be the army theater commander, but all of the services were to work together to assure a maximum effort.

On this latter point differences of interpretation soon emerged between the army and the navy. The army pointed to a naval order dated March 27, only four days after the issuance of Directive No. 40, as proof of the navy's desire to undermine the concept of unity of command in the West.[8] The portion of the order which must have upset army leaders was the section which states:

> Even if the fight for the coast extends to the coastal areas within the reach of the medium artillery [range of the army coastal artillery], control over the bombardment of targets at sea remains in the hands of naval shore commanders, who have command over coastal artillery [inclusive of Army coastal artillery] in the sector for this purpose. The naval shore commanders are under the operational command of the respective Army divisional commanders only in the battle for the coast.[9]

Within this framework responsibility for sea targets would be assigned to a naval commander, while the battle for the coast would be the responsibility of an army commander within the same sector. This duality of command about which the army was complaining therefore had a great deal of validity and it continued to hamper the effectiveness of the western defensive system for some time to come.[10]

Despite the army-navy disagreement, the ideas set forth in Führer Directive No. 40 were referred to time and again by German staff officers as the basis for defensive planning in the West.

The relationship between Directive 40 and western defensive thinking, and hence the Atlantic Wall concept, became readily apparent during the ensuing months.

The Führer entrusted the implementation of Directive No. 40 to the new Commander-in-Chief West, Field Marshal Gerd von Rundstedt. Von Rundstedt, the distinguished senior officer, in many ways personified the Prussian military tradition. He had most recently served as military commander in the Russian campaign until being relieved by Hitler after a disagreement over a withdrawal order toward the end of 1941. But less than four months later in March of 1942 the Führer asked von Rundstedt to take over as *Oberbefehlshaber West* for the ailing Field Marshal von Witzleben.[11]

Von Rundstedt and his staff set about putting the western theater on an organized basis. His staff consisted of the usual Chief of Staff and Operations, Intelligence, Transportation, Land Defense, Artillery, Quartermaster, and Personnel sections, and eventually he made two additions.[12] He sent a liaison officer (*Deutscher General in Vichy*) to Vichy after its zone was occupied by Wehrmacht forces in November 1942, and he created Panzer Group West in 1943 to oversee the training of German tank units stationed in the area.

Commander-in-Chief West also regularized procedures for transmitting its orders and instructions to the lower echelons.[13] Basic orders (*Grundlegende Befehle*) were to deal with the general, overall situation in the West. Special instructions (*Sonderanordnungen*) were to apply to concerns within the area, such as communications, reporting and supply procedures, cooperation with flying units, and so on. Specific orders (*Einzelbefehle*) were to be issued from time to time for limited matters, and more informal explanations, rather than orders sent out by *Ob West*, were to be called basic remarks (*Grundlegende Bemerkungen*).

Basic Order No. 1 of *Ob West*, entitled "Raising Combat Strength and Combat Preparedness," pinpointed what von Rundstedt considered to be the key problem in the West: the critical manpower situation. The gist of the order is made clear in the initial paragraph:

The small number of Army, Navy, and Air Force units remaining at our disposal in the West and their lack of equipment requires that absolutely every means possible be used in order to raise their combat strength and preparedness.[14]

The order went on to offer suggestions for raising the number of combat troops and also for improving combat proficiency in the area. Suggestions included using every German soldier and worker available to form improvised units (*Alarmeinheiten*), scheduling numerous war game exercises, and obtaining volunteer workers from nearby areas to free Wehrmacht troops from construction duties. Other orders from *Ob West* several weeks later spelled out special training measures for use in coastal defense duties and designated operational tasks for German divisions returning from the East, even though they were primarily to be rehabilitated.[15]

Also alert regulations were established by which *Ob West* was to transmit the signal "Extreme Danger" or "Alarm Stage I" (*Alarmstufe I*) to subordinate commands if an Allied attack were considered possible.[16] But if the situation became more critical, "Alarm Stage II" (*Alarmstufe II*) which instructed all formations in the entire area to assume a defense-ready posture, was to be declared. Other "standing operating procedures" included regulations for handling internal disorders by indigenous nationals, for dealing with espionage activities, and for assuming full control of the railway lines in case of an emergency.[17]

Commander-in-Chief West did not confine his activities, of course, to the standardizing of procedures. He also decided in May 1942 to reorganize the theater on a different basis than before. During the first year and a half of the occupation the Wehrmacht had assigned two armies—the Fifteenth and the Seventh—plus two more German divisions in the Netherlands to guard the Channel and Atlantic coasts. In the May reorganization von Rundstedt added a third army—the First—to the coastal defense set up.[18] First Army, which had maintained security in the interior of France north of the Vichy zone, was replaced by the LXXXIII Army Corps, which was renamed Army Task Force Felber (*Armeegruppe Felber*).[19]

Although the addition of First Army along the coast reduced in size the area which each army had to protect, the change did not signify any increase in the number of Wehrmacht forces assigned to von Rundstedt. In fact, the reorganization was undertaken originally to disguise from the Western Allies the relative paucity of German forces in the West.[20] What actually happened was that First Army assumed command over an army corps that had previously been under the control of Seventh Army, while Seventh Army took over an army corps that had been under Fifteenth Army.[21] The two corps continued to control the same area as before—the LXXX Corps the Bay of Biscay area, the LXXXIV Corps the Cotentin Peninsula and the Bay of the Seine region. The only difference was that these corps now had been placed under different armies. The headquarters of First and Seventh Armies had moved, but not the troops themselves. Nevertheless, the arrangement instituted by von Rundstedt did fit in well with Germany's defensive posture that was beginning to emerge, so well that it continued to function until the D-Day invasion.

The main area of concern for the Germans was that of Fifteenth Army. Since this 440-mile stretch of Channel coastline lay closest to England, it was considered the most logical place for a large-scale Anglo-American attack. As the Germans well realized, the area was within range of Allied fighter aircraft based in the British Isles, and it also provided the shortest route for British and United States forces to reach Germany and the industrially strategic Ruhr area.[22] In addition, the Channel sector contained numerous major and secondary harbors, and all of them could serve as supply *entrepôts* for an Allied attempt to establish a bridgehead on the continent. Thus, Wehrmacht staff officers, like their British and American counterparts, quickly perceived the importance of the Channel area as a possible invasion route and made their plans accordingly.

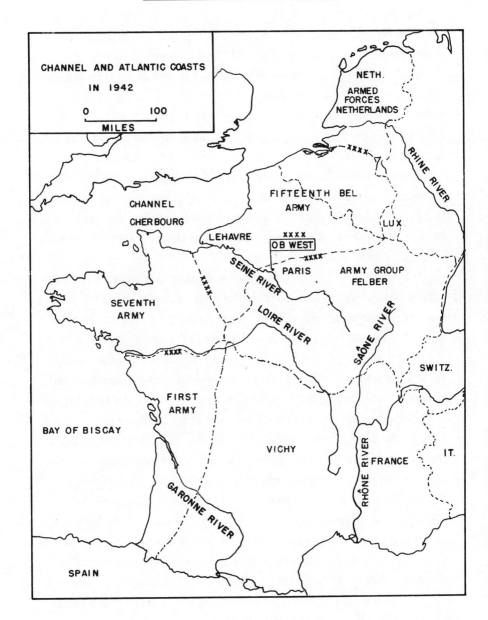

Fig. 2.1 Channel and Atlantic Coast, 1942

This coastal sector always received more attention than any other region in the West. Throughout 1942, for instance, Fifteenth Army normally had twelve combat divisions stationed in its area, which was more than in any other sector.[23] In terms of artillery emplacements, Fifteenth Army also did quite well. On July 6, 1942, it listed ninety-two permanent coastal batteries in its inventory, or over 40 percent of the batteries in the entire theater.[24] Moreover, the large offensive guns that had been constructed to strike the English coast at the time of "Sea Lion" were also located in the region. In short, the Fifteenth Army area contained proportionately more and better troops, more artillery pieces, and more defensive strongpoints than any other sector in the West.

Fifteenth Army also assumed command authority over the Dutch coastal region in case that area were in danger of attack, but under normal circumstances the Commander of the Armed Forces in the Netherlands was in charge. The Dutch coast appealed to the Western Allies as a suitable landing place for a number of reasons.[25] In 1942 it was defended by two or at most three divisions. It had several major harbors and controlled the estuary of the Scheldt in front of Antwerp. It also provided a short route to the Ruhr area. Still, a number of factors militated against an Allied attack aimed at the Netherlands: its many large cities, its numerous dikes and canals that served as natural barriers to any rapid advance, and its distance from the English coast, all of which could impair any Anglo-American attempt to sustain an attack logistically. This does not mean that the Germans were unconcerned about the Dutch coast, and they managed to build up the defenses in the Netherlands to the point that by 1944 it was generally well defended.[26]

The area under Seventh Army control had been reduced by the coastal reorganization in May, but it was still responsible for more than 900 miles of coastline, from the Bay of the Seine in Normandy around the vulnerable Cotentin and Brittany peninsulas to the mouth of the Loire River. The most threatened areas, besides the major harbor at Cherbourg, were the submarine bases at Brest, Lorient, and St. Nazaire. These bases and those at La Pallice and Bordeaux in the First Army sector had to be protected at all costs if Germany's U-boat war against Allied shipping in the Atlantic was to continue. Therefore, the Germans concentrated the bulk of their heavy construction (under the direction of Organization Todt) as well as their combat troops at these points.

The other coastal zones in the Seventh Army sector were only lightly defended. Albert Benary's unit history of the 257th Infantry Division, for example, indicates that that portion of the Brittany Peninsula which was under the division's control in 1942 was much too extensive to be defended with the troops at hand, and the division commander tried to deploy combat teams (*Kampfgruppen*) in key places to overcome the difficulty.[27] This meant that some areas were under no observation for hours at a time, and the 257th had only one battalion of mobile reserves who were to be transported if necessary in French buses driven by French civilians! But because the entire area was located a considerable distance from the main Allied source of supply in England, it was deemed more susceptible to raids or surprise attacks than it was to a big operation, a theory which the Germans felt was confirmed by the St. Nazaire raid in March. The Germans therefore continued to concentrate their efforts on the harbor areas and only slowly began to fill in the coastal regions in between.

In one other region under Seventh Army control the Armed Forces High Command anticipated a possible Anglo-American landing: the British Channel Islands of Guernsey, Jersey, Alderney, and Sark.[28] The islands were only nominally under Seventh Army's jurisdiction, for they were, in effect, Hitler's "pet project" in the West. They held a special fascination for the Nazi dictator, who was convinced that the British would attempt to get their islands back either for prestige purposes or as a base from which to launch an operation against the continent.

On October 20, 1941, the Führer ordered that "the Channel Islands are to be consolidated into an unassailable fortress through various and unremitting efforts."[29] As a result, not only did they become the most heavily defended area in the West, but they also received attention vastly out of proportion to their true worth. They were eventually defended by 30,000 to 35,000 well-trained troops attached to the 319th Division, and this number was more than twice the normal complement of a German infantry division. The thirty-one permanent artillery batteries were supported by other guns of lesser caliber, extensive flak guns, searchlights, and other up-to-date equipment. The artillery pieces themselves, most of which could fire at a rapid rate and which had a 360 degree turning capacity, ranged in caliber from the deadly 88s to 30.5 centimeter guns. The actual defensive positions were well planned to cover the most vulnerable sectors and were constructed for all-around defense.

It is understandable in these circumstances that the German commanders in the West eyed the Channel Islands as a source of possible reinforcements during critical periods, but most of their requests were denied.[30] It is also understandable that the Allies never expended the effort to attack these island fortresses in force, and they held out until the end of the war.[31]

The final 650-mile stretch of the French Atlantic coast, from the Loire River to the Spanish border, which had been turned over to the First Army in May, was lightly held by five divisions, and defense construction centered around La Rochelle and on both sides of the Gironde estuary that leads to Bordeaux.[32] Like the Seventh Army sector, the Wehrmacht expected little more than raids along this coast since it was a long way from Britain and marked by extreme tidal variations. And there was also the further question as to what the Allies would gain from a landing attempt in the area. It might arouse some support on the part of the French populace or tie down some German forces that could be used elsewhere. But an operation into southwestern France would not move American and British units any closer to the German homeland. The First Army continued to guard its area against an Allied attack, and the building of defensive fortifications proceeded, but never on the same scale as in the more endangered sectors.

Ob West realized that the setting up of coastal defense zones was insufficient in itself, and he took further steps to insure that mobile reserves could be utilized as a deterrent to any possible Allied invasion of Western Europe. This use of motorized reinforcements to bolster the admittedly weaker coastal units proved to be a cardinal feature of Commander-in-Chief West's defensive thinking throughout the German occupation.

Even before von Rundstedt had taken over as theater commander, German staff officers in October 1941 had outlined five contingency plans for possible implementation in the theater. Three of the plans were to counter any British undertaking against the Channel coast, Brittany, or the Bordeaux area. The fourth and fifth plans were a continuation of operations into Spain ("Isabella") and the occupation of Vichy France ("Attila") The plans merely stipulated that certain units, most of which would be mobile infantry formations held in reserve some distance from the coast, were to be sent into the areas under attack.[33]

During 1942 staff officers instituted a number of changes in the existing plans. Rather than being specified by area, they redesignated the various operations as *"Aufmarschbewegung"* with an appropriate number code for each.[34] They also eventually expanded the number of contingencies from five to nine, including two operations designed to help protect the Netherlands, two for the Channel coast, and one each for Normandy, Brittany, the French Atlantic coast, Vichy France, and the Iberian Peninsula.

The Germans then refined and spelled out each contingency in great detail.[35] They made preparations to move the units by road or rail, depending on the distance and the type of equipment, to areas under attack. They also worked out landing priorities and timetables for the most effective use of the railway network, and they selected the routes and mapped out rest and refueling stations for the panzer formations. They further provided road commanders and traffic controllers for all major roads near the coast and charted bypasses around the larger towns to avoid possible highway bottlenecks. In short, German forces in reserve were to be moved as quickly and decisively as possible to counter any Allied assault.

The establishment of general guidelines and the reorganization of the western theater on a defensive basis were obviously necessary first steps to help insure Germany's continued presence in the area. But even more significant from the German point of view was the amount of progress they hoped to realize during 1942 in terms of construction, armaments, and personnel.

Führer Directive No. 40 had stated that those sectors most in danger of enemy attack were to receive first priority in the building of defenses, and German planners later decided that those areas most threatened were the major harbors, the U-boat bases, and the mouths of the large rivers.[36] In some instances considerable construction had already been undertaken to protect these places from enemy attack, but they were now to be prepared for all-around defenses from both the sea and the landward sides. Again in accordance with Directive No. 40, each of these regions, called defense areas (*Verteidigungsbereiche*) or fortress areas (*Festungsbereiche*) were to be self-contained entities, dependent on mobile reserves only in extreme cases, and designed, on the whole, to take care of themselves. Within the fortress areas and also between them were to be located strongpoint groups (*Stützpunktgruppen*), which were to consist of a company or a battalion of troops; individual strongpoints (*Stützpunkte*) with up to a company in strength and possessing heavy infantry weapons and all-around protection from attack; and resistance points (*Widerstandsnester*) usually having less than a platoon and including machine guns and occasionally antitank guns among their armaments.

This type of defensive thinking was to prevail in the West until 1944; that is, keep the enemy out of the major ports and away from the submarine bases in particular and also, when possible, to try and fill in the rest of the Atlantic Wall framework.[37] Commander-in-Chief West went further and designated the exact defense of fortress areas (the terms were used interchangeably) on July 8, 1942.[38] These included Den Helder, Ijmuiden, the Hook of Holland, and Vlissingen, at the entrance to the Scheldt River, in the Netherlands; Dunkirk, Calais, Boulogne, Le Havre, Cherbourg, and St. Malo along the Channel coast; and the harbors at Brest, Lorient, St. Nazaire, La Rochelle (with the U-boat pens at nearby La Pallice), and Royan at the mouth of the Gironde along France's Atlantic coastline.

Construction on some of the defense areas as well as on a portion of the strongpoints caused the builders little difficulty; how to proceed on them was obvious. In other instances this was not the case. They were generally erected by concentrating initially on the area inside the strongpoint and then on the area around it. When necessary, local commanders ascertained the most advantageous sites for artillery and other gun emplacements. Then engineers and Organization Todt workers constructed the positions and surrounded them with trenches, earthworks, and other field-type hindrances. This step was followed by the building of quarters for the troops and supply depots either inside or outside the strongpoints, depending on the situation. Finally, engineers and laborers completed the outer defenses and made sure that the adjacent areas which could not be occupied by soldiers were at least kept under surveillance with searchlights and protected by the use of land mines.[39]

The Germans, using these methods, did realize some progress in heavy construction during the year. The amount of concrete poured by Organization Todt in Western Europe, for instance, nearly trebled between January 1942, and July, from approximately 100,000 to 300,000 cubic meters per month.[40] Moreover, the number of coastal artillery batteries listed as ready for firing rose from ninety-two in July 1941 to 208 one year later. German officials hoped to do even better in the months ahead.[41]

Not all of the emphasis was placed on large construction projects. In fact, the erection of reinforced field and field-type fortifications received even more attention.[42] German engineering officials categorized these types of installations according to the thickness of their protective walls and the material out of which they were built. A defensive barrier constructed out of reinforced concrete or of wood covered with earth and over eleven inches thick was considered a "field-type" fortification. When the walls or the roof reached three feet, three inches in thickness, the Germans defined it as a "reinforced field" position. These types of installations could be put to any use—machine-gun nests, searchlights batteries, munitions bunkers, antitank embankments, and they came to form the bulk of the defensive positions in the West.

The fortifications being erected as well as those being improved varied greatly in size and configuration, and so did the artillery pieces which were placed in them.[43] They ranged in caliber from 75 millimeters to the superheavy 16-inch guns in the Calais area, and they also consisted of numerous different types of guns, including even captured field pieces. But the basic light artillery weapons in the theater were the 105-mm gun and the 105-mm howitzer. Both of them had a maximum rate of fire of ten to fifteen rounds per minute, and with a maximum range of 17,000 yards, while that of the howitzer was 13,000. Among the medium artillery the 150-millimeter gun was most prevalent. Many of them could reach a target 24,000 yards away, although their rate of fire was only 3 rounds per minute, much less than that of the 105-mm gun. The most effective artillery pieces was the highly accurate 88-mm gun. Originally developed as an antiaircraft weapon, the Germans had found as early as 1937 that it could be adapted to land combat. With a high muzzle velocity, a range of 16,200 yards, and a firing rate of fifteen to twenty rounds per minute, it also came to be employed for coastal defense purposes.

The batteries in which the 88s and other artillery weapons were emplaced did not conform to any particular pattern. The usual three-or-four-gun layout might resemble a trapezoid or an arc or a straight or staggered line, depending on the situation. Most of the guns

were not under cover and in the open, but they were normally camouflaged and supported by other smaller weapons, such as light
flak or machine guns. Even though it has not been possible to ascertain the exact number of artillery pieces in the area in 1942, by
October 19 the Germans had 225 army and naval batteries among
their coastal arsenal.[44] If one counts 3½ guns per battery, there
were approximately 790 coastal artillery weapons emplaced in the
West by this time, and this figure does not include the field artillery
organic to the divisions (usually thirty-six pieces) or the Luftwaffe
flak. If one considers that it usually took laborers three months of
uninterrupted work to construct a battery site, then the amount of
construction obviously reached sizable proportions.

The manpower situation in the western theater in 1942 was
also quite favorable, at least on paper. The number of German
army divisions increased from twenty-four in April to thirty-five in
August and reached 43 in December.[45] Part of the rise can be attributed to Germany's fear of a Western Allied operation against
the continent in the summer, a fear justified by the Dieppe Raid in
August.

These figures are also deceptive from several other standpoints.
For one thing, many of the best infantry divisions and smaller units
which were deployed along the coast were shuttled east when the
situation on the Soviet front became critical toward the end of the
year. To be sure, they were of great help while in the West, but their
replacements were often of lesser quality and called "static"
(*bodenständig*) divisions.[46] The "static" division represented a new
concept in German planning in that they were set up specifically to
handle coastal defense duties. In reality, however, they reflected
Germany's growing problems, since they were immobile, incapable
of offensive operations, and consisted mainly of raw recruits or
inexperienced personnel. These divisions became an increasingly
prominent feature in the western landscape.

Another reason why the increase in divisions is misleading is
that a number of the formations, especially panzer divisions, only

remained stationed in the West long enough to prepare for further eastern combat. A situation report from von Rundstedt to the Army Chief of Staff in October makes clear the correlation between East and West.[47] The report stressed that while Commander-in-Chief West was responsible for defending the western flank and for building up the Atlantic Wall defenses he had other duties, which included the replenishment of worn-out eastern divisions, the exchange of western divisions for depleted eastern ones, and the removal of specific German personnel from the West to be utilized as cadres in forming up new units. And western commanders were to assist further by conducting training courses of all types for officers and noncommissioned soldiers. Taken as a whole, von Rundstedt therefore recognized that the eastern front continued to cast a large shadow on developments in the West.

At the same time that the Germans set about planning, building, manning, and in general attempting to piece together an Atlantic Wall strategy, the Western Allies were developing plans of their own. British and American leaders decided not to launch a cross-Channel attack in 1942, but they still felt they could keep the Wehrmacht off balance and assist their Soviet ally at the same time. In part they hoped to do this by an invasion of Northwest Africa. But they also thought it would be helpful to conduct a series of raids against Western Europe. For the Allies the raids demonstrated the myriad of difficulties involved in undertaking an amphibious operation. For the Germans they served to strengthen several misconceptions of Allied strategy. Hitler and his western commanders became more convinced than ever during the course of 1942 that the initial U.S.-British thrust would be designed to secure a major port and that the invasion would be directed against the Channel coast. Still the various raids did not prove altogether negative in relation to the German war effort. They did make it apparent to the Führer how susceptible the West was to attack and hence demonstrated the need to intensify the defensive effort in the theater.

With the exception that almost all of the raids were of the hit-and-run variety, they bore little resemblance to each other and did not conform to any recognizable pattern. The first British foray was in 1942 at the end of February. It was directed against a German air force radar station on Cap d'Antifer north of Le Havre.[48] In this operation sixty English airborne troops parachuted at night on the landward side of the radar complex, overran it, destroyed or captured the equipment, and then withdrew at 4 a.m. to British ships lying offshore.

The British directed a more extensive raid against the German naval base at St. Nazaire on March 28.[49] The Germans realized that the port of St. Nazaire, which is located at the mouth of the Loire River, was a high-priority target for the British, for it contained seven submarine pens and a large dry-dock, called *Normandie* Dock, which was the only berth along the Atlantic capable of holding a large battleship. (The only regular battleship still left in the German inventory was the *Tirpitz*, which had only recently escaped up the French coast to Norway.) The Wehrmacht had made certain that St. Nazaire, like all U-boat bases, was well defended. They had stationed approximately 6,000 troops in the area, and had covered the approaches with numerous artillery batteries and large and small antiaircraft guns, which could be trained against targets approaching from the sea. Searchlights also dotted the area, and several harbor defense boats and a guardship, which was anchored near the entrance to the harbor for alert purposes, were well armed with close-range weapons.

Although a British air bombardment failed to materialize on the night of the raid, mainly because of inclement weather, more than 600 commandos and naval specialists managed to penetrate the formidable St. Nazaire defenses between two and four o'clock and frontally attack this important submarine strongpoint. The results were mixed. The British failed to reach the submarine pens, and they were likewise unable to blow up the lock gates through which the U-boats had to pass to reach the open sea. But the raid-

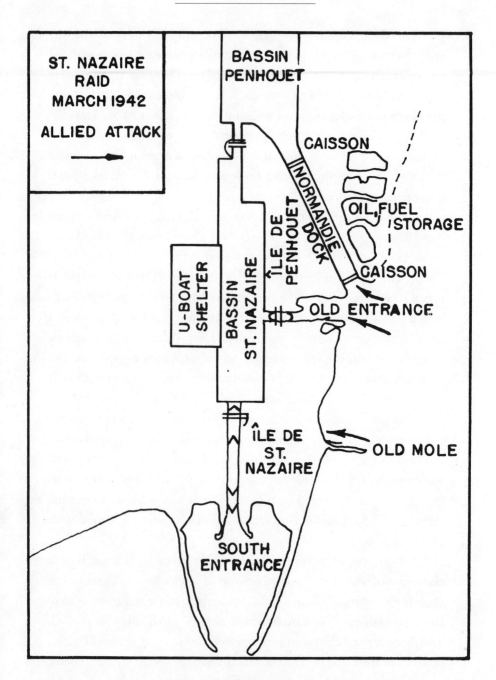

Fig. 2.2 St. Nazaire Harbor, 1942

ers were able to ram an expendable destroyer, H.M.S. *Campbeltown*, into the main gate of the *Normandie* Dock where the ship remained lodged until the next morning. At 11:35, twenty-four 400-pound depth charges armed with delay fuses went off, destroying the entire dock facility.[50] The Germans were never able to effect a satisfactory repair, and it remained inoperative throughout the war.

Losses in personnel were high for both sides. Captain Robert Ryder, the head of the British expedition, lists the total force at 630 men. Of these, 144 were killed or missing, 215 became prisoners of war, and 271 returned to England.[51] German military casualties were sixty-seven dead and 136 wounded.[52]

Both the British and the Germans claimed some degree of success. The British felt that rendering the *Normandie* Dock unusable ended the possibility of the *Tirpitz* breaking out into the Atlantic, attacking Allied shipping, and then returning to St. Nazaire. More important from the German standpoint, the entrances and exits to the U-boat area as well as the submarine bunkers themselves were still intact, and in addition, the British had suffered heavy losses and no German reinforcements had been needed.

But Hitler and some of the Wehrmacht staff officers were disconcerted about the St. Nazaire raid, for the German forces in the area at the time of the raid were already in a state of alert for a possible Allied attack. An order from Hitler on March 23, which cited numerous reports from undercover agents, stressed that this portion of the coast was in special danger.[53] He then commanded that all available reserves, in this case a panzer division and part of an airborne unit, were to move immediately into the sector west of a line between Caen and St. Nazaire. Although the units did not arrive in the area until after the raid, they would have been available for any large-scale British operation.

Moreover, seven days before the raid, on March 21, naval officers, as a result of a recent inspection trip, had pointed out to their subordinate commanders that the defenses for the submarine bases against sneak attacks were not sufficient. The report stated: "Destruction of the U-boat strongpoints, even their occupation for a short time, is truly unbearable. Above all, strongpoints Brest, Lorient, St. Nazaire, and La Pallice must remain closed off from any enemy surprise attack."[54] Yet, in spite of the increased state of readiness, in spite of the emphasis placed on protecting the U-boat harbors, the British had been able to force their way through the German defenses and cause considerable damage.

The Führer asked the Naval High Command to explain why the enemy had been able to do as much damage as it did, and he seemed satisfied when the navy said that remedial measures were being instituted in the form of increased sea reconnaissance and more off-shore patrol boats.[55] But the majority of the German military leaders, though irritated, did not seem unduly alarmed. Commander-in-Chief West's conclusion that "the enemy…had suffered a heavy defeat" (*schwere Niederlage*) seemed to reflect the thinking of the other commanders in the area.[56]

Nothing that occurred throughout the spring and summer months of 1942 shook the confidence of the Wehrmacht leaders that they could deal with any landing maneuver the Western Allies might attempt. For example, German naval craft intercepted a British landing party south of Boulogne during the night of April 21-22 and forced it to turn back before it was able to land.[57] Another small British party did effect a landing in the same vicinity of June 4, but the German defenders drove it off with little difficulty.[58]

What was significant from the German point of view was that the Wehrmacht was able to pursue its objectives on the eastern front without diverting any appreciable number of troops to the West.[59] This meant, in effect, that three-fourths of all German combat troops were engaged against the Red Army in 1942. To be sure, Armed Forces High Command did send four additional panzer divisions and one armored brigade to the western theater during the critical summer months, when an Anglo-American attack was considered most likely. But even though these armored formations were needed to help protect Germany's western flank, they were equally in need of rest and refitting after having suffered heavy losses in the Russian campaign.[60]

The Allied raids therefore failed to reduce the pressure on the Soviet Union. They did, however, tie down a portion of the German forces in Western Europe to guard against hit-and-run attacks of the St. Nazaire variety. They also accomplished one other objective: they kept German officials guessing. These lesser forays and Allied air activity assisted in keeping the German forces along the coast on edge. As a result, local commanders and their troops after a while developed what might be called an "invasion syndrome." It is a malady common to all, and especially inexperienced, military personnel who spend long periods of time on alert, waiting, anticipating, but never experiencing a full-scale attack. The soldiers saw defensive fortifications being built and took part in training and coastal exercises for the expressed purpose of repelling an enemy invasion. They reasoned it must come soon, and within this atmosphere tensions mounted throughout the summer.

Directives and orders from higher headquarters helped reinforce this feeling of expectancy. Periodic naval and army reports pointed out the most favorable times during the year for enemy amphibious landings.[61] Other orders in April stressed that "the British are determined and able to attack our extensive coastline more frequently and on a larger scale than heretofore," that "England has the capability for a large-scale operation against Europe—25–30 divisions," and that "public opinion in England is exerting pressure" for a landing of some type.[62] During the summer German intelligence sources noted a considerable number of landing craft being assembled along England's southern shores. Hitler on July 9 indicated that "Great Britain, under pressure from Russia, will stage a large-scale invasion, probably in the area of Ob West."[63] The Nazi leader went on to name those regions especially threatened—the Channel coast and Normandy—followed in priority by the southern part of the Netherlands and Brittany. He then designated that additional units be sent to the West and that local precautions should be instituted. The Führer concluded, "In the event of an enemy landing I personally will proceed to the West and assume charge of the operations from there." About a month later, however, Hitler felt that the time for a major attack had passed.[64]

Still within this general atmosphere of anticipation a small British raid took place against the eastern coast of the Cotentin Peninsula on August 14.[65] It was followed on the 19th by the Dieppe Raid, the most extensive Allied raid in 1942. In this action more than 6,000 Allied troops, most of them Canadians, attacked the French coast in five places near and in front of the seaside town of Dieppe during the pre-dawn hours.[66] The German forces in the area, part of the 302nd Infantry Division, were on alert and reacted promptly to the assault. The Allies succeeded only in destroying or neutralizing several German artillery batteries on the extreme flanks. In all other instances, including the main landing against the beaches leading to the town, the Wehrmacht forces unleashed a barrage of devastating small arms and artillery fire and quickly threw back the attackers. The Allied use of medium-sized Churchill tanks in particular proved to be a disaster, since the tanks never got off the beaches. The Canadian, British, and French forces were forced to begin withdrawing at 11 a.m., and by the afternoon it was clear that the landing attempt had been repulsed. The Western powers listed 3,610 out of 6,100 men as dead, missing, wounded, or prisoners of war. The Germans suffered only 591 casualties.[67]

The problem for the Germans after the attack was to determine its actual nature. Was it a raid or a diversionary attack or an attempt to establish a small, permanent bridgehead? Or was it rather the first step in an extensive, large-scale invasion? German officers analyzed the Dieppe experience in painstaking detail to find the answer. There were a number of imponderables. Why would the Allies use 6,000 troops and thirty modern tanks for a mere raid? Why attack a harbor in force, even a secondary harbor like Dieppe, unless one intended to stay for a while? Why were additional British troop transports being loaded in Portsmouth on the English coast

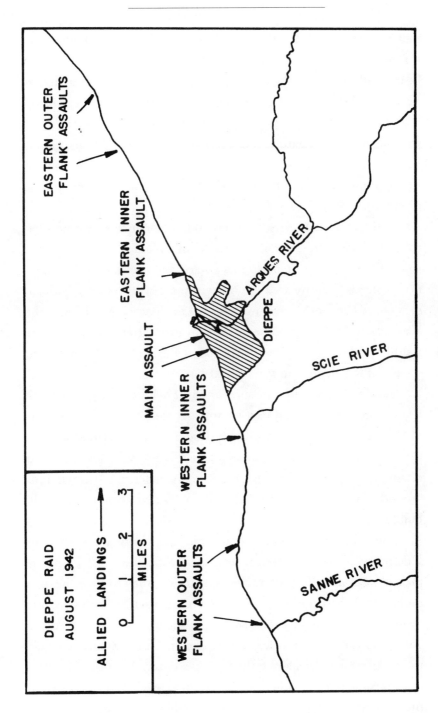

Fig. 2.3. Dieppe Raid, August 1942

DIEPPE RAID
AUGUST 1942

ALLIED LANDINGS →

0   1   2   3
MILES

EASTERN OUTER
FLANK ASSAULTS

EASTERN INNER
FLANK ASSAULT

MAIN ASSAULT

WESTERN INNER
FLANK ASSAULTS

WESTERN OUTER
FLANK ASSAULTS

ARQUES RIVER

DIEPPE

SCIE RIVER

SANNE RIVER

that same morning? On the other hand, an Allied battle plan found on the body of one of the attackers, a dead major on the Dieppe beach, indicated that the operation was a raid in force designed to occupy and destroy military objectives in and around Dieppe and then to withdraw around 3:30 in the afternoon. Still, a majority of the German investigators, including von Rundstedt and his Chief-of-Staff at the time, General Kurt Zeitzler, were of the opinion that Dieppe was more than a raid, that it was the beginning of a possible invasion.[68]

In the end the Germans accepted the evidence which pointed toward a major attack rather than taking Allied intentions at face value. One might contend in this regard that the state of anticipation which had permeated the western theater prior to the raid had influenced the Germans as much as the evidence at hand. Since the Wehrmacht leadership expected an invasion attempt, the Dieppe Raid became just that, the prelude to a full-scale Allied attack, in spite of the evidence to the contrary.

Two further conclusions surrounding the Dieppe Raid are worth noting. Since the operation was aimed at the port city of Dieppe, Hitler and other German military leaders felt confirmed in their previous belief that any future Allied landing would be directed at seizing an important harbor. Accordingly, defensive fortifications around major ports continued to be accorded a high priority in building plans.

The other conclusion is that while the Germans pointed to Dieppe as a victory, which it was, and while the coastal defense procedures, including the movement of reserves toward the area under attack, had worked adequately, German staff officers became more convinced than ever that any future attempt by the British and Americans to establish a second front in western Europe would most likely take place along the Channel coast. As in the case of a great deal of military thinking, the German analysts read more into the victory at Dieppe than was warranted by the facts.

The Allies did not completely abandon their raiding activities after the Dieppe operation. British military personnel conducted at least two more raids before the end of the year. In one of them British commandos on October 4 captured several German engineering troops during a morning fog on the Channel island of Sark.[69] In the other, English sabotage teams damaged fifteen German naval vessels with magnetic mines in the Bordeaux harbor on December 8.[70] These raids were no doubt irritating, but they were of little significance. By this time the Germans had become preoccupied with other matters in the West, including an ambitious building program.

This building program had been instituted by Hitler even prior to the Dieppe Raid, for he was well aware of growing British-U.S. military strength. On at least two occasions during the first half of August he talked about the western situation at some length. On August 2, he discussed chiefly what type of large operation the Western powers would someday conduct against the coast, and he emphasized the need for strong defenses, especially in light of the difficulty of moving mobile reserves fast enough into areas under attack.[71]

Hitler's discussion of matters with Army engineers in the West on August 13 was more specific and more instructive.[72] He started by expressing his desire to avoid under all circumstances the establishment of a second front. "There is only one battle front [the Russian front]," he noted. "The other fronts can be defended only with slight strength [geringen Kräften]." Therefore, he said, he had decided to make the Atlantic and Channel coasts into an impenetrable fortress. Those areas which were to receive special attention were, first of all, U-boat bases; secondly, large ports; thirdly, secondary harbors; and fourthly, heavy artillery batteries.

Hitler went on to discuss a number of specific points. Most significant was his desire to have 15,000 permanent defensive positions constructed by the end of the spring of 1943. To reach this figure he calculated would require approximately twenty positions per kilometer along the entire length of the coast, although he regarded ten per kilometer as tolerable. The fortifications were to be manned by 300,000 combat troops, backed up by 150,000 reserves. With 450,000 to 500,000 men, the Führer considered that the Wall could be held.

Several weeks later the head of the army engineers in the West apportioned the 15,000 projected strongpoints among the various areas.[73] Ten to eleven thousand positions were to be divided equally between the Fifteenth and Seventh Armies along the Belgian and French coast north of the Loire. Fifteen hundred to two thousand fortifications each were to be erected along the less extensive Dutch coast and in the less endangered First Army sector in southwestern France. Planning, as always, was to be accomplished by the engineering staffs in conjunction with local tactical commanders, while the actual construction was to be handled by Organization Todt. Todt officials felt that they could complete only about 40 percent, or 6,000 of the required installations by May 1943, but the Germans hoped that this number would still make the Atlantic Wall into a formidable barrier, especially in key sectors.[74]

The importance which Hitler placed in the construction effort is well brought out in a high-level meeting he held toward the end of September 1942. At the conclusion of the three-hour session, the Nazi leader remarked, "At this time the Atlantic Wall is the most decisive factor that there is. If nothing happens during the next year in the West, the war is won."[75]

In summary, 1942 was a formative year in the Atlantic Wall concept. A defensive orientation had been established, general guidelines set down, a building program instituted. Even at this early stage, the Western Allies had tested the Wall, and it had generally withstood the tests. The Germans felt they could look forward again to steady, if unspectacular, progress in the year ahead. But this picture was upset toward the end of 1942 by the disaster at Stalingrad and by the invasion of North Africa. These two events also caused a number of reverberations throughout the western theater.

Chapter 3

The Wall Extends

The Anglo-American landing in northwest Africa on November 8, 1942, obviously affected both sides. It altered Allied strategy in the West, for the commitment of men and materiel to the Mediterranean area made a full-scale invasion of Western Europe impossible in 1943.[1] But the African landing also had important consequences for the Germans with regard to the West. With the British Eighth Army pushing west from El Alamein, the Italian army in the process of deteriorating, and United States, British, and other Allied forces moving east toward Tunisia, Germany's southern flank was no longer secure. Wehrmacht leaders did not expect, for the moment, to prevent the Allies from taking over most of French-controlled Africa, which was sparsely held by Vichy forces, but they did feel obliged to strengthen their defensive posture in southern Europe. The Führer entrusted part of this task to *Ob West*. As a result, von Rundstedt was forced to divert part of his attention away from building up Germany's defensive posture along the Channel and Atlantic coast. To be sure, the erection of the Atlantic Wall continued, but at a slackened pace, and a great deal of activity in the West became concentrated in the heretofore neglected southern portion of the theater.

The activity took the form of occupying in November, with Italian assistance, the area of southeastern France, which had been under Vichy control. This was followed by an attempt on the part of the Germans and the Italians to strengthen the defensive posture in the sector. At the same time plans were revived to deal with the renewed threat to neutral Spain. Adding to these difficulties, German forces reluctantly took over Italy's zone in France east of the Rhône River, when the Italians surrendered in September 1943. The Atlantic Wall, once thought to stretch from the Frisian Islands to the Pyrenees frontier, had now been extended to include the 400-mile French Mediterranean coastline as well.

The German takeover of Unoccupied France was not a spur-of-the-moment decision. Hitler, it will be remembered, had considered occupying the Vichy zone as early as the end of 1940. Plans had been formalized at that time, and Wehrmacht formations had been held in reserve for Operation "Attila" throughout the course of 1941. By 1942, however, the western commander felt he lacked sufficient forces to occupy the rest of France.[2] The Führer himself acknowledged this situation in a directive issued on May 29.[3] In it he emphasized at least one major change in German military thinking toward France.

The change was that "because of the continual shifting of our forces in the west, and the consequent changes in the readiness for battle of our formations there," the operations to occupy the Vichy sector, now renamed "Anton," could only be carried out on an improvised basis. "Improvised" in this case meant that the German divisions which still remained in the West had other tasks to perform, such as protecting the Atlantic and Channel coasts from a British attack, and some lead time would be required to bring the formations into positions to execute "Anton." Wehrmacht planners, faced with this shortage of troops, decided to bring Italian formations into the scheme for the first time. Thus, the situation was reversed from previous occasions. The Germans were asking the Italians for help rather than the other way around. But, as before, planning for "Anton" continued to exemplify the problems which the Axis partners had in coordinating a common strategy.

Hitler's Directive No. 42 also made clear that although the situation had changed, the conditions for executing "Anton" and the objectives of the operation remained the same as they had in the past; that is, if "the situation in Unoccupied France, or in the French possessions in North Africa" so required, German forces were "to break the power of resistance in Unoccupied France and to occupy the country."

A final section of the directive stipulated that the high commands of the various services were to submit plans by June 10 for carrying out the occupation. Not until the middle of July, however, did a detailed plan for "Anton" appear.[4] According to this plan Wehrmacht staff officers calculated it would take at least ten days to prepare "Anton" for execution. The actual operation was to be a limited one in which four mobile divisions were to cross over the Vichy frontier from the north and the west and move rapidly toward a line running from Geneva through Lyons and then southwest to Toulouse. Four additional mobile divisions were to remain in reserve, and the Military Commander in France was to detach small, temporarily mobile units of reserve troops (*Landesschützen-Einheiten*) to occupy such important areas as military posts, supply points, munitions dumps, and airfields bypassed in the initial onrush. A special army combat team was to make a sudden attack on the town of Vichy and take over the governmental apparatus. The Luftwaffe, for its part, was to support the army formations and to overpower the small French air force which the Germans had allowed to continue after 1940.

Wehrmacht manpower problems become quite evident, however, when one realizes that the key element in the entire operation was not the German forces, but the Italian military units which

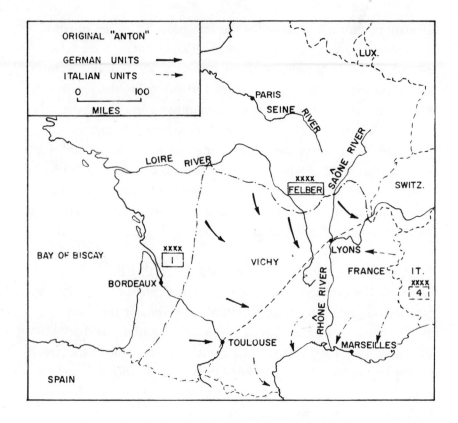

Fig. 3.1. Original "Anton"

were scheduled to take part. The Italians were to occupy the south-eastern half of the Vichy sector, which included the entire French Mediterranean coast as well as the island of Corsica, while the Germans took over the northwestern part. In addition to subsequent occupation duties for the Italian army, the Italian navy was to prevent the French home fleet and any commercial vessels from leaving port.

This type of thinking did not prevail for long, and by the end of October plans for "Anton" had changed considerably.[5] The warning time felt necessary to implement the operation remained ten days, but in most other respects the plan for taking over Unoccu-

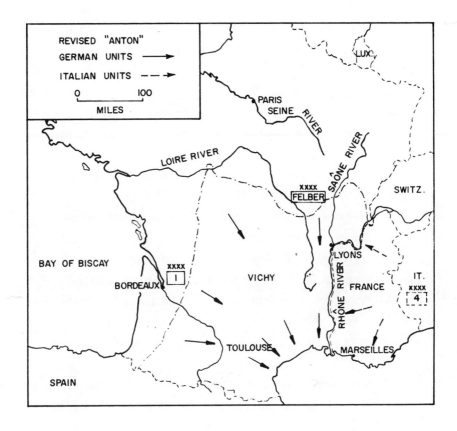

Fig. 3.2. Revised "Anton"

pied France was quite different. In particular, the role of the Italian military had been diminished from what it had been before. It is not clear whether the Italians insisted that their participation in "Anton" be reduced, or whether the Germans insisted they should be given at least part of the strategically significant Mediterranean coast. In any event, German forces were now to take over all of Vichy France west of and including the Rhône River valley, while the Italians were to occupy the area east of the Rhône. In other words, instead of dividing Vichy along a line running northeast by southwest, the Axis powers had decided to partition Unoccupied France on a more logical east-west basis.

The revised scheme for "Anton" took into account at least a portion of the original plan. German formations still were to push rapidly into the Vichy zone followed by occupation forces to take over key places in the rear. But instead of stopping at Toulouse and Lyons, the fast units were to press on to the Mediterranean coast. In the meantime the Italians were to move into the Vichy sector from the east. The initial phase of the operation was named "Anton I," and the second phase, which was to extend German control to the coast, was called "Anton II."

By this time, the fall of 1942, Hitler had decided to take over Vichy France at the first opportunity. The Allied landing in Northwest Africa, though a surprise to the Germans, merely gave him the pretext for eliminating the distinction between the heretofore Occupied zones.[6] An order sent out by First Army on November 7, or one day before Allied troops disembarked in Africa, clearly demonstrates Hitler's desire to have all of France occupied.[7]

> The Führer has determined, in order to prevent an enemy agitation and putsch attempts in the unoccupied zone, to take over…by blitz-type tactics the seat of government in Vichy and depot areas near the border. [Anton I]
>
> An occupation of the entire unoccupied area [Operation Anton II] can be joined to this undertaking [Anton I] according to the situation and in conformity with the "Anton" directive.

On the same day, November 7, the OKW War Diary noted that a British naval attack force with four or five divisions had left Gibraltar, probably headed for Tripoli or Benghazi on the Libyan coast. The War Diary continued: "On command from the Führer, orders have been given by *Ob West* for the eventual entrance of predetermined units into Unoccupied France (Operation 'Anton')."[8]

On the 8th, the operation began to be readied for implementation. Hitler heard of the North African invasion while traveling in his private train between Berlin and Munich, but he waited a few days to see what the reaction of the French Armistice Army in Africa would be before ordering "Anton's" execution.[9] By November 10, not only was French military resistance in Morocco and Algeria collapsing, but the Führer was also encountering a great deal of duplicity from supposedly loyal Vichy officials. He therefore ordered "Anton I and II" to begin the next morning at 7 a.m.[10]

The actual operation on the 11th went smoothly.[11] Three mobile divisions, the 17th Panzer, SS "Totenkopf," and 327th Infantry, which were under First Army, moved into the area from the west. Three others, the 10th Panzer, 328th Infantry, and 335th Infantry, under Army Task Force Felber, pushed forward from the north. By late afternoon all units reported good progress. Toulouse and Lyons were in German hands. Important supply points near the demarcation line and the border passes into Spain were being taken over by German occupation troops or border guards. The air force was assuming control of the major airfields, and the *Kriegsmarine* was covering the main Mediterranean harbors.[12] A possible reaction on the part of the French armistice army, or even by French civilians, had not materialized. That morning von Rundstedt himself delivered a note to Marshal Pétain at Vichy informing him that Unoccupied France was being occupied.[13] The first stage of the operation, or "Anton I," had been fulfilled.

The German forces, in part spurred on by fear of a possible Anglo-American landing attempt along the French Mediterranean coast, late that afternoon were ordered to carry out "Anton II."[14] Two of the three motorized formations under First Army, the 7th Panzer and the 327th Infantry Division, pressed on to reach the coast just before dawn the next day. The third division, SS "Totenkopf," instead of advancing toward the Mediterranean, moved across the northwest part of the Vichy sector to link up with the forces of Army Task Force Felber. Army Task Force Felber, like First Army, sent two divisions—in this case the 328th Infantry and the 10th Panzer—to occupy specific portions along the coast, while the 335th Infantry fanned out behind the lead divisions. By mid-morning of the 12th, the Mediterranean coast from the Spanish boundary to east of Marseilles was at least nominally under German control.

Meanwhile four Italian divisions had crossed over the French border and occupied without resistance the eastern sector of Vichy, thereby placing France's entire southeastern region in Axis hands.[15] Italian forces also occupied the northern portion of Corsica on November 11, but because of rough seas, they had to wait until the next day to take over the southern half of the island.

Even though the German and Italian forces had reached the coast, complete Axis control over the area was not accomplished until some days later. The Germans, because they lacked sufficient troops, had allowed French units, though under German supervision, to continue manning the artillery batteries at a number of places along the coast.[16] But Hitler's suspicions of Vichy officials did not abate, and on the 19th he ordered these French forces relieved of their duties and to withdraw into the interior. Later on the 27th all the French forces were disarmed as part of a small operation known as "Lila."[17]

The most important aspect of "Lila" was the French-held naval base at Toulon. What remained of the French fleet in Metropolitan France was stationed in the harbor area, and it included three battleships, seven cruisers, and numerous submarines and destroyers among the nearly ninety ships.[18] Because of reprisals and indignities the French had suffered at the hands of the British after the Battle of France, they made no effort during the November 11 occupation to escape to a neutral or Allied port. But they were not pro-German either. They were in fact neutral. Hitler and his advisers greatly desired to take over this "free zone in miniature." However, they came to realize increasingly that even if they captured the ships intact, which was doubtful, they could probably not make use of them. For one thing, it would take some time before German crews were sufficiently trained to sail the French vessels, and there was the further factor that heavy Allied bombing attacks against Toulon would undoubtedly limit any naval operations the Germans might wish to undertake. But they hoped at least to prevent the fleet from setting out for the recently occupied Allied harbors in North Africa.

With this goal in mind, the Germans readied "Lila" for implementation by the 27th. At four o'clock in the morning, four battle groups of the reinforced 7th Panzer Division began a surprise assault on Toulon and its environs. The attack went well with one vital exception. The main French communications center in the middle of the city was not silenced in time, and the officer on duty was able to relay word of the attack to the French ships. With the fleet alerted, there was little the Germans could do. By the time they arrived at the naval yards, scuttling operations were already underway, and most of the vessels were soon listing or sinking. The only ships which managed to escape were four submarines, one of which was interned in Barcelona, while the other three reached Allied ports in Algeria. By 8:30 a.m. the raid was over, and although the fleet had been scuttled, the Germans had gained some consolation from the fact that the last vestige of Unoccupied France was now in Axis hands.[19]

Given the worsening situation in North Africa and the recent Russian offensive at Stalingrad, it was obvious that the newly occupied area could be only lightly held. After "Lila" had been carried out, German staff officers during December and January reduced the number of combat troops in the former Vichy zone and began to allocate the military formations that still remained specific duties, Army Task Force Felber was placed in command of the German-held Mediterranean cast, and oversaw, in conjunction with First Army (whose headquarters was in Bordeaux), the Pyrenees boundary between France and Spain.[20] The Military Commander in France provided the actual border guards and he also supplied occupation forces for the area over twenty miles inland from the coast.[21] Air force and naval units took over the airfields and port facilities, and the Italians were to look after their sector, including Toulon, although the Germans stationed personnel in the area in a liaison capacity.

As soon as Hitler felt that the danger of an Allied attack against southeastern France had passed, a number of the Wehrmacht divisions, and especially the panzer formations, were returned to their pre-"Anton" positions in the West or sent to the Russian front.[22] By the first of February a fairly constant arrangement for the positioning of forces in the area had evolved. Three divisions, usually under strength and immobile, defended the coast with one or two divisions in reserve.[23] The latter formations might have been of some help in case of an invasion, but they were generally stationed in the region for rehabilitation purposes. The individual units continued to change, but the pattern of three divisions on the coast with one or two others in the interior continued into the summer of 1943.[24]

Since the former Vichy zone was occupied so sparsely, fortifications, as in the case of the Atlantic and Channel coasts, were to compensate for a lack of manpower. The Germans felt the major task along their portion of the Mediterranean coastline was to improve and add to the relatively weak French defenses. Engineers and planners followed a course of action similar to that employed early on on the Atlantic Wall.[25] Local tactical commanders decided where to position the permanent defenses in their areas; army fortress engineers then drew up building plans for the fortifications; and Organization Todt carried out the actual construction with its own materiel and personnel, though under army engineer supervision. At the same time engineering troops and labor service battalions erected field-type installations, although regular troops were often called on to assist as well.

A report in July from the commanding general in the Mediterranean sector, Hans Felber, pointed out numerous other inadequacies.[26] For the defenses to be adequate, he emphasized, there needed to be more concrete, more steel, more barbed wire and land mines, more medium and heavy artillery pieces. He asserted further that the coastal batteries remained emplaced almost exclusively along the rim of the coast and in the open. They ought to be moved rearward or put under cover. Defenses in and around the larger cities and ports were also too weak, and responsible commanders should be stationed inside each threatened sector. The naval artillery, he continued, could only be used to defend the harbor entrances and not for land warfare. Antiaircraft defenses needed to be strengthened substantially; in the Marseilles area they were pitiful (*kümmerlich*). Finally, Felber's report stated that almost all the German telephones were dependent on the French system, and hence the Wehrmacht needed to develop an independent telephone network. In brief, the German commander had found that the coast was not defense ready, and he concluded that the strength of the sector was such that a weak attack might be beaten off, but a strong assault at a single place could probably not be stopped.

Undoubtedly part of the reason why the French Mediterranean was generally neglected in comparison with other theaters was because Wehrmacht leaders during 1943 did not consider it a likely place for an Allied invasion. But if an attack ever did occur, the Germans at this time calculated it would take place either in the Narbonne regions west of the Rhône or at the mouth of the Rhône itself.[27] Both these operations, the Germans felt, would be coupled with another U.S.-British landing on the Atlantic or Channel coast.

But the consensus was reflected in an estimate sent out on July 6, 1943, by General Blumentritt, von Rundstedt's Chief of Staff. In it Blumentritt stated that at present a large Anglo-American landing in the entire area controlled by *Ob West* was improbable.[28] He was well aware of the Allied buildup in the Mediterranean, but he was of the opinion that it was designed for an assault against Sardinia, Corsica, Sicily, or southern Italy—or even a thrust into the Balkans, but not as a prelude for an invasion of the south of France.

Nevertheless, even though the former Vichy zone was not considered a prime target for an Allied landing, it still had to be incorporated into the Atlantic Wall framework. This meant an added burden for Commander-in-Chief West, a burden that continued to increase in the months ahead.

Von Rundstedt was responsible also for guarding against an Allied attack on the Iberian Peninsula, and the North African invasion once again made this possibility appear plausible. German concern about Spain, and to a lesser degree, Portugal, reflected a continuing National Socialist interest in the region, a point which Charles Burdick's several works on the subject amply demonstrate.[29] But Spain's position toward Hitler and the Reich had proved ambivalent since early in the war. Plans for the takeover of Gibraltar with German units had never materialized, mainly because of Spanish intransigence. Franco had also been cool to Operation "Isabella" for meeting a possible British invasion of the peninsula during 1941. By the end of the year the once ambitious "Isabella" plan had been so weakened by exigencies on the eastern front that it was limited to an occupation of the Spanish ports along the Bay of Biscay and the protection of the Pyrenees passes.[30] By the spring of 1942, "Isabella" remained little more than a paper operation.

Still, Hitler had not completely forgotten about Spain. On May 29, 1942, he issued Directive No. 42, calling for a new Spanish operation, codenamed "Ilona."[31] The directive emphasized renewed German concern about the Iberian area, but "Ilona" was more like a reflex action than an offensive undertaking. It was based on the premise that if the Allies attacked Spain or Portugal or even the French Atlantic coast, then German forces would have to react to the landing, especially to protect their U-boat bases in France. The immediate objective was limited to German formations occupying the southern passes of the Pyrenees and thus establishing the conditions for future operations. The operational order for "Ilona," which was issued on July 15, was to include only four divisions, two of them motorized, to implement the operation, at least in its initial phase.

Even though there were several changes in detail, the Germans did not alter "Ilona" appreciably during the remainder of 1942. In

September the operation was renamed "Gisela," but that change was the result of a junior officer reportedly losing his briefcase which contained the "Ilona" plan, rather than indicating an entirely new operation.[32]

The Allied invasion of northwest Africa, of course, heightened German apprehension regarding Spain, and in this context Hitler ordered "Gisela" reactivated on January 7, 1943.[33] The revived "Gisela" plan was more ambitious than the 1942 German operation for the area in that three mobile divisions were to move into north central Spain, and, after being reinforced, to proceed against the Anglo-American invaders, while three other divisions and a motorized regiment were to occupy the harbors along the northern coast.

But German anxieties over a possible Anglo-American landing attempt in January and February faded during the spring when Allied troops became heavily engaged with reinforced Axis forces in Tunisia. Admiral Karl Dönitz, the newly appointed head of the German navy, did try to revive a Spanish operation in May so that his U-boats would have better access to the Atlantic, but Hitler recognized that the time was past, at least temporarily, for any Iberian project.

On June 14, the Armed Forces High Command replaced "Gisela" with a strictly defensive plan, "Nuremberg," which was designed merely to send reinforcements to help the German border guards in protecting the mountain passes.[34] With one exception, the Germans hereafter considered the Pyrenees front to be relatively unimportant.

This exception came about early in 1944. At this time Hitler seemed to be anticipating an Allied landing almost everywhere in Western Europe, and Wehrmacht planners therefore devised yet another Iberian operation (*2. Fall aa*).[35] This scheme was extremely ambitious, and resembled the "Gisela" operations of the year before. As many as fourteen army divisions, including six panzer formations, and numerous navy and air force units were to take part.

The operational aspect of the plan stipulated that some of the German mobile forces were to take over the north Spanish harbors, while other formations, notably three panzer divisions, were to move into Central Spain and engage the advancing enemy.

But by the end of March, the Germans had once again converted the proposed plan, redesignated "New Gisela" (*Gisela Neu*), into a holding action across the French-Spanish border rather than a full-scale attack.[36] An interesting feature of the new "Gisela" plan was that for the first time it was to take place with or without Spanish assistance. In other words, the Germans at this late date had finally decided, if necessary, not to respect Spanish neutrality.[37] But as we know, nothing came of "New Gisela," and it remained a contingency plan with little chance of ever being implemented. In effect, Spain had ceased to play a role in Germany's defensive strategy in the West.

The various German plans for Spain and the Axis occupation of Vichy France as well as the subsequent construction tasks in the Mediterranean region had forced von Rundstedt and his staff to devote a great deal of attention to their exposed southern flank during the first half of 1943. To his displeasure, Wehrmacht activity along the French Mediterranean did not abate during the second half of the year.

Part of the reason why southern France continued to be an area of German concern was because of the increasing presence of British and American forces. But an equally important factor was the defection of Hitler's chief European ally, Italy. Nazi officials were not unaware of Mussolini's deteriorating position, for the depleted Italian forces had been suffering ruinous defeats for some months. Hitler had therefore had the OKW staff in May 1943, draw up plans for German troops to occupy the Italian Peninsula if that proved necessary (Operation "Alarich"). Events in Italy began to move rapidly after the Anglo-American invasion of Sicily on July 10, and two weeks later leading Italian officials and generals conspired together to overthrow the Fascist dictator.

What followed in the Italian situation was a period during which the new government under Marshal Pietro Badoglio was still formally allied with Germany, but informally negotiating with the Allies to seek a way out of the conflict. The secret negotiations finally led to an Italian surrender on September 3, the same day that the British landed troops on the southern tip of the Italian mainland. But not until September 8 was Italy's capitulation made public.

During these six weeks of protracted talks the Germans managed to move a substantial number of troops into Italy and into Italian-held areas in the Balkans and in France east of the Rhône. Extreme southeastern France, it will be remembered, had come under Italian military occupation during the takeover of the Vichy zone in November 1942. In the ensuing months four or five divisions under the Italian Fourth Army had occupied the area, which, although predominantly mountainous, included the significant Toulon naval base as well as the resort beaches along the famous French Riviera.

During August, after the Sicily landing and Mussolini's downfall, the Germans increased the number of troops moving through the area into Italy, and they also brought additional Wehrmacht units into the area itself. These movements were often indistinguishable, and there was little the commander of the Italian Fourth Army, General Vercellino, could do, even if he wanted to, as long as Germany and Italy were still nominally allied. In some cases the German forces supposedly bound for Italy lingered in the Italian zone of France before moving on.[38] In other instances Wehrmacht formations designated by *Ob West* to help accelerate the troop movements into Italy remained in the area. On yet another occasion the Germans sent additional naval personnel to shore up the Italian defenses at Toulon.[39]

On August 29, after an agreement between top-level German and Italian officers, four German divisions under the command of Army Task Force Felber, which had been redesignated Nineteenth Army, began to replace the Italian formations stationed on the coast and in the interior.[40]

Thus, by the time the Italian surrender was announced on September 8, the German occupation of Italian-held France was well advanced.[41] The next day, when German troops started taking over the Italian Peninsula by force as part of Operation "Achse," German formations in southeastern France had little trouble extending effective control over the entire area.

The actual disarming of Italian forces and the establishment of complete German domination east of the Rhône took the form of two separate undertakings. One operation consisted of three German divisions securing the Mediterranean shoreline, which extended 185 miles from the Rhône River to the French-Italian border. At the same time German troops cordoned off the border to prevent the Italians from leaving the area.[42] The disarming of Italian formations proceeded with little difficulty, and by the evening of the 9th, only one day after "Achse" had been put into effect, the French Riviera region was securely in Wehrmacht hands.[43]

The second operation, German control of the Mont Cenis railway tunnel that linked Lyons and Turin across the Alps, proved to be a more formidable task. The small German units entrusted with the undertaking ran into difficulties when the Italian forces guarding the tunnel refused to give up the exit on the Italian side.[44] The Armed Forces High Command ordered portions of the 157th Reserve Division in Grenoble, and the SS Division "Leibstandarte Adolf Hitler" in Turin, to converge on the Mont Cenis area.[45] The special force from Grenoble reached Mont Cenis first on September 11, and after a discussion with the Italian commander, took over the tunnel exit without a fight.[46] During the next two weeks the Germans used the Italians as prisoners to repair those places in the tunnel wrecked by explosives during the brief period of Italian resistance.[47]

With the takeover completed, German officials separated the 41, 057 Italian soldiers who had remained on French soil into three groups: those volunteering for service in the German military (*Kampfwillige* or *Arbeitswillige*), those volunteering for supply or construction work, but not as military personnel (*Hilfswillige*), and those

Construction of the Atlantic Wall: a coastal battery in France in 1942.

Construction on the waterfront at Biarritz, May 19, 1943.

Atlantic Wall construction, 1943.

German soldiers on the Atlantic Wall, 1944.

Anti-landing devices on the beach in Normandy, 1944.

Artillery along the Atlantic Wall in April 1944.

U-Boat repair docks under construction at St. Nazaire, June 30, 1943.

Albert Speer *(second from right)* visits the Atlantic Wall on November 24, 1942.

German sentry on duty on the beach in Normandy.

A bunker along the coast.

The huge "Batterie Todt" was often used as a propaganda tool in German newsreels.

German soldiers on a drill in Atlantic Wall bunkers.

A mine tied to an anti-landing pole.

German soldiers planting anti-landing poles in the sand on the Normandy coast, 1943.

Albert Speer returns on another inspection tour of the Atlantic Wall with Org. Todt officials on May 15, 1943.

Inauguration of the *Lindemann* battery, 1942.

who did not want to fight or work for the German side (*Militäringternierte*). Nazi officials considered the military interns to be war prisoners, and sent 10,225 of them to Germany to work in the armament factories.[48]

Immediate German defensive measures in the region east of the Rhône followed a pattern similar to that employed previously. Wehrmacht engineers reconnoitered the area to ascertain where defensive positions were needed (the Italians had constructed some fortifications, but not nearly enough). They then drew up plans for building permanent installations, and in the meantime work battalions began to erect new antitank ditches and other field-type defenses and to improve the existing ones.[49] In terms of personnel, Nineteenth Army now extended its control to include the entire French Mediterranean coast and was allotted five divisions plus a division in reserve to defend the region. After the situation stabilized, the Germans had the mobile units that had participated in "Achse" and the better infantry divisions transported out of the area.[50] The divisions that remained were under strength and contained numerous older and foreign troops. By the end of October, the Germans had once again relegated the French Mediterranean to a position of secondary importance.

The fact that the Germans expended a great deal of energy on the southern portion of the theater during 1943 should not lead one to conclude that all other military commitments in Western Europe came to a halt. The building up of the Atlantic Wall moved ahead, and, at least during the first six months, the Channel and Atlantic coasts experienced a considerable amount of troop and construction activity.

This activity had both a positive and a negative aspect—positive in the sense that a substantial number of new fortifications were completed, but negative with regard to the rapidly worsening personnel situation. This deterioration in the number and quality of German forces was caused primarily by the continual loss of divisions and smaller contingents of troops to the east, and this, in turn, resulted in the large-scale infusion of older and less able German soldiers as well as foreign troops into the depleting German tanks.

In relation to the East-West troop movements the western theater in 1943 continued to be a training ground for new soldiers and a rehabilitation area for worn-out formations before being re-deployed to Russia and other fronts. A detailed report from von Rundstedt in October 1943 stated that fifty-three divisions were "given away" to other theaters during the past year.[51] This number of divisions, he pointed out, was greater than the total number of divisions in the West at any one time during 1943. And he added that many of the remaining formations had lost a portion of their personnel for other assignments, and that the new divisions which were formed were often under strength. In some instances replacements did take the place of departing personnel, but on other occasions none was forthcoming.[52]

Germany's manpower problems in the West in 1943 led to a large influx of less qualified military personnel into the Wehrmacht formations. These individuals might be foreign volunteers from Eastern Europe or ethnic Germans who lived outside the boundaries of the Reich but who were given conditional German citizenship (*Volksdeutsche*). Or they might be older recruits from the homeland (more than 36 years of age) or very young. The necessity of utilizing such personnel in combat formations quite naturally affected adversely the proficiency of the German units.[53]

The foreign troops in the main were from Russia and called *Osttruppen*.[54] They consisted of such various ethnic groups as Cossacks, Armenians, Georgians, Ukrainians, Azerbaijanis, and Turkomans, all of whom had suffered injustices at the hands of the Soviet regime. The Wehrmacht formed these groups into separate battalions under German commanders, and for religious and ethnic reasons the groups were not to be mixed under any circumstances. The Germans, many of whom tragically believed their racial propaganda, treated the *Osttruppen* as second-class soldiers and doubted whether these units, which began to be shifted west in the fall of 1943, would fight even if given the chance. Nonetheless, by the end of the year there were one or two *Ost* battalions in almost every German coastal unit.

Another curious foreign group that became deployed in the area of *Ob West* was an Indian Legion.[55] This group, which eventually numbered 2,500 troops, was composed of Indian prisoners captured in the North African campaigns and followers of the militant Indian nationalist, Subhas Chandra Bose, who resided in Berlin for awhile during the war. German officials stationed the unit in the First Army sector along the Atlantic coast, but they never considered it battleworthy.[56] In fact, it never engaged in combat.

The Germans also questioned the combat value of the *Volksdeutsche* soldiers.[57] Wehrmacht officers integrated these German-speaking East European into reserve formations, some of which helped to defend the coasts, but still the *Volksdeutsche* soldier was often discriminated against in terms of rank.

This type of restriction did not apply to the older Reich Germans and the eighteen-year-old recruits who began to arrive in the western theater in increasing numbers. Even though they lacked military experience, they came to make up twenty-five percent of the army troops in the area by the end of the year, and they served in various capacities to alleviate the personnel shortage. Many of the older personnel became attached to fortress cadre units (*Festungs-Stamm-Abteilungen*).[58] The Germans set up these units in 1943 out of reserve divisions in the Reich, and their primary function was to maintain and service the stationary artillery pieces that were located within the defensive strongpoints. Each *Abteilung* had its own commander who was responsible to the division commander of that sector. By July 1943, fortress cadre units had been established in the main coastal harbors from Ijmuiden to Marseilles.

Also by the middle of 1943, the Atlantic, and to a much greater extent the Channel coast, had begun to assume a fortress-like appearance. In this respect, the Germans continued to consider the most endangered areas to be the major ports. Especially during the first six months of 1943 the Germans focused a great deal of attention on building up these defense areas (*Verteidigungsbereiche*). A basic orders from *Ob West* stipulated that they were to have munitions reserves that could last for three to six weeks, a food supply for over a month, and a source of drinking water that could not be cut off.[59]

By the middle of the year, the defense areas had begun to conform to a general pattern, even though they exhibited local variations depending on the terrain and the nature of the sector being protected.[60] The typical *Verteidigungsbereich* usually extended a number of miles along the coast and featured two major types of fortifications—perimeter and strongpoint defenses. The perimeter defenses consisted of land hindrances, such as earth embankments, antitank ditches, and personnel trenches, which were used to help protect the area from both the sea and landward sides. In addition, naval units set out sea barriers in the form of underwater minefields and steel nets, and both of these obstacles proved effective against enemy ships or torpedoes attempting to penetrate the harbor sea.

Interspersed among, but normally behind, the perimeter defenses were the strongpoints. They were often self-contained areas within the entire defense area. Around the outside of the strongpoints were numerous machine gun nests, barbed wire ensnarements, antitank walls, and other similar types of obstacles. Several roads with guardhouses at the entrances led into the strongpoint itself.

The main feature inside was usually an artillery battery of three or four guns with a fire-control center positioned in the middle of the emplacements. The artillery pieces normally ranged in caliber from 15 to 21 centimeters, though some might be larger, and some of them had an effective range of fire of up to 18 miles. They generally were located within a few hundred yards of the shore and set in round or rectangular, reinforced concrete bunkers. Inside the bunkers, in addition to the guns, were ammunition rooms and a sleeping area for the alert crews. The sides of the bunker were 6½ feet thick, and if covered, the roof usually had a thickness of 10 feet. Most of the guns were not covered, however. This made them vulnerable to air attacks and naval gunfire, but this disadvantage was offset to a degree by antiaircraft weapons mounted on both sides of each site. The gun crews not on duty lived in nearby barracks, and a battery usually consisted of between 80 to 150 men.

Supplementing the artillery units was the usual complement of buildings and shelters, including additional living quarters, a radio communications center, an underground munitions bunker, a decontamination area, an orderly room, a canteen and eating area, an officer's mess, and a supply store. A well-protected hospital and water storage tank were set some distance from the gun emplacements, and each strongpoint had its own source of power. The entire strongpoint was further protected by infantry troops and other forces utilizing small caliber artillery weapons, mortars, antitank guns, flamethrowers, and the like. These strongpoints combined with the perimeter defenses and other scattered fortifications to form the bases of the defense areas.

An extreme example, but one which indicates the length to which the Germans could take strongpoint construction, is provided in the case of the mammoth 40.6 cm. (16-inch) guns at Sangatte.[61] This was one of the batteries designed to hit targets on the English coast across the Straits of Dover, and its effective range was nearly 30 miles. The entire battery complex, which measured approximately 1,250 by 1,040 yards, was surrounded by minefields, and inside the minefields, except for road and rail connections, had been placed a wide band of heavy barbed wire. Behind the wire were the perimeter defenses, which consisted of sixteen concrete machine gun nests, nine light antiaircraft batteries, a heavier 88-millimeter emplacement of six guns, and an antitank ditch faced with concrete.

Inside the strongpoint the Germans had placed several additional minefields and had surrounded all of the buildings, such as living quarters, recreational facilities, and a bombproof hospital, with wire. The command post for the battery was located 450 yards in front of the three guns, which were laid out in the shape of a huge triangle. Circular wire and an electrified fence as well as four machine guns for each site protected the large guns from close-in attack. One of the structures which housed the guns and the gun crews and shells had three floor levels and was 53 feet in height, or the equivalent of a five-story building. The entrance at the rear of the structure was at the top floor, and the bottom half was embedded in the side of a limestone hill. The overhead concrete cover and side walls were 11½ feet thick.

Most of the construction, of course, was not of this magnitude, but the rate of construction in 1943 did accelerate in accordance with the extensive building program which had been set forth the previous autumn. Several examples make clear the degree to which the western defenses improved. In December 1942 *Ob West* listed 5,120 permanent installations (*ständigen Ausbau*) as having been built.[62] By June 1943 the number had risen to more than 8,000, or an increase of about 3,000 constructed fortifications over a six-month period. If one adds to this the fact that Organization Todt in April 1943, poured more concrete—876,000 cubic meters—and had more workers employed—260,000—on the coasts of Western Europe than in any other month during the war, it becomes obvious that the Germans made substantial progress in defense construction during this period.[63]

Furthermore, if one counts the number artillery pieces emplaced along the coasts in 1943, it is also evident that Germany's western defenses had become more formidable. By November the number of antitank weapons in the West had increased to 2,354, and the number of guns over 75 millimeters reached 2,692.[64] In this context, the heavily defended Fifteenth Army Channel sector alone had 1,174 artillery pieces in August, or nearly as many as there had been in the entire western theater in 1941.[65]

But the German building program did not keep pace in the second half of 1943. Part of the reason was because National Socialist officials began to shift Organization Todt laborers to other projects, including the repair of dams in the Ruhr area, the construction of a bauxite mine in southern France, and even the actual mining of wolfram at a site in the west of France.[66] As a result, current high priority items in the erection of the Wall, such as the covering and camouflaging of permanent fortifications, barely advanced beyond their initial stages at this time.

Another reason why Commander-in-Chief West's building plans suffered during this period was because certain Reich business firms involved in the construction effort failed to live up to the terms of their contracts.[67] On these occasions when extremely poor workmanship was found, a work stoppage ensued until a new German firm could be engaged to send construction experts to oversee the completion of the project. Problems such as these no doubt could be overcome, but they do indicate a variety of causes in the construction slowdown.

The year 1943 as related to the Atlantic Wall therefore turned out to be one of frustration. Allied moves in North Africa had forced *Ob West* to devote a considerable amount of his attention to the southern portion of the theater, and the integration of the area into the western defense complex was still far from complete. Building activity along the western coast of France and in Belgium and the Netherlands had slowed in the face of ever-increasing commitments, and developments on the eastern front had led to a steady deterioration in the number and quality of military personnel available in the West. This slowdown in construction and the progressively worsening troop situation plus the growing prospect of a large-scale western invasion prompted von Rundstedt in October 1943 to frame his annual inspection report in the form of a warning to higher headquarters that these conditions must change. But before discussing his lengthy report in some detail, it is necessary to examine another problem which had at least some effect on German thinking in Western Europe. That problem was the interservice frictions which existed in the theater among the army, navy, and air force.

Chapter 4

Interservice Frictions and a Warning

F riction among the various branches of the armed forces is not, of course, something unique to the Wehrmacht. It exists to a degree in all sizable military establishments, and it may produce beneficial as well as detrimental results. While serious interservice controversies were present in varying degrees throughout the German military structure, they took the specific form they did because of their association with National Socialism.

The fundamental Nazi concept of the *Führerprinzip*, or leadership principle as personified in Hitler, lay at the heart of the problem. The leader was the key element, and the supreme leader was Hitler. The National Socialist ruler had under him a group of secondary leaders, and they had, in turn, a number of subordinates under them, and so on down the leadership ladder. As one might expect, there was a great deal of "empire building" among the ambitious lesser leaders within the structure of National Socialist society. This often led to controversies among the lesser leaders, but when this happened, they turned to Hitler for the ultimate solution. Because of their belief in him and his ideas, they accepted his judgments as final.

Still in many instances Hitler perpetuated the centuries old principle of divide and rule among his minions by issuing imprecise rulings or by not making any decision at all, thus heightening his own control in the process. Examples of infighting among Hitler's functionaries were evident in all spheres of National Socialist society, from the production of war materials to the selection of school textbooks, from espionage and intelligence activities to hunting and fishing privileges. The army, navy, and air force too became caught up in various types of conflicts such as those which abounded in the civilian sector.

These conflicts never reached critical proportions in the western theater, but they did hamper the defensive effort to some degree. The controversy which has subsequently received the most attention took place between army and navy officials over the positioning and command of the coastal artillery batteries. From this disagreement, as in most other instances, the German air force remained aloof. The only exception was in the distribution of materials for building purposes, and in this case all of the services became involved. By 1944, however, when the danger of an invasion appeared imminent, the army's authority had become virtually unchallenged.

In the West, as in every German land theater, the Luftwaffe and the *Kriegsmarine* were tactically subordinate to the army, and in this instance to *Ob West*. Nevertheless, there were complicating factors. The complication as applied to Western Europe stemmed from developments which had occurred following the projected German invasion of Great Britain in 1940. To carry out this amphibious operation across the channel, the navy and the air force had naturally been allocated a prominent role. But after the Luftwaffe failed to destroy the Royal Air Force and gain control of the air, the bulk of the frontline army and air force units were moved east in preparation for the Russian campaign, and the West became a secondary theater.

However, a substantial portion of the navy stayed behind, and their duties in the West remained fundamental to the German war effort.[1] The main task of the *Kriegsmarine* was to sink any ships, including neutral vessels, which might be of assistance to the British cause. And the occupation of numerous harbors along France's western coast as well as the limited use of some of Spain's ports for supply purposes, allowed the Germans to intensify the submarine campaign. Although not of the magnitude of the war on merchant shipping, the navy also had the additional duty of keeping its own sea-lanes open, especially near the coasts, and free from enemy harassment.

To accomplish these tasks the *Kriegsmarine* needed a number of shore-based naval forces as well as shipboard personnel. Naval bases had to be maintained and protected, and navy troops were also trained to man some of the artillery batteries along the coasts. These guns were often of large caliber and designed to fire primarily at sea targets, thereby helping to protect friendly shipping along the coast. Therefore, as long as the Battle of the Atlantic raged, and as long as Axis ships continued to utilize sea lanes close to shore, the navy, even though tactically under Commander-in-Chief West, insisted on having a say in the running of this less important theater.

The problem was that from 1942 on the West was increasingly a possibility for an Allied attack, and if it were a large-scale invasion, army priorities would have to take precedence. In certain instances the measures necessary to defend the coast against an invading enemy coincided with those employed for safeguarding coastal shipping, but at times the measures were not the same. It was a recurring dilemma for the Germans to decide whether navy or army requirements should receive priority.[2] Was it more important to protect coastal traffic and to keep away enemy raiders, or was it more important that the primary emphasis should be to prepare for the eventual Allied assault? More specifically, should coastal artillery be placed in the open near the shore and directed primarily against naval targets? Or should it be positioned further inland and under cover so that the guns could fire only indirectly at Allied ships, but still be of use against an enemy landing force? Should one sacrifice an all-around field of fire for battle-hardened, bomb-proof, gun emplacements? Could nonvisual sighting be effective against fast moving targets? Around these issues the army-navy controversy in the West revolved.

In 1941 and early 1942 the main issue was whether naval or army commanders should control the coastal artillery batteries. Hitler's Directive No. 40 of March 1942 had clarified this point: *Ob West* was to select one commander for each coastal sector. In most instances this meant that a local army divisional commander was put in charge, but in certain areas, especially at naval strongpoints, *Kriegsmarine* officers assumed control.

Even though the Führer had settled the question of command responsibility, the problem of target priorities for coastal artillery persisted. The navy wanted artillery batteries emplaced primarily to fire at sea targets; the army desired them for use against an invading enemy. Even if the differences could be reconciled and artillery positions erected to satisfy both the requirements of naval and land warfare, yet another issue would have to be resolved. What was an artillery commander to do if he had to fire at Allied ships and against an enemy landing force at the same time? Which alternative should he choose?

German military leaders in the West again looked to Hitler for an answer. The Führer at first equivocated, and his final decision in 1943 provided little help. The navy was to be in control when firing at sea targets. However, if the enemy succeeded in reaching land, an army artillery officer was to assume command. In theory Hitler's solution appeared to be an acceptable compromise, but in practice it simply would not work. Several unanswered questions still remained. If the Western powers gained a foothold at one place, but failed in another area covered by the same battery, was the navy or the army in control? Or at what moment did one decide in essence that an enemy assault was successful?

The coastal artillery problem resolved itself not because of the Führer's ruling, but rather because of the turn of events in the West. By mid 1943 the navy for all practical purposes had lost the Battle of the Atlantic, and German U-boats, under their own separate command, were no longer capable of destroying Allied shipping on a large scale. With the role of the navy's chief offensive striking threat greatly diminished, all of the functions that remained for the navy in the West were defensive in nature and connected with the anti-invasion effort.

The defensive naval tasks were not under submarine commanders, but under Naval Command Group West (*Marine-Gruppen-Kommando-West*).[5] Naval Group West counted among its missions escort services for the Axis merchant vessels which still used the shipping lanes along the French coast, patrol duties, naval reconnaissance, laying and sweeping minefields, and in general guarding the area near the coast. To perform these tasks the elaborately organized naval group had to rely mainly upon smaller craft, such as torpedo boats, minesweepers, and patrol boats, although its commander, Admiral Theodor Krancke, did have five destroyers at his disposal, and he could also call upon some small submarines in case of an emergency.[6] In addition, the *Kriegsmarine* continued to have its personnel manning the naval artillery batteries and some antiaircraft positions.

The significant point, however, is that all these duties were associated with defensive, not offensive, operations. This defensive effort, as with all questions pertaining to Fortress Europe, was in almost all cases under army command. The ration strength figures in 1944 bear this out. Of the 1,400,000 servicemen listed by Commander-in-Chief West on February 1, more than 800,000 were army troops as compared with 96,000 naval personnel.[7] In brief, the Germany navy, which never became a balanced force before or during the early stages of the war, lost its chief *raison d'être* in the submarine campaign which followed. By 1944 army and naval commanders might continue to fulminate occasionally about the inordinate demands of the other service, but in fact the navy retained little voice in the defensive thinking that was being pushed forward in the hope of turning back the Anglo-American invaders.[8]

It is rather surprising that the Luftwaffe did not become involved in a controversy similar to the one that embroiled the army and the navy. After all, the German air force owed its existence to the National Socialist movement, and it was not tainted in Hitler's eyes with the defects of "traditional services." Here was an organization that was favorably disposed toward Nazism, an organization that might well come into conflict with the older branches.

Yet in spite of the serious frictions that existed at higher command levels, conflicts between the Luftwaffe and the other services did not exist to any large degree in the West.[9] To be sure, the air force was organized as elaborately as the other two branches in France and the Low Countries, with its own supply channels and administrative apparatus. But the Third Air Fleet (*Luftflotte 3*), which oversaw air force matters in Western Europe, accepted its subordinate position much more readily than did the navy. Part of the reason was that after the Battle of Britain subsided, the Luftwaffe no longer played a primary role in the West and had shifted its attention to the East.

Another reason was that as the war progressed, the proficiency and performance of the German air force on all fronts steadily declined. Even though aircraft production within the Reich continued to mount until the end of 1944, fuel shortages and the high casualty rate among flying personnel eventually put severe limitations on German's air capabilities.[10] These restrictions, combined with Hitler's decision early in the war not to concentrate on building up a strategic bomber force, relegated the Luftwaffe quite early to a subordinate position in Western Europe. The German air force did manage to institute what was called a "Baby Blitz" against England in February 1944, but it was soon abandoned because of heavy losses.

Field Marshal Hugo Sperrle's Third Air Fleet, therefore, concentrated most of its effort on supporting the defensive posture being promulgated and guided by Commander-in-Chief West. By 1944 the Germans were employing almost all of their approximately 500 operational airplanes in the West in a variety of anti-invasion activities, such as air defense, logistical support, aerial minelaying, and reconnaissance missions. Even though future Luftwaffe plans called for transferring large numbers of aircraft, especially fighter planes, to air bases in France as soon as an amphibious assault began, the major function of the newly arrived units was still to be defensive.

The other significant aerial activity which involved air force units in the West was also defensive in nature—manning the antiaircraft batteries that dotted the entire area of Western Europe.[12] Over 100,000 of the 337,000 Luftwaffe personnel in the theater served as members of the antiaircraft groups, and all these formations, when threatened by an invasion, were to come under the jurisdiction of the local army or navy commander. The air force flak units were well aware that their chief mission was to support the land forces against aerial and ground attacks, and air force commanders further realized that to accomplish their task required close cooperation with the other services.

Thus the Luftwaffe more readily accepted its subordinate position in the western theater than was the case with the navy. Nevertheless, by 1944 neither the navy nor the air force was in a position to challenge the dominant authority of the army.

One further problem, the problem of allocating laborers and materials for reconstruction purposes, probably caused more interservice friction than any other issue in the West. Like the issue revolving around the control of coastal artillery, this conflict resolved itself more by the turn of events than by a resolute command decision. In this case each branch felt that the other services were undermining its specific building priorities. The army was especially adamant on this point.[13] The Luftwaffe, according to army staff officers, was receiving too many workers for air field construction. The navy was getting more cement than it deserved for submarine base installations, and the army was not receiving its faire share. One army divisional commander records that naval latrines were being made bombproof at the same time numerous coastal artillery batteries remained uncovered and in the open. In other words, the army was complaining that higher headquarters was neglecting its construction projects in the theater in favor of the other services.

Much of the blame, the army insisted, should be borne by Organization Todt. This agency, which had built the famous autobahns as well as the West Wall prior to the war, had subsequently been responsible for carrying out large-scale building schemes in all parts of Hitler's Europe.

The Todt organization, which formed part of Speer's Ministry for Armaments and War Production after 1942, preferred big projects for several reasons. It had been set up originally to handle large construction undertakings, and its first important projects in Western Europe had been to build the formidable long-range artillery emplacements in the Pas de Calais sector. After completing this task, the Todt agency devoted a significant part of its energies to erecting submarine pens and improving harbor defenses along the Channel and Atlantic coasts.[14] It was therefore understandable if Todt organization leaders wanted to continue the same kind of work with which its workmen, many of whom were foreign laborers, were familiar.

Another reason why Organization Todt favored building large permanent defenses was that it did not have enough motor vehicles to move often from place to place.[15] This lack of vehicles made Organization Todt officials reluctant to undertake projects away from major supply centers and railheads. The army might decry this practice, but they did not exercise direct control over the Todt agency. Army planners could only suggest projects; they could not dictate them. And as long as the navy and the air force, with their own building needs, retained some influence in the theater, they demanded some say in the allocation of Organization Todt materiel and personnel.[16]

But more significant than the army's exasperation with Organization Todt was the fact that the Germans simply had too few workers and too little materiel for the building tasks they wished to complete. Time and again Wehrmacht officers reported that only a portion of the projected construction undertakings could be finished within the time specified because they lacked sufficient resources.[17] Construction in the West also suffered because of the many other projects which required immediate attention inside the Reich and in the more hardpressed theaters. Toward the end of 1943, however, German planners were well aware that more of the total construction effort had to be shifted to the West since an Allied invasion was in the offing. By this time the navy and the air force had clearly been relegated to a subordinate position, and the army had become the dominant voice in preparing for the long-anticipated Anglo-American attack.

Commander-in-Chief West, his staff, and his subordinate commanders had all become genuinely alarmed by the fall of 1943 about military developments pertaining to Western Europe. The autumn months had brought with them not only the normal chill in the air; they had also brought the sobering realization that a full-scale Allied invasion was not far off. A number of signs led von Rundstedt to this conclusion.[18] The Allies were deploying more and more aircraft to bases in the south of England. Increasing numbers of American and British troops were being placed near embarkation points along the southern and eastern English coasts. The theater commander estimated that as many Allied divisions were stationed in Britain and poised to assault the continent as there were German forces, including noncombat units, in all of Western Europe. As von Rundstedt pointed out, "The enemy can attack from England across the Channel at any time. His military preparations for the most part have been completed."[19] It was only a matter of time until the Allied invasion would assuredly take place.

This atmosphere of anticipation coupled with the previously mentioned slowdown of construction and the continual exodus of the more able German troops from the West during the summer of 1943, made von Rundstedt's fifty-page situation report especially timely, when it was forwarded to the Armed Forces High Command on October 28.[20] Each year at this time Commander-in-Chief West issued an overall estimate of the situation in theater, but this particular estimate was more significant than the 1942 version, for the 1943 report was clearly an attempt by the field marshal to alter German policy toward Western Europe.

The actual report took the form of a thoroughly prepared staff study and was based on facts and figures compiled after an extensive inspection of the area. It is an extremely important document from several standpoints. Not only is it a warning calling for an intensified effort in the West; it is also a proposal to give this warning a definite direction in the months ahead. To be sure, there is little new in the report. But the study is so forcefully presented that it gives the old ideas a new sense of urgency. Von Rundstedt's report marks the beginning of a new phase in Germany's strategy for the West.

In the initial portion of the report von Rundstedt presented an estimate of the enemy's capabilities and its possible courses of action. British and American striking power, he asserted, was quite formidable. With a powerful array of forces stationed in the United Kingdom, the Allies would assuredly attempt to establish a second front in 1944. The only question was when and where the attempt would take place. The western commander figured that the attack would probably not begin until early spring because of the weather, but he did not want to rule out a partial operation even during the winter months, for "the technical equipment of the Anglo-American forces even permits a landing at this time of the year."

As to where the Allies would invade, von Rundstedt, like most German military experts, continued to consider the Channel coast as the most likely possibility. He also warned that the Western Allies might well attempt to couple the main assault with one or more small-scale operations in other sectors. A limited attack of this nature could tie down a sizable number of German troops, and thereby make it easier for additional British and American combat units to invade across the Channel. Von Rundstedt further pointed out that these small operations might be devised with additional objectives in mind. By establishing a bridgehead on the Cotentin or the Brittany Peninsula, for example, Allied forces would have the use of a major port, and, in the case of Brittany, would eliminate two German U-boat bases at the same time. Or the Allies might decide to institute simultaneous attacks on France's Atlantic and Mediterranean coasts designed eventually to link up around Toulouse and thus cut off German access to Spain. Another possibility was an Allied landing near the mouth of the Rhône River, which could be used in conjunction with either a large-scale Channel or Atlantic coastal operation. Therefore, even though von Rundstedt anticipated an invasion across the Channel, he fully realized that the United States and Britain had other alternatives at their disposal, and German forces must have the flexibility to meet any Allied course of action.

The second section of the report dealt with how in general *Ob West* proposed to counter the various Allied strengths and capabilities. The enemy, von Rundstedt reiterated, possessed the advantage of being able to select the time and place of attack. This fact placed the German forces in a difficult position, for the mere length of the coast precluded defending it everywhere in depth. Hence, the field marshal stressed again that flexibility was the key principle if one expected to repel an Allied invasion. The main goal, he asserted, was to try at all costs to disrupt and defeat the enemy at the water's edge. In fact, if possible, German forces should attempt to destroy the invader before he ever reached shore. But if the enemy succeeded in gaining a foothold, local reserves ought to begin an immediate counterthrust (*Gegenstoss*) to confuse and weaken the Allied attackers. "Every hour is costly," von Rundstedt emphasized.

"If the enemy gets the time to establish himself, it will be most difficult to bring about his expulsion." The local counterthrust was to be followed by a strong German reserve force, which would launch a counterattack (*Gegenangriff*) against the most exposed positions of the enemy until he was annihilated.

He went on to evaluate how the Wehrmacht might best make use of its defensive setup when opposed by an enemy possessing naval and air superiority. Even though permanent fortifications built out of concrete and well-constructed, camouflaged, field-type installations were essential for the impending battle as well as for propagandistic purposes, von Rundstedt warned that one should not be deluded into thinking that these obstacles made the Atlantic Wall impregnable. They could be overcome, and the western commander once more declared that flexibility was the most logical means of surmounting Allied materiel predominance. Certainly, coastal artillery batteries ought to continue to be erected and existing ones improved, but he pointed out that German infantry troops and their heavy weapons should not disappear into thick bunkers. They, too, must be made mobile to meet any situation, even against British and American paratroopers who might attack from the rear. By making his forces more mobile, the theater commander felt that he could minimize the probability of Allied success in the West and thus accomplish an objective of decisive importance in the overall conduct of the war.

To carry out this task, however, von Rundstedt emphasized that he would need more and better-equipped personnel. In the third section of his report he depicted how both the number and the quality of German military forces in the western theater were woefully inadequate to face the growing might of the Allies.

In terms of numbers, the field marshal declared that the strength of the *Kriegsmarine* and the Luftwaffe formations was clearly insufficient to counter Allied air and sea superiority. Furthermore, the naval and air force artillery units, whose crews were working in close conjunction with the army, lacked the necessary ammunition and equipment to reach and maintain the desired level of effectiveness.

The army, too, von Rundstedt asserted, was weak and needed to be revitalized. There had always been too much area to cover in the West with the forces available, and the situation had deteriorated even more during 1943.[21] In October 1942 twenty-two infantry divisions had been deployed along the coasts. All these units had been well equipped, and most of them had three, fully trained regiments and a full complement of thirty-six artillery pieces. In reserve were seven panzer and motorized divisions of excellent quality, plus six more infantry divisions.

By contrast, in October 1943, although twenty-seven divisions were stationed along the coastal front, German troops had 400 additional miles of Mediterranean shoreline to defend, and many of the formations were much too weak in artillery and consisted of only two, inexperienced, largely immobile, infantry regiments. Of the reserve forces, all six armored and motorized divisions were still in the process of being formed initially or were being refitted after serving on the eastern front. The seven infantry units in the interior consisted of two reserve divisions of only marginal combat value, two divisions in the course of formation, and three reinforced regiments. This force was simply inadequate to meet a full-scale Anglo-American invasion.

Another factor, according to von Rundstedt, was that a total of fifty-three divisions had been moved out of the West to other theaters during the course of 1942. This transfer of troops must cease if Western Europe were to be defended successfully. Not only did the number of troops have to be increased, but *Ob West* also stressed the need for a considerable upgrading in the quality of personnel. He pointed out that most of the divisions now contained numerous foreign troops, *Volksdeutsche*, and inexperienced German personnel among their ranks. This situation had to be remedied if Wehrmacht forces were going to be able to repel a large Allied landing.

According to von Rundstedt, armaments were also in need of improvement. German divisions in the coastal sectors had at least ten different types of artillery guns in their inventories plus numerous captured weapons of foreign make. It was difficult enough to obtain sufficient ammunition for this large variety of guns, let alone to build up stockpiles in reserve. Furthermore, if German forces expected to have any prospect of victory against the well-equipped British and American soldiers, weapons shipped to the West had to be up-to-date and not of World War I vintage. This situation could be remedied only with a substantial increase in the number of modern weapons being allocated to the western theater.

Von Rundstedt then concluded in the final section that basically two things were needed to raise German defensive capabilities in the West. First of all, the divisions manning the coast had to be strengthened to the normal complement of three infantry regiments, including one with heavy guns; sufficient antitank weapons; and adequate supply personnel. Just as importantly, substantial portions of these divisions had to be made mobile. Mobility, in von Rundstedt's view, was the key concept, for by being made mobile these formations would naturally be more flexible in coping with whatever invasion plan the Allies might select.

Flexibility through mobility was also the chief notion behind Commander-in-Chief West's second specific proposal. He advocated that a sizable number of combat-ready, fully mobile, motorized reserve formations remain poised behind the coastal front to deal a devastating blow to any large-scale enemy attack that might arise.

> These units must not be dependent on the railway network and must be established as a strong, decisive shock force which would operate in a rapid, coordinated manner, be it to overrun a major airborne attack, or be it to destroy an enemy penetrating inland from the coast...

Von Rundstedt contended that nine first-rate armored divisions would be required if this mobile reserve were to be made into an effective fighting force. His plan was therefore quite simple; offset the Allied advantage of being able to strike the continent when and where they wished by establishing a strong, well-drilled mobile army.

To be sure, Commander-in-Chief West's proposals contained nothing novel, but they did clarify his position on several points. They showed that he was not optimistic that a static system of defenses alone could ward off a large-scale Allied assault. For the Atlantic Wall concept to be effective, it had to include a mobile striking force in reserve as well. The other point von Rundstedt wanted to emphasize was to warn Hitler that immediate steps were called for if the Wehrmacht expected to counter the Allied threat from the West.

One additional circumstance surrounding von Rundstedt's report is worth mentioning. It concerns the way in which *Ob West* submitted the report and supports the notion that the manner of preservation may be as important as the contents themselves. Von Rundstedt knew that Hitler made all of the basic decisions, and he wanted to make sure that the Führer himself looked over this estimate of the western theater. Therefore, when von Rundstedt forwarded his report to Armed Forces High Command headquarters, he sent with it an accompanying cover letter to Field Marshal Keitel.[22] In the letter von Rundstedt entreated Hitler's pliant armed forces chief to have the Führer read the report in its entirety so that he was fully aware of the critical manpower and materiel situation in the western theater.

Ob West also had his Chief of Staff, Blumentritt, submit another cover letter, in this instance to Blumentritt's Armed Forces (OKW) and Army High Command (OKH) counterparts, Generals Jodl and Zeitzler.[23] The missive to the OKW and OKH Chiefs of Staff was an extension of von Rundstedt's comments to Keitel. The attached estimate of the western situation, Blumentritt wrote, is extremely significant. It gives an "unadorned picture" of the true situation. Do not be misled by Theater Command West's Basic Order No. 32, which also deals with the inspection of the western area, for it is intended for general dissemination and for bolstering troop morale.[24] Von Rundstedt's more detailed report describes conditions as they really exist, Blumentritt concluded, and it should be considered in this light. Thus, in essence, von Rundstedt was making every effort to assure that his estimate of the western theater received a proper hearing at the highest command level.

Although German high command officers might have contended that von Rundstedt's report was unduly pessimistic in places, the fact remained that, in his opinion, the West was soon to become a major theater of war. Responsible staff officers now had at their disposal a relatively objective assessment of Germany's military objective assessment of Germany's military posture in Western Europe. The question was, what position would Hitler take toward the report? Would it prompt the Führer to act?

Von Rundstedt and his staff did not have long to wait. Less than a week later, on November 3, 1943, Hitler issued Directive No. 51, which dealt with developments in the West as related to the overall war strategy.[25] This new Führer Directive, for the most part, echoed von Rundstedt's position in his recently submitted estimate and serves as one more example that, although Hitler made the decisions, he accepted the advice of his field commanders more often than his military critics have been willing to admit.

The initial portion of Directive No. 51 set forth the reasoning behind Hitler's change of policy toward the western theater. For the past two and a half years, the directive began, German forces have concentrated their energies in the life-and-death struggle against the Bolshevik menace in the East. But the situation has changed. "The threat from the East remains, but an even greater danger now appears in the West: an Anglo-Saxon landing." If necessary, as a last resort the directive continued, space can be sacrificed in Eastern Europe and still not deal a mortal blow to Germany's chances for survival.

Not so in the West! Here, if the enemy succeeds in breaching our defenses along a wide front, consequences of staggering proportions will follow within a short time. All signs point to an offensive against the western front of Europe, at the latest in the spring, perhaps even earlier.

For that reason, I can no longer justify the further weakening of the West in favor of other theaters of war. I have therefore decided to strengthen the defenses in the West...

Hitler had thus decreed a basic change in Germany's strategy toward the western theater. No longer was it to be considered of secondary importance, and the defensive effort was to be intensified for the impending Anglo-American assault. The alteration in German policy that von Rundstedt had hoped for had become a reality.

The second section of the directive also closely paralleled Commander-in-Chief West's proposals. The Führer, like von Runstedt, at this time expected the main attack to take place in the Channel sector, but he felt the enemy would probably elect to undertake additional diversions or holding operations in other areas, even possibly in Denmark. Every resource, the Führer continued, ought to be strained to strengthen the coastal fortifications, especially in the most threatened regions, so that the invasion attempt could be repulsed before the Western Powers were able to establish a beachhead.

But what if the Allies succeeded in gaining a foothold? Once again, Hitler's solution was a carbon copy of the proposal advocated by von Rundstedt a few days earlier.

Should the enemy nevertheless force a landing by concentrating his forces, he must be hit by a counterattack delivered with all our might. The problem is to make the large number of units available to us into a first-rate, offensively oriented, and fully mobile reserve through intensive training. A counterattack by these units will prevent the enlargement of the beachhead, and will throw the enemy back into the sea.

In addition, carefully worked out and detailed emergency plans must be drawn up so that everything we have at home and in the coastal areas which have not been attacked can be thrown immediately against the invading enemy.

In the third and final portion of the directive, Hitler issued more specific instructions to the various services to upgrade the defensive posture in the West. The army was to make maximum use of the modern weapons that were to be shipped to France and the Low Countries. Army divisions, particularly mobile forces, were rapidly to be brought up to full armed strength. Reserve formations within the Reich were to be prepared to move west within forty-eight hours after being notified. Air force formations in the West were to be dispersed to a number of airfields to lessen the effect of enemy bomber attacks. Naval forces were to assemble as many vessels as possible to oppose the Allied landing fleet.

Most important, the Führer asserted that "no units or formations stationed in the West and in Denmark,...are to be withdrawn to other fronts without my approval." Western Europe was to move away from the position of a stepchild in relation to the other theaters. In fact, Hitler felt that a victory in the West in 1944 might well prove decisive in the outcome of the war.[26]

Chapter 5

Command Conflicts

F ührer Directive No. 51 led to a flurry of activity by German staff planners in the western theater during the last two months of 1943. Commander-in-Chief West, for example, laid out plans for making his coastal divisions mobile, as well as for upgrading the panzer formations in the area.[1] The theater commander also set forth an ambitious building program for 1944 that included the erection and improvement of numerous permanent and field-type fortifications.[2] And the navy took steps to add more ships, mines, and artillery pieces to its defensive arsenal.[3]

Although these plans brought few tangible results before the end of the year, von Rundstedt was still satisfied that progress was being made and was confident that the tempo of change would accelerate early in the new year.[4] Part of von Rundstedt's optimism undoubtedly stemmed from Hitler's demonstrated concern about the gravity of the situation in the West. In fact, the Führer went so far as to send his famous Afrika Korps commander, Erwin Rommel, in November 1943, to inspect the defenses in the western theater.

The fifty-two-year-old field marshal had been quite ill during part of 1943, but he had still managed to serve in several different capacities since the conclusion of the African campaign in May. In July, Rommel was named head of Army Group B, which had been reconstituted in Germany after its staff had been withdrawn from the Russian front. At the end of the month, Rommel's group was put in charge of German defensive preparations in northern Italy, a task that took on added significance when large numbers of Wehrmacht troops began moving into the area after the overthrow of Mussolini. This timely influx of German forces was an important factor in confining the Allies, who invaded the Italian mainland in September, to the southern portion of the peninsula during the autumn months. The Führer rewarded Field Marshal Kesselring, the German commander in southern Italy, for his work by naming him commander over all the German forces in Italy. Rommel thus became expendable. (An added factor was that Rommel and Kesselring did not get along.)

On November 5, 1943, only two days after Hitler had issued Führer Directive No. 51, Rommel received orders to begin inspecting "the defensive readiness of the German-occupied coasts" in the western theater.[5] The order stated that Rommel and part of his Army Group B staff were to reconnoiter first Denmark; then the Channel area, including Brittany; and finally any other sector which the Führer might later designate. During the inspection Rommel's group was to offer suggestions and to draw up plans for the best way to meet an Allied invasion in the West. Rommel left for Denmark on November 21, and he began checking the defenses along the Danish coast early in December, finishing his work there in about ten days.[6] He and his staff then moved to northern France to start inspecting the Channel sector.[7]

By this time, the middle of December, several problems had arisen regarding Rommel and his anomalous position in the western theater. To begin with, what exactly was his position in the West? Clearly, he was responsible to the Führer and not subordinate to von

Rundstedt. How long was Rommel to have privileged access to Hitler without having to go through *Ob West?* Would this situation continue as long as Rommel remained in the area? Both Rommel and von Rundstedt agreed that Rommel's status ought to be clarified.

The National Socialist dictator decided the issue on January 1, 1944, when he placed Rommel and his entire Army Group B staff under *Ob West*.[8] Hitler's order singled out two exceptions, however. The former Afrika Korps commander and his headquarters personnel were to be available (1) if the enemy launched a large-scale attack on Denmark, or (2) if the Führer found it necessary to occupy Hungary. But in all other circumstances the head of Army Group B was to be subordinate to von Rundstedt.

Rommel's position in the West was further clarified on January 15. On this date, Rommel, who was already one of the most celebrated field commanders in the German army as a result of Josef Goebbels' propaganda effort, was officially given control over the coastal region that stretched from the tip of Holland to the Loire River, or that area defended by Seventh and Fifteenth Armies and the Netherlands command.[9] What this assignment meant was that, while von Rundstedt remained overall theater commander, Rommel had been entrusted with overseeing the defensive effort in that sector considered most likely for an Allied assault.

Even though the problem of finding a place for Rommel in the western command structure had been resolved, a second problem persisted; that is, what strategy was Germany to employ with regard to its panzer forces in the West? More precisely, the issue has been depicted as a conflict in strategy between Rommel's idea of defeating the enemy on the beaches by positioning strong armored forces near the coast, and von Rundstedt's notion of placing the mobile reserves further inland but still capable of dealing a crushing blow against the Allies once they had landed.[10] It has therefore become known as the Rommel-Rundstedt controversy. Many writers have read into the controversy more than a disagreement over strategy. They have seen it, in addition, as an excellent illustration of Hitler's divide-and-rule technique and as an example of the tensions that existed between the old and the new in Germany, or in this instance, between the traditional, Prussian military caste as epitomized by von Rundstedt, and the new, aggressive National Socialist officer as typified by Rommel. While there is some truth in these allegations, they do need to be qualified, and an examination of these assertions in greater detail will give us a more accurate picture of the entire command controversy as well as of the command situation in the West.

No doubt, areas of tension did exist between von Rundstedt and Rommel. But the conflict over strategy was more bitter and prolonged between Rommel and General Baron Geyr von Schweppenburg, the head of German panzer forces in the West, than it ever was between the two field marshals. To be sure, von Rundstedt, both in October 1942 and a year later in 1943, had proposed a strong mobile reserve.[11] Yet he made other pronouncements on the subject which indicate that his preference for a strategic mobile force was not the only approach he advocated, nor was it an inalterable decision. On several occasions during these years *Ob West* exhorted German forces to destroy the enemy if possible in the water, or "at the latest to smash him after reaching the coast."[12] "The goal," von Rundstedt emphasized, "must be to meet the enemy on the same day he lands and throw him again into the sea."[13] Even in his October 28 report von Rundstedt did not opt solely for the mobile reserve alternative.[14] He stressed that every effort ought to be made with the existing coastal defenses to throw back the invading enemy before he ever reached shore. But if the Allies succeeded in breaching the German defenses, local reserves were to begin a counterthrust as soon as possible. Then a strong mobile striking force was to destroy what remained of the enemy. In brief, von Rundstedt did not tie himself exclusively to any one solution. He was attempting to strengthen the coastal defenses, increase the number of local reserves, and build up the mobile armored formations all at the same time and thus to retain operational flexibility.

Rommel's position was more straightforward and never deviated during the entire period prior to the Normandy landing. To Rommel, since the Allies possessed air superiority and Germany could not afford another front, the main line of resistance (*Haupt-Kampf-Linie*) had to be the coast. The invading enemy was to be engaged in force on or near the coastline and prevented at all costs from establishing a bridgehead.[15] To accomplish this task Rommel advocated a number of measures, including the extensive use of naval and land mines, beach obstacles, and antiaircraft guns, as well as continuing to strengthen the strongpoint defenses.

In addition, panzer divisions were to be placed as far forward as possible so that they could launch an immediate counterattack against any major Allied assault. "The battle for the coast will probably be over in a few hours, and if experience is any judge, the rapid intervention of forces coming up from the rear will be decisive."[16] One should not conclude, however, that Rommel was opposed to a strategic mobile reserve, for he was not. But he felt strongly that large armored forces positioned near the coast should be given first priority.[17] In fact, Rommel doubted if the Allies could be defeated—at least in open battle—once they had established themselves on the continent.[18]

General Geyr von Schweppenburg disagreed.[19] The head of Panzer Group West, who was directly subordinate to von Rundstedt and had served as a tank commander on the Eastern Front, was convinced that placing mobile reserves near endangered sectors along the coast would merely have a splintering effect. It would be more effective, according to Geyr, to concentrate strong German panzer forces further to the rear, forces that could strike a decisive blow once the main Allied landing had been identified. After all, Geyr pointed out, it was an open question as to where the Anglo-American forces could be expected to attack. In this regard one might well anticipate a series of small enemy operations and deceptions before being able to pinpoint the exact location of his major effort.

Geyr, along with other Wehrmacht leaders, acknowledged that a large Allied assault in certain coastal regions could not be prevented. Would it not therefore be better, Geyr asked, to have strategic motorized formations prepared to counterattack in force at a critical moment than to have a mobile reserve dispersed behind several different coastal fronts? Geyr conceded that some armored divisions might have to be deployed during the "battle for the coast" to prevent an Allied breakthrough. But as soon as German commanders had determined the area of the main enemy attack, "all fast units—even those engaged on nearby fronts—should be led together into battle "to deal the Western Powers a devastating defeat."

The Rommel-Geyr dispute did not abate during the spring of 1944. Both commanders held fast to their original positions regarding the use of mobile reserves, even though both of them should have been more amenable to compromise. For they were well aware that the British and Americans possessed vast naval and air superiority, and that the Allies would, in all likelihood, use airborne troops in conjunction with the main landing attempt.[20] In the instance of Allied naval and air superiority, of course, it would be preferable to have the mobile units stationed near the coast, while in the case of airborne forces, strategic reserves located further inland would be a better solution to the problem.

Logically the quarreling commanders expected von Rundstedt to settle the controversy, and *Ob West* at this junction tended to favor, though not exclusively, Geyr's solution. On February 24, 1944, von Rundstedt insisted that Wehrmacht formations defending the coast were to be backed up by three distinct echelons of reserve forces.[21] The first echelon was to be made up of tactical reserves under the local divisional commanders, and these troops were to begin an immediate counterthrust if the Allies succeeded in gaining a foothold.

If the Western Powers were still able to move a portion of their forces past the coastal zone, they were to be met by additional reserves under the direction of the specific army or corps commander responsible for the area. This intermediate reserve force was to be positioned initially as close to the coast as possible, depending on the terrain and the range of the enemy's naval guns. The placement of these reserve units coincided more with Rommel's thinking, with one important exception—they were not to be armored divisions. The panzer formations, in von Rundstedt's view, were to make up the third echelon and were to be placed behind the army or corps reserve as part of Theater Command West's reserve group, which was led by General Geyr. Von Rundstedt stressed, however, that these armored divisions were to be ultimately under his control and were to be deployed "so that they can attack the coast within the shortest possible time, [but] without being committed prematurely into combat against my instructions." Thus, Commander-in-Chief West's position regarding the use of panzer units accorded with Geyr's view with one difference. Whereas Geyr preferred placing the mobile forces further inland in order to meet the enemy in open battle, von Rundstedt wanted them positioned nearer the coast.

Neither Geyr nor Rommel was completely satisfied with von Rundstedt's solution, even though his decision was clearly an attempt on his part not to upset unduly either of his subordinate commanders.[22] He felt that although Rommel and Geyr had different goals in mind, both were competent commanders, and both were pursuing objectives with which he concurred. With Rommel devoting his tireless energy to strengthening the coastal defenses, and with Geyr busy training the panzer forces for strategic employment, especially to execute such maneuvers as nighttime combat and antiairborne tactics, von Rundstedt undoubtedly hoped his decision would signal an end of the dispute.

But Rommel and Geyr remained dissatisfied, and both attempted to enlist other influential Wehrmacht leaders to side with them. Geyr, for example, received support from General Heinz Guderian, at this time overall Inspector of Armed Forces, and Guderian agreed with Geyr that German armored formations ought to be positioned in the interior.[23] Rommel, on the other hand, at a meeting on March 20, went so far as to request the Armed Forces High Command to place all mobile forces in the West under his command and to allow him tactical control over all military units in the theater, including those formations south of the Loire River.[24]

Von Rundstedt proceeded after the conference to meet Rommel halfway in his requests. On March 24, von Rundstedt ordered that all motorized divisions located in the region commanded by Rommel were to participate in training exercises conducted by Army Group B, and that he could also move these divisions within his area of responsibility upon approval from both *Ob West* and OKW.[25] Most important, Rommel was to receive tactical control over part of Commander-in-Chief West's armored reserve, although the exact number of divisions was to be determined by von Rundstedt. In addition, "to do justice in preparing the head of Army Group B for other possible command duties," von Rundstedt instructed Rommel to inspect the defenses south of the Loire and along the French Mediterranean coast and to report back to him any suggestions Rommel might have for upgrading the defensive posture in that area.[26] In other words, von Rundstedt was asking Rommel, who had already been in the south for a few days in February, to acquaint himself further with this portion of the theater so that, if necessary, he could assume additional command responsibilities in southern France.

Von Rundstedt's action, of course, left him in ultimate control of the panzer forces while dividing tactical responsibility for these units between Geyr and Rommel. The theater commander's directive also allowed him to strengthen his intermediate reserve force, or those formations deployed between the coast and the strategic reserve further to the rear, by giving his tactical commander, in this case Rommel, control over some of these units. Moreover, it seems clear that even though tensions did exist between von Rundstedt and the head of Army Group B, the former was greatly impressed by Rommel's leadership ability and felt that he deserved more authority.[27]

Von Rundstedt was hopeful at the end of March that the compromise worked out over the command controversy would prove to be permanent. According to the compromise, *Ob West* still retained final supervision over all the armored units in the theater. Rommel would be given a mobile reserve force for use near the coast, and Geyr, though his command authority had been decreased, would continue to direct those armored formations positioned further inland.

The problem was that Rommel and Geyr were still upset, and at this stage of the controversy both commanders urged the Führer to become directly involved.[28] On this occasion, as in so many other instances during the war, Hitler's intervention proved decisive. On April 9, the Nazi leader declared that he was in agreement with von Rundstedt's solution regarding command relationships in the West. But in the next sentence Hitler revived the controversy again by asking if "all or only part of the fast units should be made subordinate to Army Group B in all respects."[29] On this issue the Führer said he himself would render a decision.

Hitler's final ruling nearly three weeks later on April 27 closely resembled von Rundstedt's earlier solution with one crucial exception.[30] This exception concerned the strategic reserve. Of the ten armored divisions stationed in the western theater, three were to be placed under the tactical control of Army Group B; three were to be given to the soon-to-be-formed Army Group G, which was eventually to direct Germany's defensive effort in the south of France; and four were to continue to function as a strategic reserve.[31] These four armored divisions, however, instead of remaining under *Ob West* supervision, were to be subject to Hitler's personal command as part of an OKW-Reserve. They could not be moved or sent into battle except by direct order from the Führer. What Hitler had done, in essence, was to eliminate von Rundstedt's control over the strategic reserve that the latter had worked so hard to create.

It was this decision that probably prompted an embittered von Rundstedt to tell a Canadian interrogator after the war: "As Commander-in-Chief West my one authority was to change the guard in front of my gate."[32] The decision did not please Rommel either, and the head of Army Group B continued to agitate for more control over the panzer units. His last attempt came in May. In this instance, von Rundstedt, after receiving a telephone call from a member of the OKW staff, notified Rommel that he was to strengthen the defenses in the Normandy and Brittany sectors.[33] Rommel used the occasion to press that the OKW-Reserve be used for this purpose, and that it be put under his command.[34] *Ob West* turned down the proposal as a premature commitment of these mobile units, and Hitler quite naturally backed von Runstedt, for Rommel's request would have had the effect of doing away with the Führer's control over the strategic reserve in the West.

Was Hitler's final decision, then, a classic example of the Führer's divide-and-rule technique? And did his earlier inaction during the first four months of 1944 serve the same purpose? The answer to these questions is a qualified yes. To be sure, Hitler's failure to step in at first tended to heighten the frictions between von Rundstedt and Rommel, or more properly between Rommel and General Geyr, and the latter two commanders looked to Hitler for a ruling. Eventually the German commanders in the West grudgingly agreed to Hitler's solution with the result that his military decision-making power in the theater was strengthened.

Nevertheless, Hitler's decision did not completely consolidate his hold over the commanders in Western Europe, for the decision tended to alienate a number of them. In fact, many of them felt that the Führer's decision to take over control of the strategic reserve merely substantiated further the notion, already widespread in military circles, that Hitler's egomania was leading Germany toward ultimate disaster. In the end, Geyr, and an increasingly disenchanted Rommel were won over to the necessity of removing the National Socialist dictator. Although von Rundstedt was unwilling to join actively in the plot against Hitler, the fact that *Ob West* allowed such talk and plans to go on in his vicinity would indicate that he was fully aware of the changes being sought by the conspirators.[35]

In light of the small but growing opposition to Hitler, one might ask further why the combat commanders in the West did not become more actively involved in the plot against Hitler. At least part of the answer can be attributed to the pressing military situation in the western theater. The Germans had anticipated an Anglo-American invasion since the middle of February. By this time, in May, it could be expected at any moment. Von Runstedt and the other military leaders in the West realized that they had to reconcile themselves to Hitler's decision regarding the strategic reserve as well as to subdue their own differences if they hoped to meet the Allied Powers with any hope of success.

On May 8, von Rundstedt called together his most important subordinate commanders, including Rommel and Geyr, for a final meeting on strategy before the impending battle.[36] Von Rundstedt, in his brief remarks, stressed that the battle for the coast was now considered decisive and must be won at all costs. Everything must be in readiness to strike at the enemy while he was still in the water or on the beaches, and all remaining efforts should be made with that objective in mind. He went on to conclude that he was confident of victory over the Allied invaders, especially with the recent bolstering of the coastal defenses. In this regard von Rundstedt said he wished especially to thank Field Marshal Rommel for his initiative and his energy in improving the defensive posture along the coast. With this conciliatory gesture toward the head of Army Group B, von Rundstedt doubtless hoped to unify his commanders for the imminent enemy attack.

The senior commander's praise of Rommel should not lead one to conclude, however, that no areas of tension remained between the two field marshals. As pointed out earlier, von Rundstedt and Rommel disagreed in certain instances over strategy, and they also differed in outlook as well as in their style of command. But to depict these differences as leading to an irreconcilable conflict between the two men would be misleading.

In terms of outlook, there was the normal conflict between the younger and older generations. Von Rundstedt had been a professional soldier for nearly 50 years.[37] Since he had been brought up in a Prussian family and had served in the army since 1893, fellow German officers looked upon him as a symbol of a bygone age, as a figure out of the glorious Imperial past. Many of his associates viewed him further as the epitome of the Prussian military tradition—polite, taciturn, religious, outwardly cosmopolitan—a personification of the last Teutonic knight.[38] Yet they respected him as a keen strategist and as a person who knew his trade well.[39]

Rommel, on the other hand, was thought of as the new breed of German officer. He, too, was a professional, but of a different mold.[40] He was the son of a Württemberg schoolmaster and was not tied so strongly to the past. His contemporaries considered him brave, aggressive, willful, a brilliant tactician, a master of the technical aspects of modern warfare. He was most famous for his exploits in the North African campaign, and the German people thought of him even during the war as a superior field captain and as a soldier's general. According to National Socialist propaganda, Rommel exemplified everything an officer in the Wehrmacht ought to be.

There was also another basic distinction between Rommel and von Runstedt, the difference in their command style. The older field marshal was a staff commander. He normally stayed near his headquarters and delegated a great deal of responsibility to his staff and his field commanders, giving them as much latitude as possible in carrying out his orders.[41] He was a stickler for conformity to general principles, but left details to his subordinates.

Rommel was more dynamic. He led from the front and inspired his men by his example. He drove his troops hard and himself even harder. He was interested in detailed instructions as well as in strategy and was more at home on the front lines than in a staff headquarters. Both methods of command, of course, can be effective, even though in this situation a preference for one technique or the other did lead at times to frictions between the two commanders and their respective staffs.

Still the differences between von Rundstedt and the head of Army Group B can be exaggerated. Both individuals enjoyed the military life, and believed strongly in duty to the state. While von Rundstedt was unwilling to associate himself with the July 20 conspiracy against Hitler, and Rommel by 1944 was more willing, both willingly served in Hitler's army. Finally, they respected each other, although Rommel on occasion became impatient with his immediate superior in the West.[42]

This respect between the two field marshals, especially von Rundstedt's respect for Rommel, led to an alteration in the command structure in Western Europe during the first five months of 1944. *Ob West* gave Rommel considerable command responsibility, but Rommel wanted more control over the strategic motorized units held in reserve. He appealed to Hitler to intervene, but the Führer's decision—to take over the ultimate direction of the panzer formations himself—pleased neither of the two commanders. In effect, von Rundstedt had had his command authority in the West greatly diminished, and Rommel had not received any additional control over the armored divisions.

In the meantime, a new echelon of command—Army Group B under Rommel and another army group, Army Group G under General Johannes Blaskowitz, south of the Loire—had been created. These two new army groups brought about a new division of tactical command authority in the western theater. Commander-in-chief West was still in overall command, but subject to more control by OKW.[43] One army group was to look after the less endangered Atlantic and Mediterranean coasts of southern France. The other, Rommel's Army Group B, was responsible for the German defensive effort in the highly threatened sector along the Channel coast. Rommel, with the backing of von Rundstedt, was to become the driving force in this effort.

Chapter 6

Strengthening the Wall and Waiting

B y the end of 1943, both Rommel and von Rundstedt, as well as the other commanders in the theater, agreed that an Allied invasion was certain to take place within the coming year. More specifically, they felt it was only a matter of months, perhaps six at most, before British and American forces would launch a full-scale assault against the continent. Their most pressing problem was how to stop a thoroughly prepared and well-equipped enemy from gaining a foothold in Western Europe.

They also realized that if the Atlantic Wall concept was to have any meaning, they would have to do more than merely strengthen the existing fortifications along the coast. They would also have to ensure a substantial upgrading in the number and quality of personnel and weapons in the area. Any one of these undertakings, let alone all three, was an exceedingly formidable task for the Germans by this stage in the war. Yet they did realize considerable progress in all of these areas during the first six months of 1944, and the improvement would have been greater had not a number of problems intervened. These problems, which included the use of laborers for other high-priority projects and a series of crises in the other theaters, tended to detract from the western buildup.

The buildup was most noticeable in terms of coastal fortifications, and building plans for 1944 called for a number of different types of construction programs.[1] One consisted mainly of improving the existing permanent defenses, although the Germans were not opposed to erecting, if necessary, completely new installations. A second program was to construct a system of secondary defenses some fifteen to twenty-five miles inland from the coast. And a third program, and the one with which Rommel became most closely associated, called for a substantial increase in the number of field-type fortifications being placed on or near the beaches. In this way the Germans felt the Atlantic Wall would become more than a series of knot-points interspersed along the coast, and instead would become a truly comprehensive system of fortifications. In all three instances, whether they were permanent, secondary, or field-type defenses, the main task was to build them as fast as possible with every resource available.

In terms of permanent fortifications, the Germans continued to concentrate a substantial portion of their heavy construction work near the major ports, and Hitler went so far as to declare eleven of them "fortresses" (*Festungen*) on January 19, 1944.[2] The areas singled out were Ijmuiden and the Hook of Holland in the Netherlands; Dunkirk, Boulogne, and Le Havre in the Fifteenth Army sector along the Channel; Cherbourg, St. Malo, Brest, Lorient, and St. Nazaire in the Seventh Army zone; and the Gironde River estuary that led to Bordeaux in the first Army area. Wehrmacht staff officers added three more fortresses—the Channel Islands and the coastal harbors of Calais and La Pallice-La Rochelle—during February and March.[3] Their designation as *Festungen* was rather hollow, however, for most of them had already been declared defense areas in July of 1942 and had therefore been given considerable attention.

What the Germans hoped to do now was to make them into defense-worthy installations in every respect.[4] Both inside the fortresses and in the strongpoints along the coast, engineering troops and Organization Todt workers proceeded to start covering the heavy infantry weapon positions, the command posts, and even machine gun nests as well as many of the coastal artillery batteries which still lay in the open. They also began moving artillery pieces so that they would be less susceptible to Allied air and ship bombardments. And in other instances the engineers cleverly camouflaged existing batteries and constructed dummy positions to deceive the enemy.

Local commanders lent a hand by lowering the number of hours that troops spent in combat training and had them assist in the construction effort. The soldiers used every resource available—sea walls, ship canals, old ramparts—to help build the strongpoints into truly impregnable barriers. Interspersed among these hindrances the Germans placed numerous field-type defenses, such as minefields, bogus minefields, barbed wire ensnarements, antitank ditches—in short, anything that might strengthen the perimeter or interior defenses.

Since the major harbors were to be held to the last person, the Germans wanted to stockpile enough supplies so that these ports would be self-sufficient even in case of a prolonged enemy attack. But if Allied troops succeeded in penetrating the fortress defenses, *Ob West* directed that measures by instituted to assure that the port facilities and the surrounding transportation network be destroyed or rendered unusable.[5]

By effectively utilizing the men and materiel at their disposal, the Germans made considerable strides in building up the defenses prior to D-Day. During the first four months of 1944, for instance, the number of cubic meters of concrete laid by Organization Todt doubled from 357,000 to 722,100 per month.[6] The Germans also erected more than 5,000 permanent installations (including the French Mediterranean coast) between January and the end of May.[7]

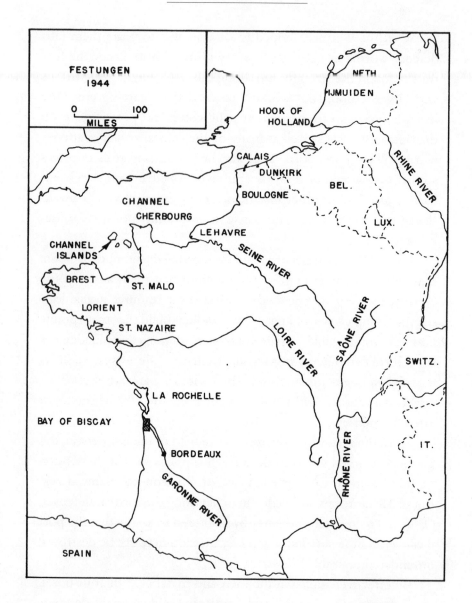

Fig. 6.1 *Festungen*

This latter figure is particularly impressive when one considers that from 1941 to the end of 1943, construction workers built 8,478 concrete structures along the Channel and Atlantic coasts, while during 1944, in a period of only five months, labor crews in the West erected over 4,600 permanent fortifications, or more than half of the total number constructed during the previous 2½ years.

By this time the differentiation in defenses for each coastal sector had become quite evident. An evaluation conducted by United States artillery experts after the war estimated that the Germans in 1944 had emplacements for 495 coastal artillery guns of 15 cm. (6-inch) or larger caliber in the Fifteenth Army area along the Channel.[8] By contrast, in the Seventh Army sector, which covered twice as much coastline, including the eventual invasion zone, the Germans had erected positions for only 211 medium and heavy artillery weapons. The contrast becomes even more pronounced along France's Atlantic coast, where there were a mere sixty-five artillery emplacements for guns of over 15 centimeters.

The same contrast holds true in terms of the total number of coastal batteries constructed in each region. The Netherlands area had ninety-seven batteries to house its coastal artillery guns, and the Seventh Army region only seventy-nine batteries. But the Fifteenth Army had 236 batteries in its sector, making it by far the most heavily fortified area in the western theater.

No matter how great the contrast among the various coastal regions, von Runstedt was well aware that the Atlantic Wall defenses lacked depth. He ordered the local commanders in October 1943 to begin constructing a number of secondary positions (2. *Stellungen*) in the sector lying more than ten miles inland from the coast.[9] He stressed that these positions should not be a rigid, inflexible line, but should take advantage of the already existing strongpoints, such as airfields, ammunition dumps, and military posts located in the rear areas. Then new fortifications and hindrances should be erected among the strongpoints to form a system of secondary defenses.

Although work started almost immediately on these positions, and foreign laborers did build some field-type fortifications and obstacles behind the coastal zone, the Germans never released enough men and materiel to construct an effective line of interior defenses.[10] In other words, by 1944, other, more pressing priorities prevented them from carrying through a project of this magnitude in such a short period of time.

The rise in the number and types of field-type hindrances along the coast was more substantial and more spectacular. This program was advocated by Rommel, and it had von Runstedt's enthusiastic support.[11] It included a variety of measures by which to disrupt an Allied landing, such as laying land mines, flooding low-lying areas, and placing foreshore obstacles and anti-airborne stakes on or near the coast. Rommel persistently pushed forward all aspects of the program, and by June he could point to considerable progress.

With regard to flooding, the Germans flooded some stretches of low ground immediately behind the beach areas. Although the amount of ground inundated was considerable, especially in Holland and Belgium, it was not as extensive as it might have been.[12]

Rather than flooding large areas, which might tend to hamper the Germans as much as the Allies, Rommel preferred the extensive use of land mines.[13] In the two years prior to October 30, 1943, German engineering specialists had laid 1,992,895 antitank and antipersonnel mines in the West.[14] By May 30, 1944, within a space of seven months, the number had risen about 3½ times to 6,508,330 mines.[15] This figure fell far short of Rommel's own estimate that at least 50 million mines would be necessary to establish a continuous defensive belt around the western theater, but the Germans could still feel they had accomplished a great deal since the beginning of the year.[16]

The most important new defensive technique introduced by Rommel was the use of foreshore obstacles.[17] These obstacles, placed along the beaches, were designed to serve a number of purposes. They would fill in the defensive gaps between the strongpoints.

They would help protect the more remote beaches along the coast. And there was even some hope that the obstacles might lead the Allies to postpone their landing for a short time in order to put their troops through additional training, thus allowing German units to gain precious time in the defensive buildup.[18]

The plan was to position the underwater obstructions in three to six rows along the beaches, so that they could disrupt an amphibious operation, whether it came at high or low tide. Fortunately for the Allies, whose D-Day attack took place on a rising tide, only three of the projected six rows of obstacles, or those obstructions closest to shore, had been laid along the Normandy beach that was invaded.

The actual obstacles consisted of a number of ingenious devices. The simplest was an 8 to 10-foot wooden or concrete stake driven into the beach and angled toward the sea. Some of the stakes had mines or grenades attached, and all of them, when submerged, could damage the bottom of a landing craft advancing rapidly toward shore. The same was true of numerous V-shaped, ramplike structures, which the Germans sloped toward the sea and armed with mines or old artillery shells designed to explode on impact.

A third type of obstacle was the concrete tetrahedron. This pyramid-shaped object was six feet high, weighed nearly a ton, and it, too, could be mined or could tear a hole in the bottom of a landing craft. Another effective hindrance was an obsolete tank obstacle called the "hedgehog." It was made up of three 7-foot steel girders bent at right angles and welded together in the middle so that it resembled a jackstone used in the game of jacks. The sharp points that extended in all directions from the center acted like a "can opener" on incoming amphibious craft.

Finally, there were Belgian gates, which, as the name implies, looked like gates that would mark the entrance to a country estate. In reality they were heavy, steel, antitank structures erected by the Belgians before the war and placed along their border with Germany. Standing about nine feet high and measuring nine feet across, a few of them had mines attached, and these mines were often coated with tar to make them impervious to water.

The number of hindrances placed along the coast did not come up to Rommel's expectations (in part because the Germans ran out of steel antitank obstacles in April and had to start relying almost exclusively on ones made of wood and concrete).[19] But by the middle of May, Wehrmacht staff officers could still point to more than 500,000 foreshore obstacles having been positioned on the Channel beaches, and 31,000 of them of them had been fitted with mines.[20] Laid further out to sea, but still complementing the beach obstructions, were a variety of shallow-water mines, which exacted their toll on Allied shipping both during and after the invasion.[21]

To complete the system of smaller defenses, the German field marshal also had installed behind the coast another innovation called "Rommel Asparagus."[22] This antiparatroop and antiglider device consisted of tall, pointed stakes driven into the ground and spaced so that an area which had once been flat terrain and in the open took on the appearance of a field of wooden spears. German engineers further planned to put captured shells at the top of some of the stakes, and all the shells were then to be connected by a tripwire so that if an airborne troop or glider hit the wire, the shells would detonate. At the time of the invasion, however, the stakes had not been wired together or fitted with explosives. These obstacles, as well as the others, were perhaps not as effective as the Germans would have liked, but they still represent a considerable effort.

The amount of progress in defense construction would have been even more extensive had it not been for the diversion of workers and materiel to other tasks, including the construction of V-weapon launching sites and the repair of damage being inflicted increasingly by enemy bombing attacks and by Resistance sabotage activity.

The V-weapons, or vengeance weapons (originally called "experimental" weapons but changed to "vengeance" weapons for propaganda purposes), were designed by the Germans to strike at enemy targets several hundred miles behind the front lines.[23] The V-1 was essentially a pilotless monoplane developed by the air force which could reach speeds of up to 400 miles per hour. It could, moreover, be launched from the ground or from an aircraft, and the British labeled them "buzz bombs" or "doodlebugs" because of the noise made by their jet engines while flying through the air.

The V-2, on the other hand, was a large, fast sophisticated rocket developed by the army to compete with the V-1. The army version could reach a maximum speed of 3,600 miles per hour on the way to the target, and it was launched from an upright position. Both the army and the Luftwaffe, quite naturally, tried to persuade Hitler to select its particular weapon for use against the Allies.

The Führer decided that both the V-1 and the V-2 should be made operational, and that these new "secret weapons" should be directed against targets in England from permanent positions near the Channel coast. Although von Rundstedt and the tactical commanders in the theater had little to do with the actual firing of the V-1s and V-2s, the job of erecting the weapon sites fell originally in 1943 on the air force administrative units (*Luftgaukommandos*)in the area. The first sites were for the V-1 weapons and were called ski sites because they resembled a large ski. Work crews built them quickly, often with local labor and with little regard for security. When the Allies, who were well aware that the Germans were working on a jet propelled rocket system, found in reconnaissance photos that new, odd-looking installations were being constructed near the coast in northern France, they soon concluded that the installations were tied in with V-weapon developments. The Allied commanders proceeded to bomb the ski sites with the result that most of them were put out of commission.[24]

As a result, at the beginning of 1944 the Germans began to build another type of launching site. They were less elaborate than the ski sites, but easily constructed, well concealed, and difficult to detect. Once discovered by British and American flyers, they were still very poor targets because of their small size.[25] The Germans also tightened security measures while building these new installations, and at times the Wehrmacht supervisors intentionally misemployed French workers on the old ski sites.[26] Germany's success in erecting the new sites became apparent when they started dropping flying bombs on England on June 13.

No doubt, the V-1 and V-2 weapons were important in Germany's attempt to change the balance of the war in her favor. But the significant point regarding the V-weapon launching areas as they pertained to the defense of Western Europe was that had not the Wehrmacht allocated a substantial number of laborers to work on the sites, they might well have been utilized in building up the Atlantic Wall.

The same problem applied to the effort expended by the Germans to repair the damage inflicted by enemy bombing and sabotage activity. American and British bombing missions conducted against Western Europe prior to 1944 had generally been confined to purely military targets, such as submarine pens, ammunition dumps, personnel barracks, and the like. In 1944 the Allies not only increased the number of air attacks directed against France, Belgium, and the Netherlands, but they also began attacking many additional types of targets.

Allied pilots, in their desire to isolate the invasion area and still not tip off the Germans as to where the landing would take place, found the transportation network to be especially vulnerable. As a result, British and American bombers and tactical fighters succeeded in disrupting rail lines, destroying bridges, and damaging roadways on a vast scale prior to the Allied assault. On June 3, just three days before the invasion, Army Group B reported that "rising enemy air activity has made the transporting of supplies by rail very difficult," and that "1,700 rail cars destined for the West remain in rear area depots."[27] The report went on to relate that many bridges had been destroyed and that truck transport could be carried out only on a limited basis.

Supplementing the Allied bombing raids on the transportation system were an increasing number of acts of sabotage undertaken by the French Resistance.[28] In addition to interfering with rail traffic, the Resistance movement by 1944 began to set up other such terrorist activities as cutting telephone and telegraph lines and sabotaging war industries. Factory laborers also aided the Resistance, and at the same time demonstrated their disdain for the German occupiers by slowing down their work pace or by instituting work stoppages.[29]

All these activities, whether in the form of passive resistance or sabotage or aerial bombing, obviously had a harmful effect on the effort being expended to build up the Atlantic Wall. It meant a reduction in the amount of construction materials that reached the coastal area. It also signified that more and more workers had to be shifted to repair the damages being inflicted on the transportation and communication systems and the industrial plants. The Germans, in fact, started using every kind of labor available, from German technicians sent out from the Reich to Indochinese workers and Senegalese soldiers who had been caught up in the fall of France, in an effort to keep the rail, road, and communications lines open.[30] In terms of labor crews working specifically on the Atlantic Wall, *Ob West* removed 18,000 Organization Todt workers in March 1944, to perform railroad maintenance, and in May he requested 47,000 more laborers be withdrawn.[31] Although von Rundstedt received permission from OKW to take off only 10,000 additional workers, it still shows how critical the repair work problem had become.

With regard to military personnel in the West in 1944, the rise during the first half of 1944 was steady rather than spectacular. On October 4, 1943, Commander-in-Chief West listed thirty-eight divisions ready for combat and thirteen additional divisions in the process of formation.[32] The number of ready divisions toward the end of December had increased to forty-one with seven more being formed or refitted.[33] By April 1944, the total figures had climbed further to fifty-five divisions, almost all of which could be used at least on a limited basis, and this number reached fifty-eight just prior to the invasion.[34]

Forty-six of the fifty-eight divisions were positioned along the coast.[35] The most threatened Fifteenth Army sector had eighteen divisions under its command. The Seventh Army zone, which by April and May was thought to be highly vulnerable, had fourteen divisions, and the less endangered Netherlands command in the north had three divisions stationed in its area. In the south, four divisions under First Army provided a thin defensive line along the Atlantic coast, and seven divisions under Nineteenth Army guarded the French Mediterranean region. Two reserve divisions were located in the interior.

The remaining ten divisions were the armored formations which von Rundstedt had worked so hard to bring into the area after October 1943. Three of the panzer divisions were stationed north of the Seine, three between the Seine and Loire Rivers, and the other four in the south of France.

The composition of the German panzer divisions varied so widely at this time that they are difficult to characterize.[36] In general, however, the typical division had four battalions of infantry (six in an SS formation), one tank regiment of two battalions, an antitank battalion (usually armed with assault guns), an armored reconnaissance battalion, and an artillery regiment of three or four battalions plus additional support troops. The actual number of personnel in these divisions ranged from 13,000 to over 21,000 men.

The heart of the armored formations was the tank regiment, which was to have at least one battalion of Mark IV and one battalion of Mark V Panther tanks. This meant that each division was to have a complement of 176 tanks if fully outfitted, but five of the ten divisions had less than 100 tanks each (the 17th SS Panzer Grenadier Division had no tanks at all), and only the Panzer Lehr Division with 183 tanks was up to strength. The next closest was the 2nd Panzer Division with ninety-four Mark IVs and sixty-seven Mark Vs.

The Mark IV was a medium tank of twenty-three tons with a 75-mm. gun, and the Panther weighed forty-five tons and had a high-velocity 75-mm. gun. Of the more than 1,300 tanks in the theater at the end of April, 420 were the lighter Mark IIIs, 674 were Mark IVs, and 514 Mark Vs. There were also some captured French or Russian models. The tank forces were further augmented when a battalion of Mark VI Tiger tanks arrived in the West on June 1.[37]

The influx of panzer formations was part of the continuing effort to have firepower compensate for the lack of manpower. The Germans also tried to meet this problem by altering the composition of their infantry divisions. The conventional Wehrmacht infantry division between 1939 and 1943 had had at full strength 17,200 troops.[38] The Germans decreased this number to 13,656 late in 1943, and in January 1944, they lowered the number again to 12,769 soldiers. But this loss of personnel in the new 1944 division was to be offset by almost twice as many automatic weapons, and hence much greater firepower, than its earlier counterpart.

Contrary to what one might expect, the reduction in the number of troops per division actually had a beneficial effect in that some of the coastal divisions which had become depleted during the last two years now received additional personnel and better equipment.[39] Moreover, a number of the reserve divisions, now upgraded to regular units, also benefited from the increase in troops and weapons.[40]

Admittedly, these forces, no matter how well equipped, were not of the fighting quality of the German formations in 1940 and 1941, but nowhere in Europe in 1944 were they equal to their predecessors. Included among their ranks were soldiers of every description—combat veterans and raw recruits, Germans and foreign nationals, air force and navy (some of them serving in ground combat units) as well as army personnel.[41] But the Germans hoped that this force would be sufficient to turn back the Allied invasion.

As impressive as the rise in manpower was, the increase in the number of artillery weapons had continued to mount throughout the German occupation until by the time of the invasion there were more than 3,300 light, medium and heavy artillery pieces, or more than three times what there had been in 1941.[42] The Wehrmacht also transported large numbers of antitank guns into the west in 1944. A special group sent to inspect the Seventh Army area came away with the impression that the 2,027 antitank weapons in the area could prevent even a strong enemy panzer force from effecting a successful landing.

But this increase in the number of weapons as well as in the number of personnel never reached the proportions that the Germans had expected or had hoped. The chief reason was that Allied pressure from both the east and south never allowed OKW to shut off completely the flow of personnel to other, more immediately critical war theaters. The Allied landing at Anzio in January, the Wehrmacht occupation of Hungary in March, the critical situation on the southern flank of the eastern front at the end of the month, and the renewed Allied offensive toward Rome in May—all of these affected the western theater adversely in both a direct and an indirect way.

The direct effect was that OKW had to remove three panzer and one infantry division plus a number of assault guns from Western Europe during the course of the spring, although one of the armored formations—the Panzer Lehr Division—returned to France in good shape in May.[43] Indirectly, German forces stationed in other areas but scheduled for deployment in the West were rushed to meet the new emergencies on the Russian and Italian fronts. These troop movements along with the shifting of units within the western theater itself could not help but disrupt, at least to a degree, the preparations that were being instituted for the Allied invasion.

In spite of the disruptions and the fact that the Germans were never able to achieve the type of defensive presence in the West they would have liked, by late spring of 1944 they could still commit a fairly respectable force behind a fairly formidable defensive barrier. In this light Hitler and the other German military leaders could actually face the prospect of an Anglo-American landing not so much in a state of apprehension as in a state of anticipation.

There was nothing novel about the mood of anticipation which permeated Western Europe during the first half of 1944, but the atmosphere of expectancy reached new heights because of the impending Allied invasion. The question Wehrmacht leaders had on their minds was not if the British and Americans were coming, but rather where and when they would attack.

The German guessing game as to Anglo-American intentions had begun in 1942, and it continued even after the D-Day landing, since German commanders, who never had precise information regarding Allied plans that they could depend on, still continued to expect another landing in the Fifteenth Army area. In the six months prior to June 6, however, German thinking with regard to the invasion went through three different phases.[44] During the first phase at the end of 1943, Hitler and the other military leaders generally confirmed in their own minds, as they had all along, that the landing would take place along the Channel coast somewhere between the mouth of the Scheldt River and the tip of Brittany. But during January and February, they became uneasy and began to prepare for other possible Allied moves against the continent. By March the German military once again returned to its original conviction that the Western Powers would attack across the channel, and this opinion prevailed during the third phase until D-Day itself.

The new psychological buildup for the invasion began with von Rundstedt's report of October 1943, and his views, in a sense, reflected the consensus of the tactical commanders in the West at this time.[45] He warned that the impending battle could be expected within a matter of months and that the most likely place was the Channel coast, probably in conjunction with a smaller attack in some other area.[46]

Hitler agreed with his theater commander and forcibly expressed his opinion to his generals after the Allied conferences at Teheran and Cairo in November and December.

I have studied most of these documents [reports of the Teheran and Cairo meetings]. There is no doubt that an attack in the West will come in the spring. There's absolutely no doubt about it. I have the feeling that they want to operate on very broad fronts.[47]

The National Socialist dictator went on to declare that the Allies would "catch hell" when they invaded Western Europe. There was a great deal of difference, he maintained, between landing in North Africa and being opposed by Vichy French units and "Italians who mostly sit in their holes and don't fire a shot, and landing in the West where there is really going to be shooting. As long as our batteries can fire, they will fire, that's certain."

In January, Hitler and von Rundstedt continued to stress that the Channel coast was the most likely place for the main Allied landing, but they became concerned about the possibility of other operations being conducted at the same time.[48] In all probability these Allied actions would take the form of a series of small attacks designed to draw German forces away from the Channel area. But the military leaders were fearful that British and American forces might even attempt a major landing in the Balkans or in northern Italy.

The Germans therefore made plans to meet any contingency the Allies might select, whether it was aimed at Norway or Denmark or the Balkans or within the western theater itself.[49] In February, Ob West and OKW as well became particularly apprehensive about a possible allied attack in southern France or Portugal and moved several additional divisions into the area south of the Loire.[50] Wehrmacht fears about its southern flank subsided after the Germans learned that the Allies had transferred a number of combat-experienced divisions from the Mediterranean theater to Great Britain. But the idea that British and American forces would initiate several diversionary attacks before or during the main assault phase had become deeply implanted in the minds of the German leaders.[51]

As German intelligence began to evaluate more and more information concerning Allied intentions in the West, it became clear to them by the spring of 1944 that the main attack would be somewhere along the Channel. But, handicapped in particular by their inability to provide continuous reconnaissance coverage of the English coast, the Germans were still in a quandry as to its exact location.[52] They were well aware that most of the thousand-mile Channel coastline was within range of American and British fighter aircraft, and the Armed Forces High Command calculated that this factor would be of major importance in any choice the Allies made for a landing.[53]

Since they had no clear indication, however, the German generals continued to speculate throughout the spring months. Their consensus was that it would probably come between the mouth of the Seine and the Pas de Calais area, but they did not rule out at least small-scale operations on the Cotentin and Brittany Peninsulas. Only Admiral Krancke, the German naval commander in the West, consistently dissented from this view. Krancke and his staff based their estimate on tidal considerations, the availability of a major harbor, and the pattern of enemy minelaying activity in the Channel. They concluded, as it turned out correctly, from 1942 on that the region between Cherbourg and Le Havre was the most logical place for an Allied attack.[54] But all of the military leaders, including Hitler, were at least in agreement that the coastal sector between the Scheldt estuary and Brittany was critical.[55]

The reports and orders that shuttled between the western theater and higher headquarters during the final forty days before the invasion give an excellent picture as to where Hitler, von Runstedt, and Rommel figured the invasion would take place. These reports are significant in several respects. Not only do they reveal the slight changes that occurred from week to week in the German estimate of where American and British forces would land. They also bring out when Hitler and his western commanders expected the Allied assault to come about, and they further indicate how the atmosphere of tension continued to mount in the West just prior to D-Day itself.

On April 26, von Runstedt declared that he anticipated an attack within the next few weeks and that plainly the strongpoint (*eindeutigen Schwerpunkt*) of the invasion would be the Channel front between the Scheldt and Brittany.[56] Later that day von Rundstedt received an order from Hitler to move two parachute divisions, the 3rd and the 5th, into Brittany to guard against a possible airborne attack in the area.

Commander-in-Chief West made sure that Hitler's decision was carried out, and it is interesting to note that his weekly estimate on April 29 for the first time mentioned Normandy (by which he meant the Cotentin Peninsula) and Brittany as possible primary Allied target areas.[57] The reason, von Rundstedt noted, was because the British and Americans were concentrating in southwestern England large number of troops that could logically be used for an operation against these two vulnerable peninsulas.

No one has quite figured out why the Führer became so concerned about Normandy and Brittany, although Warlimont, who played a key role on the OKW operations staff, contends that Hitler's decision was based on a combination of factors, including the location of American troops in England, a report of an invasion exercise in Devon (Slapton Sands) where Allied units landed on flat and open terrain similar to that in Normandy, and the belief that the attack would be near a major port, in this case Cherbourg.[58] But it might also have been the result of one of Hitler's famous "intuitive" flashes. In any event, the activity during the first week in May was designed to reinforce those areas which lay within the Seventh Army region. On May 2, Hitler indicated that Brittany and Normandy were in extreme danger of attack and that the Channel Islands were also threatened.[59]

On the 4th, Rommel proposed that the four armored divisions in the OKW-Reserve be brought into the endangered sector and put under his command.[60] Although both von Rundstedt and Hitler turned down Rommel's request, they did move an airborne division (in effect, it functioned as an infantry division), and a number of artillery and assault gun battalions into the Cotentin Peninsula.[61] When one added to this total the two parachute divisions which had already been rushed into Brittany plus two panzer divisions that were newly stationed nearby, the increase in manpower and firepower in the Seventh Army area becomes quite substantial.

Ob West in his reports of May 8 and 9 pointed to the strengthening of the defensive posture in Normandy, and he also reiterated that an Allied attack would probably come in the middle of May with the coastal zone between Boulogne and Cherbourg as the most likely place.[62] The most threatened ports within the Channel area, von Rundstedt emphasized, were first of all Cherbourg and Le Havre, and secondly Boulogne and Brest.

This view of probable Anglo-American intentions persisted with some slight variations until the end of the month. On the 15th, Commander-in-Chief West stated that the probable strongpoint of the enemy invasion "remains as before the Channel front between the Scheldt and Normandy," but by this time he had relegated Brittany to a partial operation.[63] On the 22nd, using Allied air activity as the basis, Rommel and von Rundstedt once again felt Brittany was endangered, and one week later they continued to expect an enemy assault around Brest as well as in the sector between Calais and Cherbourg as possible.[64]

The final ten days before D-Day can be viewed in general as a period during which the Germans continued to anticipate an Allied assault, but also as a time during which Wehrmacht leaders hoped that the waiting and uncertainty would come to an end.[65] On May 28, the western commanders noted with alarm that U.S. and British bombing raids had destroyed or rendered unusable all of the Seine River bridges between Paris and Rouen, thus eliminating all rail traffic from crossing the Seine north of Paris and concluded that these raids signaled the final preliminary phase before the invasion.[66] *Ob West* immediately detailed work crews to try to repair several of the less damaged bridges, but without success, and neither he nor Rommel and their staffs were able to pinpoint the exact location where the Allies would land. They fully realized that the attacks on the Seine bridges had cut the Channel front in two, virtually isolating the Bay of the Seine and Normandy south of the Seine from the area north of the river. Von Rundstedt even acknowledged that this situation could mean the enemy intended to build a beachhead in Normandy. But they agreed that counterbalancing this possibility was the fact that Allied air activity, including reconnaissance flights, along the Channel coast had not singled out any one place for special emphasis.

The weekly estimates submitted by Army Group B and Theater Command West on June 5 indicate the same sense of frustration.[67] It was obvious to them that Allied aircraft were pursuing a quite effective interdiction campaign against the transportation network in preparation for the invasion, but Rommel and von Rundstedt still had no firm information as to where the actual assault would take place. They would simply have to wait.

The Germans were taken by surprise operationally when the invasion occurred the next day.[68] In part their surprise can be attributed to the poor weather conditions that prevailed over the Channel, a factor that took some of the psychological edge off the possibility of an Allied attack. But in part it was also because German officers believed that British and American bombing raids against coastal fortifications had not reached sufficient intensity to warrant taking extreme precautions. Some of the divisional and other commanders in the Seventh Army zone, where the landing took place, had even departed for a war game exercise to be held in Rennes in Brittany on the morning of the 6th, and Rommel himself was at home for several days of leave and to celebrate his wife's birthday before going to see Hitler and then returning to the West. But now the Allied invasion had intervened. The waiting was over.

Chapter 7

Normandy and Provence

E ven though the Normandy and Provence invasions form a coda to our study of the Atlantic Wall, they are obviously important in adding to our understanding of Germany's defensive system. Although the Wehrmacht's defenses failed to hold back the invading enemy, this is not so much the fault of the Atlantic Wall as it is Germany's far greater miscalculation of becoming involved in a prolonged war against overwhelming foes, a war which after 1941 it could not expect to win.

The Germans had continued to build up their western defenses to the day of the invasion. In fact, von Rundstedt had not put the theater on full alert (*Alarmstufe II*) in May because such an action would have brought about a work stoppage on the coastal defenses.[1] The western defense complex by June 6, while not as strong as the German military would have liked, was nonetheless strong enough to cause the Western Allies a great deal of concern. Wehrmacht leaders at this time could point to over 13,000 permanent installations supplemented by a much larger number of field-type defenses:

3,300 artillery pieces, 1,343 tanks, and a total of 1,873,000 troops in fifty-eight divisions, including ten panzer divisions, plus other smaller combat units. Complementing the army forces were those of the navy, which had five destroyers stationed in the Bay of Biscay, four torpedo boats, twenty-nine motor torpedo boats, and 500 small patrol boats and minesweepers ready to oppose the enemy assault. Added to this were thirty-five small submarines located at Brest and the Atlantic harbors which could be used for anti-invasion duty.[2] The Third Air Fleet listed 919 aircraft (510 were operational) as of the last of May, but the lack of German air activity on the day of the landing would indicate that the actual number in commission was much smaller than the Luftwaffe dared to admit.[3]

Allied forces in England, on the other hand, consisted of 1,440,000 troops in thirty-nine divisions—twenty-four infantry, eleven armored, and four airborne formations.[4] The real discrepancy between Allied and German forces was in the area of sea and air power. Although many of the Allied seacraft were noncombat transports, 6,939 ships and landing craft were in the opening phase of the invasion, as compared with the total of 561 that the *Kriegsmarine* had at its disposal.[5] In terms of aircraft, the Allies had 12,837 planes of all types facing 919 German aircraft, or a ratio of fourteen to one.[6]

These then in brief were the forces opposing each other on June 6. The Germans had the advantage of a system of coastal defenses reinforced by highly mobile tank formations in the rear. Facing them were the Allied invaders, whose well-equipped army and vastly superior air force and navy had the additional advantage of being able to concentrate their forces at a single point.

The long-awaited invasion began shortly after midnight when British and American airborne troops began landing directly behind the Normandy coast. German patrols in the region were confused at first, since the paratroop and glider forces in several instances were dropped over widely scattered areas. Several hours later Allied planes and ships unleashed a heavy bombardment of the coast, and this was followed starting at 6:30 a.m., by the main task force, which began

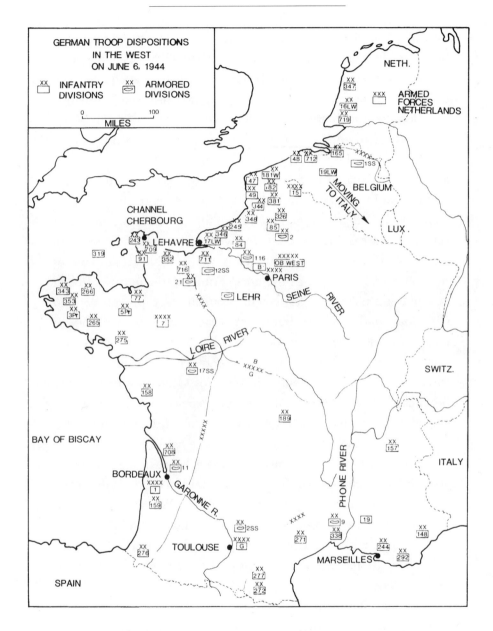

Fig. 7.1. German Troop Dispositions in the West, June 6, 1944

assaulting French beaches in five different places along a 60-mile front between Cherbourg and Le Havre in the Bay of the Seine region.[7]

German defenses in the invasion sector were inadequate, even though Wehrmacht staff officers had always considered Normandy as a definite possibility for an Allied landing. Hitler, it will be remembered, had gone so far as to reinforce the Cotentin Peninsula and the Bay of the Seine area in April and May, but this had been accomplished mainly by moving additional formations into the area rather than by constructing new fortifications. Part of the reason for the lack of defenses stemmed from the fact there was no major port in the area. But the Germans were not completely bereft of weapons, since they had positioned more than 200 artillery pieces of over 88-mm. caliber in the area.[8] Some of the guns had been covered and placed in permanent installations, especially around Cherbourg and Le Havre, but the majority of them were mobile or located in field-type fortifications. In addition to the artillery weapons, the Germans also had the usual complement of firing trenches, foreshore obstacles, and other hindrances located on or near the beaches. Still the Wehrmacht defensive barrier in Normandy was considerably weaker than in some of the other areas along the coast.

The Wehrmacht troops stationed in the battle sector were also not of the quality the Germans would have liked. In the immediate area under attack they had five infantry divisions, the 716th, 711th, 352nd, 709th, and 91st Airborne, and the 21st Panzer Division and the 6th Parachute Regiment. Of these seven units, the 21st Panzer and the 6th Parachute Regiment were considered excellent, but the infantry divisions, with the exception of the 352nd, were not first-rate formations.

On the other hand, the German tactical commanders who directed the fighting in the area were of good quality, since the British, American, and Allied forces landed for the most part in the LXXXIV Corps sector, which was under the command of the highly respected General Erich Marcks.[9] The only part of the invasion zone not under Marcks' control was the extreme eastern portion,

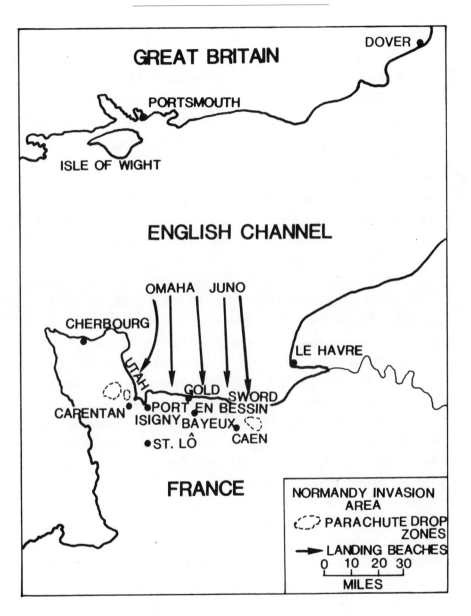

Fig. 7.2. Normandy Invasion Area

which was under LXXXI Corps. The LXXXI Corps was responsible, in turn, to Fifteenth Army, while the LXXXIV Corps was
under Seventh Army. Field Marshal Rommel, whose capabilities
were well known, was the overall tactical commander of the area.

The initial Allied assault forces started disembarking just after
dawn on a rising tide with the Americans landing in the western
portion of the invasion zone, British and Canadian soldiers in the
eastern sector. Because of their exposed position, the Allied troops
at first experienced some difficulty moving across the wide expanse
of beach. However, most of the units were soon able to advance
off the beaches and secure small bridgeheads against relatively light
opposition.

The one exception was at Omaha Beach, where the 352nd
German division greeted the U.S. 1st and 29th divisions with such a
withering barrage of artillery and smaller arms fire that it threatened to push the American forces back into the sea. The situation
was so critical at one point that the American commanders, who
were directing the overall invasion effort from a command ship
offshore, thought the Omaha assault had been repulsed. But about
eleven o'clock, with the help of naval gunfire, American troops
slowly began advancing off the beaches and securing a foothold on
higher ground. By 11 o'clock the American commanders could
breathe easier because they no longer considered the situation at
Omaha precarious and felt it could be held.

In the meantime, special United States, British, and Canadian
engineers, often in the face of extensive German artillery and small
arms fire, had started clearing the invasion beaches of obstacles so
that troop reinforcements and supplies would not be jeopardized.
The clearing operations did not progress as quickly as Allied officials had hoped because of determined German resistance, the rapidly rising tide, and congestion in the unloading areas. But in spite
of these problems the Allies still managed to land a considerable
quantity of personnel and equipment during the first, critical hours
and thus hastened the movement inland.

In some instances the Anglo-American troops were able to advance inland without any help, especially when they succeeded in gaining control of a road or draw that led through the steep cliffs or over ponds of stagnant water which often lay between the beach areas and the interior. In other instances Allied assault forces managed to link up with the airborne units which had been dropped behind the coast the night before.

Throughout the afternoon Allied forces proceeded to consolidate their positions and, except at Omaha Beach, to advance steadily inland. By nightfall some of the British and American divisions had penetrated as far as six miles from the coast. Although this distance was still short of several of the D-Day objectives, such as the capture of Caen, which was over eight miles inland, Allied commanders could justifiably feel relieved and even elated at the progress the first day, during which they landed and airdropped approximately 155,000 troops.[10]

It is rather surprising that the Germans response was not more decisive. The Germans may have been deceived to some extent by the various allied diversions, which ranged from misleading radio traffic and feint attacks against the Dutch and Norwegian coasts to dummy paratroopers landing in areas away from the assault zone. But more telling in the long run had been the fact that the Wehrmacht commanders, having anticipated the invasion for so long, could not actually believe it had finally begun. Many of them, including Rommel, who arrived back in the theater on the night of the 6th from being on leave, were convinced that the Normandy assault would soon be followed by yet another invasion along the Channel coast.[11]

This misappraisal of US-British intentions persisted throughout June and July because German officers, partly as a result of faulty intelligence information, continued to overestimate the number of allied divisions stationed in the United Kingdom. Therefore, they believed that British and American forces would strike a second blow somewhere between the Somme and the Scheldt rivers.[12]

As a result, the static coastal divisions in the Fifteenth Army, instead of being utilized against the Allied bridgehead in Normandy, remained deployed in the Pas de Calais area anticipating an invasion which never came. Not until the end of July, after the United States forces had broken out near St. Lô, did Wehrmacht commanders acknowledge that "a second large-scale enemy landing on Europe's western coast no longer appears likely."[13]

The Germans also misjudged the Allies with regard to the latter's intention of immediately attempting to seize a major port. Wehrmacht leaders failed to realize that the Allies, rather than relying on normal port facilities, had decided to set up ingenious, artificial harbors, called "Mulberries," which would allow the British and Americans to supply their forces "across the beaches" during the initial, critical phase of the Normandy operation.[14]

The only major German counterattack on the first day was undertaken by elements of the 21st Panzer Division, but it was driven back almost to its original starting point. More crucial for the Wehrmacht had been its failure to move two of its other armed formations, the 12th SS (*Hitlerjugend*) Panzer Division and the Panzer Lehr Division, toward the battle area. Since these two armored formations were positioned between forty and ninety miles from the invasion zone, they were probably not close enough to make their presence felt on the first day. But their prompt intervention still might have proved extremely costly for the Allies.[15]

Von Rundstedt and his staff, even though they were skeptical that this particular Allied assault was the main landing, had reacted with dispatch, for they realized that the enemy would be quick to exploit any success he might achieve. *Ob West* had therefore ordered the two panzer divisions to begin moving toward the Normandy coast early on the morning of the 6th. But these divisions were not directly under his command. They were OKW-Reserve formations. At 7:30 that morning Jodl, who was at OKW headquarters, ordered their movement stopped until official authorization could be obtained from Hitler. Von Rundstedt did not argue and proceeded to carry out Jodl's order, though the western commander did send additional messages during the morning requesting that the armored units be placed under his control. When word finally came from Hitler to release the two panzer formations, it was 2:30 p.m., and by this time Allied air activity was so heavy that they had to delay until after dark.[16] Because of Jodl's timidity in not disturbing Hitler, most of the combat elements of the 12th SS were not committed into battle until June 7 and Panzer Lehr not until June 8-9.

At the end of the first day of fighting, it was still too early for the German commanders to make a complete appraisal of the situation, but at least three points stood out.[17] First, the attack was the beginning of the long-anticipated Allied second front. Perhaps this particular operation was only the initial preliminary step, to be followed later by additional invasions in other sectors, but there was no doubt that the crucial battle for Western Europe had commenced.

Second, it was also obvious that the Allies had had little difficulty in overcoming the beach defenses and in securing sizable lodgments along the Normandy coast. This now meant that every possible effort must be expended to contain and eventually destroy the British and American bridgeheads before they could be strengthened.

And third, although the Germans had realized before D-Day that Allied naval and air superiority would limit their maneuverability, it was proving even more devastating than they had anticipated. This painful fact was to become even more apparent in the days and weeks ahead.

Allied plans during the immediate post-invasion phase called for British, Canadian, and United States forces to consolidate their positions by eliminating the German pockets of resistance that had been bypassed in the initial onrush and then to enlarge the bridgeheads into a single lodgment. Allied troops generally accomplished these tasks between June 7 and 9. The town of Bayeux, an original D-Day objective five miles inland from the coast, fell to British units on June 7. British and American invasion forces were able to effect a juncture the next day near Port-en-Bessin, and on the 9th the Americans captured Isigny and launched a two-pronged attack on Carentan, which was designed to join the two United States sectors together.

By this time the Germans had begun moving considerable reinforcements toward the battle zone. In addition to the 12th SS *Hitlerjugend* and Panzer Lehr Divisions, theater commanders ordered the 2nd Panzer, 1st and 2nd SS Panzer, 17th SS Panzer Grenadier, 77th Infantry, and 3rd Parachute Divisions, plus a number of smaller combat units, to start converging on the Normandy area. At this point Allied air power proved decisive, for repeated British and United States air attacks, coupled with French Resistance measures, delayed the arrival of German units at the front for several days and sometimes for as long as a week.

German commanders after the war were unanimous in their praise of the British and American air forces, and never was Allied control of the air more in evidence than during early phases of the Normandy campaign. Not only did the Allied bombers and fighters slow down the German flow of reinforcements and supplies being moved toward the battle lines. They also rendered effective assistance in protecting their own supply lines and depot areas and in supporting the fighting troops at the front. The weak German Third Air Fleet found it virtually impossible to oppose openly Allied air strength, and the relatively few planes that the Germans received as reinforcements from the Reich were confined in general to defensive activity well removed from the Normandy beachhead. Geyr von Schweppenburg, who had been given command of an important sector in the combat zone, declared on June 13 that the enemy did not possess "air superiority" (*Luftüberlegenheit*), but rather "air mastery" (*Luftherrschaft*) in his area.[18]

The German navy soon found itself in a position similar to the Luftwaffe. German submarines and torpedo boats achieved a limited degree of success during the first days of the invasion, but U.S.

and British ships and aircraft began pursuing *Kriegsmarine* destroyers and other vessels so relentlessly that they were, except for occasional minelaying operations, driven off the sea. British bombers dealt German surface flotillas a further setback on June 14 and 15 when they destroyed a large proportion of the remaining torpedo boats in two raids on the harbors at Le Havre and Boulogne. The German fleet had become an almost negligible factor in deterring Allied naval activity in the Channel.

The German army had been unable to prevent the consolidation of the various Allied beachheads into a single lodgment, but they had prevented the enemy from advancing into the interior. The Germans realized that the next Allied tactical objectives would be to take the large port city of Cherbourg and the key railroad center of Caen, and Wehrmacht commanders therefore concentrated most of their reinforcements to shore up the defenses in these two vital sectors.

In the case of Caen, German forces, including armored divisions brought into the area, were able during the remainder of June to drive back repeated British attacks and to keep them from taking Caen as well as frustrating a possible Allied breakthrough into open country leading toward Paris. The Germans were not so fortunate in the instance of Cherbourg. United States forces fought through the difficult-to-traverse hedgerow country and strong German resistance to seal off the Cotentin Peninsula by June 17. From this point on the Americans began to invest the isolated Cherbourg fortress, which they captured on the 26th and 27th. The Allies did not get the harbor intact, however, since German engineering crews as well as some Allied bomb attacks effectively destroyed the port facilities. It took several weeks before the harbor was of any use at all to the Americans, and only in September and October did it become a major supply depot for Allied goods arriving on the continent.

During June, Hitler met with Rommel and von Rundstedt on two different occasions. At both conferences—one at Margival in northern France on the 17th, and the other at Berchtesgaden on the 29th—the Führer continued to advocate, against the advice of his two top western commanders, no withdrawal and no retreat in the West. There was no need to retreat, Hitler explained, since it would not be long until the V-weapons would change the course of the war. The atmosphere at the Berchtesgaden meeting became especially heated, and both field marshals "expected to be relieved of their posts," though only von Rundstedt was replaced on July 2.[19] Rommel kept his job, but was severely wounded when his car was hit by Allied aircraft on July 17. He never saw combat again. He was, however, indirectly implicated in the July 20 plot against Hitler and was forced by Nazi generals to take his own life on October 14.

German forces in the West kept Allied forces fairly well in check throughout most of July, although British forces did take Caen after heavy fighting on July 8. Then, toward the end of the month American troops broke out near St. Lô and started moving rapidly toward the Seine River and Paris. The battle for France was moving into another phase.

By this time the Atlantic Wall concept had been largely discredited. Reports, which began coming in from German technical and operational experts, found little to commend in the Atlantic Wall effort.[20] The minefields, antitank ditches, barbed wire entanglements, and other hindrances had been rendered ineffective by Allied bombing and naval gunfire. The foreshore obstacles, they pointed out, had proved of little worth since the enemy had landed just after low tide, although the Germans acknowledged that they did assist in slowing down the Allied rate of reinforcement on the beaches. Even the coastal artillery, except those batteries which were covered, had not fulfilled their expectations.

But these pessimistic reports overlooked one other aspect of German activities, operations, and planning in the West during June and July. This development was Hitler's decision to hold onto the major Channel and Atlantic ports at all costs.[21] In a discussion with Jodl on July 31 he was quite explicit on this point.

We must be clear with each other, Jodl. Which places do we want to hold under all circumstances because they provide additional supply possibilities for the enemy? We cannot throw away the harbors that can keep the enemy from having unlimited manpower and material at his disposal. Thus, if the enemy is no longer able to get a number of the productive ports, then that is about the only brake we can put on his already almost unlimited possibilities for movement...we must therefore make up our minds that a certain number of troops are simply going to have to be sacrificed to save others.[22]

This was an extremely logical, if ruthless, move on the Führer's part, for by 1944 these areas had become truly formidable defensive bastions. Hitler's policy meant, of course, that a number of troops would be isolated from the bulk of the German forces as the Allies pushed across France and the Low Countries, and many of the harbor defenders would eventually be killed or forced to surrender. But it also meant that the Western Powers would be denied access to those ports which they considered critical for maintaining adequate lines of supply. After the fall of Cherbourg on June 27, no major harbors fell into Allied hands until the first of September, when St. Malo, Dieppe, and Antwerp were captured, but in the case of Antwerp, its approaches were not cleared of German forces until November 3.[23] Therefore, German reluctance to part with the Atlantic and Channel harbors was at least part of the reason why British and American forces were unable to sustain an offensive into Germany in the fall of 1944. To be sure, there were other factors, such as the unexpectedly rapid Allied advance in August, which also figured into the logistics problem. But at least in terms of the major ports, the Atlantic Wall did prove of some worth and helped to prolong the war in 1945.

The Allies had noticeably less trouble overcoming that portion of the Atlantic Wall which protected the Bay of Biscay and Mediterranean coasts in southern France. The Wehrmacht had not wanted to concern itself with this region south of the Loire, but events in 1942 and 1943 had forced them to devote more attention to the south of France than they would have liked. The real alteration in German military thinking toward southern France came, however, as it did throughout Western Europe, with von Rundstedt's report in October 1943, and the Führer's subsequent directive in November. Since these directives pointed out that the threat of an Allied invasion had become very real, Wehrmacht staff officers desired to bring about a strengthening of the southern portion of the theater similar to the effort being planned for the Atlantic and Channel coasts. But the problem was that they lacked the necessary resources to fulfill both tasks equally at the same time. Clearly, they reasoned, the more endangered French and Belgian Channel sector should receive first priority. Even within southern France itself priorities had to be taken into account with the result that the Biscay coast, which by 1944 was considered too far from the main Allied base of supply to be in great danger, was generally neglected in favor of the Mediterranean front.[24]

Still, the Germans accomplished more along the French Mediterranean coast during the first part of 1944 than one might reasonably expect. At the time of the Normandy invasion the Germans had had 954 permanent fortifications erected in the Mediterranean area as compared with only 341 at the end of January.[25] Many of these defensive installations contained heavy artillery guns, which had been emplaced in concrete casemates (though seldom covered) or in several instances concealed within seaside villas. In addition, a combination of combat troops and engineering personnel had laid 62,486 land mines, and these troops plus Organization Todt workers had interspersed the usual antitank defenses, barbed wire, firing trenches, and machine gun nests between and among the larger fortifications.[26]

The Germans also managed to some degree to build up the troop strength in southeastern France prior to June 6. At the end of 1943, *Ob West* had listed five infantry divisions and one more in reserve along this 400-mile stretch of Mediterranean coastline.[27] By June 1944 the number had risen to seven infantry divisions, and two armored divisions formed a mobile reserve.[28] Although a number of the divisions were "static" formations, and thus capable only of defensive actions, the commanding officers in the area considered five of the seven infantry divisions to be "completely fit for service." The two panzer formations, the 9th Panzer and 2nd SS Panzer Division (*Das Reich*), "while not up to strength," had over 160 tanks at their disposal.

Wermacht leaders effected a further improvement in all of southern France by altering the command structure. The First and Nineteenth Armies, which exercised tactical control over the Atlantic and Mediterranean coastal sectors, were now placed under an intervening command, Army Task Force G (*Armeegruppe G*), rather than directly under *Ob West*.[29] Von Rundstedt himself had actually instigated the reorganization, and it helped him in several ways. It integrated German forces in southern France more fully under one command, and it also set up two army groups, *Heeresgruppe B* under Rommel in the north, and *Armeegruppe G* under General Blaskowitz in the south, thus allowing Commander-in-Chief West more freedom to oversee the entire theater.[30]

This general strengthening of the German defensive posture along the French Mediterranean coast prior to D-Day started to deteriorate once the Normandy invasion had taken place. The deterioration took several forms. For one thing, there was a weakening in the number and quality of Wehrmacht units in the area. During June and July and then into August, the Germans moved out three of their best infantry divisions—the 271st, 272nd, and 277th—and both panzer divisions plus a sizable number of artillery and antitank guns.[31] They replaced these formations with the 716th Infantry Division, which had suffered heavy losses in Normandy, the 198th Reserve Division, a rehabilitated formation from the Russian front, and the 189th Reserve Division, which had been stationed in the French interior.[32] One of the panzer divisions was never replaced. Moreover, help that might have been forthcoming from the four divisions deployed nearby along France's Atlantic coast was no longer available, since two of the divisions had been moved north, and the other two were absolutely necessary to defend the 600 miles of shoreline.[33]

Even more decisive than the losses in personnel and weapons was the phenomenal rise in sabotage activity that occurred in southern France after June 6. The Resistance movement had always been strongest in this former Vichy area, and now with the Allied landing, the terrorist organizations redoubled their efforts. They stepped up their attacks against troop convoys, continued to derail trains, and in general disrupted the German communications and supply networks. By July, German officers reported that "traveling outside of cities and areas controlled by the Wehrmacht was impossible except under heavy escort."[34] Another German report in August indicated that "the resistance movements are becoming more and more like battle groups."[35] In effect except for the coastal zones and a few key cities and transportation routes, open warfare was raging throughout southern France.

The Germans were also aware by August that Britain and the United States had plans underway to invade the French Mediterranean sector.[36] Reports from agents, enemy troop movements, and Allied air and naval activity all pointed in this direction. This time there was little guesswork involved. The Germans knew it would take place east of the Rhône River in the zone once occupied by Italian forces.[37] The date was also well known, since the French populace discussed openly that the Allied assault would commence on August 15.[38]

The German problem was that they were in no position to stop the invasion no matter when or where it took place. Other than recalling the 11th Panzer Division from Toulouse and stopping the movement of the 338th Infantry Division out of the area, there was little else they could do.[39] The other combat zones were also critical, and therefore could not be expected to render any assistance. Wehrmacht leaders could not count on any air and sea power

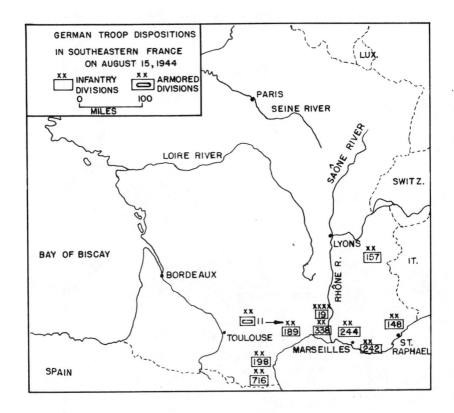

7.3 German Troop dispositions in South-eastern France,
August 15, 1944

to be of help either, for by this time they consisted of seventy-five small ships and 175 aircraft. They would simply have to face the Allies with the approximately 60,000 combat troops they had manning the coast, along with the additional 200,000 personnel that were at hand in the entire Mediterranean sector.

Following the pattern of the Normandy operation, British, American, and some French airborne units started landing behind the Provençal coast at 3:15 on the morning of August 15. Some five hours later, after a heavy aerial and naval bombardment and with the support of several commando missions west of the main assault area, United States and French forces began coming ashore

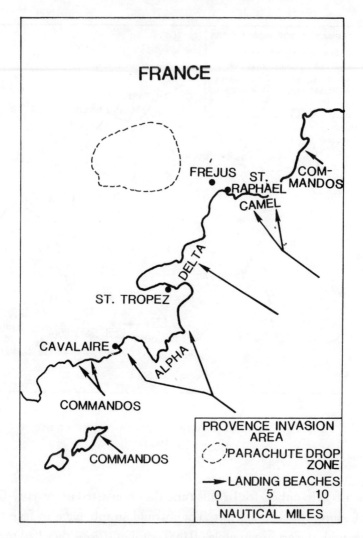

Map Fig. 7.4. Provence Invasion Area

at 8 a.m. along a 45-mile stretch of the French Riviera coast from Cavalaire to east of St. Raphael.[40] The resistance offered by the Germans was not what it had been in Normandy, and Allied troops, aided by overwhelming air and naval superiority, for the most part advanced inland against only token opposition.

One exception occurred along a heavily fortified portion of Camel Beach in the eastern portion of the invasion area, where a series of devastating German artillery barrages forced the oncoming American assault craft, while still in the water, to turn around and land on another section of the beach. These United States forces soon made up for lost time, however, and captured their original invasion objective, the town of Fréjus, on the 16th. The German formations defending the invasion sector, the 148th Reserve Division and elements of the 242nd Infantry Division, were simply no match for the well-equipped, mostly battle-hardened Allied troops. The Allies put ashore 86,000 men on the first day, and these forces soon linked up with the paratroop formations and began moving quickly along the coast and into the interior.

General Blaskowitz, the head of Army Task Force G, found himself in a dilemma. Not only were enemy forces invading along the Mediterranean coast, but Allied units advancing rapidly across northern France also posed an equal threat, for they threatened to cut off the outmanned German forces south of the Loire. The Armed Forces High Command some weeks before the Provence landing had actually considered withdrawing German troops from the south of France, but had delayed making any decision. Now, with enemy pressure from both the north and the south, Wehrmacht formations in the area faced the definite prospect of being cut off, surrounded, and forced to surrender.

Therefore it was with a sense of relief that Blaskowitz received orders from OKW on August 17 and 18 to withdraw Army Task Force G units from all of southern France.[41] The orders stipulated that troops were to be left behind to hold the "fortresses" at Marseilles, Toulon, La Rochelle, and the Gironde estuary to the last person, and several reserve divisions were put under the control of the German command in Italy. But other than these exceptions, Wehrmacht forces along the Atlantic and Mediterranean coasts were to pull back and link up with Army Group B, which was withdrawing into eastern France.

A few days later German units began pulling out in the face of Allied troops advancing from the coast as well as being harassed by

Resistance groups in the rear. By August 28, special French combat teams, after encountering stubborn resistance, had taken Toulon and Marseilles, but the Allies were unable to trap the other German columns, which were executing a skillful retreat toward the Vosges Mountains. By September 11 and 12 the formations under Army Task Force G had succeeded in stabilizing a defense line that ran through Dijon on the southern flank of Army Group B.[42] Although the Germans stubbornly held out in several isolated pockets along the French coast, the Atlantic Wall had obviously ceased to play a role in Germany's military strategy.

Chapter 8

In Retrospect

A lthough the Germans could have met the invasions more effectively, especially in Normandy, this should not detract altogether from the Atlantic Wall effort itself, for it did represent a considerable achievement. It consisted in part of large numbers of concrete fortifications, as attested by the fact that the Germans had poured 17,600,000 cubic meters of concrete along the Channel, Atlantic, and French Mediterranean coasts by the end of July 1944.[1] But for the Atlantic Wall concept to be effective, it had to consist of more than permanent defenses and field-type hindrances and barbed wire entanglements. It also required large numbers of effective soldiers and up-to-date weapons with which to "protect" Western Europe from Allied aggression. Therefore these three elements—fortifications, firepower, and manpower—constituted the basis of Germany's defensive network in the West.

The Atlantic Wall concept as it evolved was a practical solution to a practical problem which was forced upon the Germans as the war took on added dimensions, and their idea was to build up a defensive barrier that would withstand a British and American assault against the continent. In this way National Socialist leaders hoped to retain German hegemony over Western Europe.

The effectiveness of this defensive system was determined to a large degree by factors outside the control of the Wehrmacht, such as developments in other theaters and the many military alternatives at the Allies' disposal in attacking Germany's western flank. As a consequence, the Atlantic Wall never became what it might have been had the Germans been able to concentrate their energies solely on building up their defensive posture in the West. The German military machine became involved in a prolonged war on a number of fronts that eventually strained German resources to the breaking point. The result was that the effectiveness of the Atlantic Wall varied from period and from area to area according to the overall war situation.

Wehrmacht thinking as related to the western theater essentially went through three different phases. The first or pre-Atlantic Wall phase lasted from October 1940, when the Führer "temporarily" postponed the German invasion of Britain, to December 1941, when Wehrmacht reverses on the eastern front forced Hitler to alter his military timetable. During this time the Germans emphasized primarily offensive rather than defensive thinking in the West, including plans for a vigorous pursuance of the U-boat war; preparations to take Gibraltar and/or portions of Northwest Africa; and a proposal to "help" Spain and Portugal ward off any British operation aimed at the Iberian Peninsula. Plans were also kept in readiness in case the Führer decided to return to the possibility of invading England. Defensive precautions were undertaken in the West, but they were confined mainly to protecting the submarine bases and to guarding the coasts from possible British commando raids.

The crisis in the East left Hitler with no alternative but to switch to a defensive orientation in Western Europe, and this change of emphasis ushered in a new phase in the area. The second period lasted from December 1941, to October 28, 1943, and it was marked by the formulation of the Atlantic Wall concept as well as by an attempt to build up the Wall itself. The idea was to set up a system of fortifications that would make it possible for the Wehrmacht to free most of its troops for other, more urgent tasks. In short, defensive installations and firepower were to serve as a substitute for manpower in the West.

The buildup was only partially successful because military commitments elsewhere forced the Germans to follow a policy of expediency. This meant that if they thought the West was in danger of being attacked, they took steps to augment a defensive posture in the area. If, on the other hand, they saw no reason to fear an immediate allied landing during this two-year, middle period, they neglected parts of the Atlantic Wall building program in favor of more pressing projects.

As a result, the construction of the Wall went through various vicissitudes between 1942 and the end of 1943. At first, early in 1942, the impetus received from the Führer in his Directive No. 40, which set forth the general guidelines for the western defensive system, had been sufficient to propel the construction program ahead. During the summer months Wehrmacht leaders had become concerned that Western Europe was in danger of attack, and the Armed Forces High Command had proceeded to supplement the Atlantic Wall installations, many of which were in the process of being built, by moving panzer forces into the area. Although the Germans did not have to employ any of their armored divisions against the Western Allies at this time, the Germans still felt that the Dieppe Raid had justified their fears, and they therefore expended more effort than ever before in building up the western defenses.

But by the middle of 1943 it became clear that the chief Anglo-American threat was in the Mediterranean theater, and construction work on the Atlantic Wall did not keep pace. Toward the end of October 1943 von Rundstedt warned that this lag in the building program had to cease if the Wehrmacht expected to cope with the anticipated Allied invasion in 1944.

Von Rundstedt's warning began the third phase, which was to last until the Normandy landing. Hitler and his staff concurred with von Rundstedt, and the Germans during this final period used every means they could conceive to strengthen their defensive posture along the Channel, Atlantic, and Mediterranean coasts. By June 1944 the German military, in spite of its dwindling resources, had assembled a fairly impressive combat force behind a substantially improved line of coastal defenses, a defensive system which they hoped would be sufficient to turn back the Allied invaders.

Just as the effectiveness of the Atlantic Wall concept varied from period to period, its effectiveness also varied from area to area within the western theater. As one might expect, the highly vulnerable Fifteenth Army sector, which in mid-1942 extended from the Dutch-Belgian border to a line west of Le Havre, received the most attention, and by 1944, the Germans had achieved defense in depth in the area.

The Wehrmacht felt that the other sectors were less threatened, and they therefore accorded them proportionately less consideration. The Netherlands area was rather well defended, but it was not thought to be a likely choice for a major Allied assault with its built-in system of water and dike defenses. The Seventh Army zone, with its jagged coastline, including the Cotentin and Brittany peninsulas, was considered the second most endangered sector, and by the time of the invasion, it possessed a fairly adequate system of beach and especially harbor defenses.

First Army, which occupied the more distant French Biscay coast, defended its area with what can be termed at best a "paper" defense. Fortifications along the Pyrenees border with Spain received an even lower priority and consisted almost solely of field-type defenses designed to block the mountain passes. The situation in the Nineteenth Army zone that covered the French Mediterranean coast was different, for it had only come under direct Wehrmacht control in late 1942 and 1943. Although the Germans attempted to build up their defensive presence in the area, particularly in 1944, they always considered it questionable if the defenses were sufficient to withstand a large-scale Allied landing.

The French Mediterranean sector also exemplified the problem of adjusting the conditions in the West to the ever-changing war situation. No matter whether it was the occupation of Unoccupied France or rushing men and materiel to meet a crisis in Russia or in northern Africa or Italy, it affected the western theater in some way. German military leaders were never able to develop a set program for erecting the Atlantic Wall for the simple reason that its construction was contingent upon so many other developments. In this light, it is perhaps remarkable that the Wall became as formidable a defensive barrier as it did.

Two other factors that influenced the effectiveness of the Atlantic Wall at least to a degree were the interservice frictions and the command conflicts which existed within the German military establishment in the West. The interservice friction between the German army and the air force was of only minor significance, since the Luftwaffe generally accepted its support role within the theater. The conflict between the army and the navy was of greater consequence, but the frictions which centered around defensive building priorities and the positioning of coastal artillery weapons, never reached crisis proportions. The navy wanted to place the coastal batteries so that they could be concentrated against sea targets, while the army preferred using the artillery pieces against beach and land targets. The controversy resolved itself by 1944 in favor of the army primarily because the depleted German navy no longer possessed the relative power position to challenge the dominant influence of the army in the West.

The command controversy, which lasted from November 1943, to May 1944, was supposedly between Field Marshals von Rundstedt and Rommel, the latter by 1944 being one of von Rundstedt's subordinate commanders in the West. The issue has been depicted as one in which Rommel advocated deploying the motorized armored formations near the coast, while von Rundstedt, in contrast, purportedly favored positioning them further inland for a more coordinated effort once the main Allied attack had been identified.

But this controversy was more correctly between Rommel and General Geyr von Schweppenburg, the head of German panzer forces in the West, than it ever was between the two field marshals. Although there were differences of age and outlook and in style of command, it was Geyr who most enthusiastically endorsed the idea of a strong mobile reserve located some miles from the coast and on this point he and Rommel violently disagreed. Neither of the quarreling commanders would accept the compromise solution worked out by von Rundstedt, and they turned to the Führer to render a decision. Hitler in April 1944 decided not to favor either commander, but to strengthen his personal control over military matters in Western Europe by placing four of the ten mobile divisions under his direct command. His final ruling embittered a number of the German commanders in the West, including Rommel, Rundstedt, and Geyr, but they had little choice but to accept it at the time. Hitler's intervention had once again proved decisive.

The Normandy invasion in June and the Provence landing in August led to a general discrediting of the Atlantic Wall concept, but there was one area in which it can be considered at least a partial success. This was in relation to the major ports. Almost from the inception of the Atlantic Wall at the end of 1941, the Wehrmacht regarded the Allied capture of an important harbor as a necessary prerequisite for sustaining a second front in the West. By June 1944 the Germans had transformed the harbors into veritable fortresses

The *Lindemann* battery at Cap Griz-Nez in France, 1942.

Soldiers relaxing at a bunker along the French coast.

A breathtaking view along a Normandy beach.

German fortified battery at Vierville-sur-Mer.

A pillbox in Normandy.

Fécamp, where the costal area was off limits and could not be photographed.

A French 155 mm gun operating on a swivel platform frequently used by the Germans.

Inside a fortified German artillery position in Normandy.

On his birthday, April 20, 1944, Adolf Hitler is congratulated by his military leaders.
From the left: Marshal Keitel, Admiral Dönitz, and Heinrich Himmler.

Marshal Erwin Rommel *(second from left)* on an inspection tour in Normandy, January 7, 1944.

Marshal Gerd von Rundstedt, Commander in Chief
of the Western Front since March 1942.

Marshal Rommel *(center)* inspecting the Atlantic Wall near Caen with General Marcks to his left.

Marshal von Rundstedt with SS Colonel Meyer, commander of the *Hitlerjugend* division in Normandy.

General Dwight D. Eisenhower, Supreme Allied Commander, in 1943.

The military leaders of the Supreme Headquarters Allied Expeditionary Forces (S.H.A.E.F.).
From the left, General Omar Bradley, Admiral Sir Bertram Ramsay, Air Marshal Sir Arthur Tedder
(Deputy Supreme Commander), General Eisenhower, General Sir Bernard Montgomery,
Air Marshal Sir Trafford Leigh-Mallory, and General Walter Bedell Smith

American gliders dropped off by C-47 aircraft landing behind
German lines on June 6, 1944.

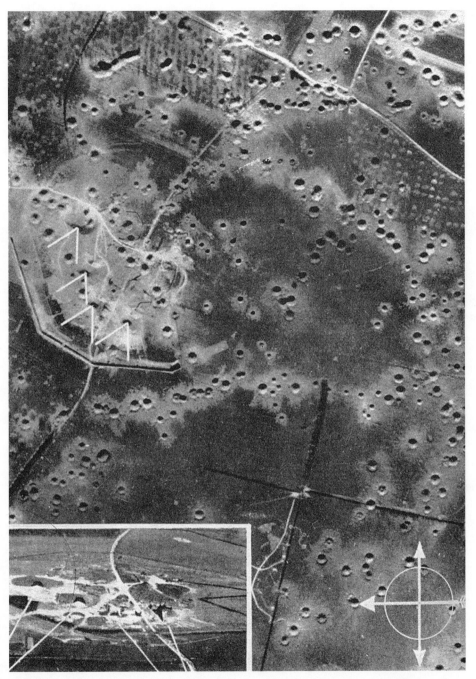

Bombing results over Merville: out of 1,000 bombs only 50 were dropped within range and only 2 actually hit German artillery batteries.

D-Day: June 6, 1944. The U.S. Army hits the Normandy beaches.

that had been prepared not only to repulse an invasion from the sea, but also to hold out against a possible enemy siege from the landward side.

The Wehrmacht's policy of holding on to the ports at all costs did not prevent the Western Powers from establishing and maintaining a beachead, for the Allies set up artificial harbors to serve as supply *entrepôts* during the initial critical period following the Normandy landing. But after the United States' breakout at the end of July, Hitler ordered the retention of specified German units inside a number of the harbor fortresses. These valiant harbor defenders realized that Hitler's decision isolated them from their sources of supply, since Allied tactical airpower, which had proved so decisive before, and after the invasion, made it virtually impossible for the Luftwaffe to fly in reinforcements from the outside. Cut off and dependent upon their own resources, many of these beleaguered German forces still held on tenaciously before finally surrendering to the Allies. These actions helped to cause a severe logistics crisis during the late summer and fall of 1944. To be sure, other factors, such as the British and American failure to plan on a rapid advance across France in August resulted in a holdup in supplies that enabled the Germans to survive through the winter and even to launch the Ardennes counteroffensive in December.

One final observation that needs to be made in evaluating the effectiveness of the Atlantic Wall is the feeling of the Allies toward Germany's defensive system in the West. In general, the Western Powers had a good idea of the makeup of the Wall, and they believed it could be breached if they could direct a sufficient amount of force against it before the Germans were able to mount a major counterattack.[2] But Allied planners realized it would be a difficult operation, partly because of the problems inherent in amphibious warfare, and partly because of the formidable defensive network that the Germans had erected.

The Allies therefore prepared with extreme care to make certain that the invasion was a success. If it were not successful, and a

Western front were not opened up, not only would all of the months of preparation and planning be lost, but, more importantly, the Allied effort to defeat Nazi Germany would have suffered a severe setback. When one looks at the Normandy operation in retrospect, the Western Powers may have been overly cautious and assumed that the Atlantic Wall was more substantial than it really was, but from their vantage point in 1944, a successful landing was not as inevitable as we have since presumed it to be.

Notes

Introduction

1. Hugh R. Trevor-Roper, ed., *Hitler's Secret Conversations, 1941–1944*, trans. Norman Cameron and R.H. Stevens (New York: Farrar, Strauss and Young, 1953), 451. The date of the conversation is May 13, 1942. Republished in 2002 by Enigma Books as *Hitler's Table Talk 1941–1944*.
2. Percy E. Schramm, et al., eds., *Kriegstagebuch des Oberkommandos der Wehrmacht, 1940–1945* (4 vols. In 7 parts; Frankfurt/Main: Bernard & Graefe, 1961–65) (hereafter cited as KTB/OKW), I 1262–1264.
3. As cited in Basil H. Liddell Hart, *The German Generals Talk* (New York: W. Morrow, 1948), 236. See among others Bodo Zimmermann, "France 1944," in *The Fatal Decisions,* Eds. Seymour Freiden and William Richardson, trans. Constantine Fitzgibbon (New York: W. Sloan Associates, 1956), 195–196; and Feldmarschall Gerd von Rundstedt, "OB West, Command Relationships, Commentary on MS# B-308," Foreign Military Studies, 1945–1954 (hereafter cited as FMS), MS# B-633, 24–25.

4. See, for example, Charles P. Stacey, *The Victory Campaign, The Operations in Northwest Europe, 1944–1945,* Vol. III of the *Official History of the Canadian Army in the Second World War* (Ottawa: The Queen's Printer, 1960), 48; and Samuel Eliot Morison, *The Invasion of France and Germany, 1944–1945,* vol. XI of the *History of the United States Naval Operations in World War II* (Boston: Little, Brown, 1957), 48.

5. As cited in Bertil Stjernfelt, *Alerte sur le Mur de l'Atlantique,* trans. Rolf Gauffin (Paris: Presses de la Cité, 1961), 21.

6. Günther Blumentritt, *Von Rundstedt, The Soldier and the Man,* trans. Cuthbert Reavely (London: Odhams, 1952), 131.

7. For a penetrating analysis of the need to study World War II in all of its ramifications, not merely its "one-sided military dimension," see Hans-Adolf Jacobsen, "The Second World War as a Problem in Historical Research, *World Politics,* XVI (July 1964), 620–641.

Chapter 1

1. Andreas Hillgruber, *Hitlers Strategie; Politik und Kriegsführung, 1940–1941* (Frankfurt/Main: Bernard & Graefe, 1965), 1944ff.

2. Walter Ansel's work, *Hitler Confronts England* (Durham: Duke, 1958), goes too far in stating that "England was a partner, not an enemy in Hitlerian mythology" (p. 320).

3. The text of the directive is contained in Walther Hubatsch, ed., *Hitlers Weisungen für die Kriegsführung, 1939–1945* (Frankfurt/Main: Bernard & Graefe, 1962), 61–65. The resume of the Battle of Britain is drawn from Peter Fleming, *Operation Sea Lion* (New York: Ace Books, 1957); Asher Lee, *The German Air Force* (New York: Harper, 1946); and especially, Ronald Wheatley, *Operation Sea Lion: German Plans for the Invasion of England, 1939–1942* (Oxford: Clarendon Press, 1958).

4. Ibid., 96. See also Basil H. Liddell Hart's *History of the Second World War* (London: Cassell, 1970), in which the famous British

military expert sees Hitler's failure to carry through against Britain as one of the most serious strategic blunders of the war (p. 709).

5. United States Navy, Office of Naval Intelligence, *Führer Conferences on Matters Dealing with the German Navy, 1939–1945*, 41; II (Washington: U.S. Navy Department, 1947); Francis H. Hinsley, *Hitler's Strategy* (Cambridge: University Press, 1951), 112; and Hillgruber, *Hitlers Strategie*, 273–277, 323–325.

6. Ibid., 325; and Gerhard L. Weinberg, "German Colonial Plans and Policies, 1938–1942, "in Waldemar Besson and Friedrich Freiherr Hiller von Gärtringen, eds., *Geschichte und Gegenwartsbewusstsein; Historische Betrachtungen und Untersuchungen: Festschrift für Hans Rothfels zum 70. Geburtstag* (Göttingen: Vandenhoeck & Ruprecht, 1963), 472–474, 479–483.

7. The following two paragraphs are based on John L. Snell, *Illusion and Necessity: The Diplomacy of Global War, 1939–1945* (Boston: Houghton Mifflin, 1963), 62–69; and Gerhard L. Weinberg, *Germany and the Soviet Union, 1939–1941* (Leiden: Brill, 1954), 103, 114–117.

8. Hillgruber, *Hitlers Strategie*, 277.

9. See Werner Warmbrunn, *The Dutch under German Occupation, 1940–1945* (Stanford: Stanford University Press, 1963); and Viscount Chilston, "Belgium," in Arnold J. and Veronica M. Toynbee, eds., *Hitler's Europe*, Vol. IV of the *Survey of International Affairs, 1939–1946* (London: Oxford University Press for the Royal Institute of International Affairs, 1956), 479–480.

10. Alfred Cobban, "Vichy France," ibid., 365; and Robert O. Paxton, *Parades and Politics at Vichy: The French Officer Corps under Marshal Pétain* (Princeton: Princeton University Press, 1966) 7–9.

11. Marinegruppenbefehlshaber West (Chefsache), "Kriegstagebuch," 8.7.1940, German Naval Records, British Reference Number PG-37485 (hereafter cited by appropriate PG number), Imperial War Museum.

12. Robert Aron, *Histoire de Vichy, 1940–1944* (Paris: Fayard, 1959), 185.

13. For a description of the early German war economy, see Berenice Carroll, *Design for Total War; Arms and Economics in the Third Reich* (The Hague: Mouton, 1968). Carroll's conclusion is that during the pre-1939 period "the German economy was fairly heavily directed toward war, …without meeting the popular conception of a total war economy" (p. 84).

14. Deutsche Waffenstillstands Kommission, DWStK Nr. 207/40 g.k. Chefs., "Der Vorsitzende der deutschen Waffenstillstands-Kommission," 14 Sep. 1940, National Archives Microcopy T-77 (Records of Headquarters, German Armed Forces High Command) (hereafter cited as T-77), Roll 851, Frames 5596202-5596212. Heinrich von Stülpnagel succeeded his cousin, Otto von Stülpnagel, as Military Commander of France in February 1942. Otto was active in the military opposition to Hitler. When the July 20 plot was unsuccessful in 1944, von Stülpnagel attempted suicide, but failed, losing only his sight. He was condemned to death on July 30.

15. "Die Lösung 'geordenete Schwächung Frankreichs' ist durch die Wirklichkeit bereits weit übertroffen."

16. Alan S. Milward, *The German Economy at War* (London: Athone, 1965), 52. A latter work by Milward, *The New Order and the French Economy* (Oxford: Clarendon, 1970), presents convincing that France's contribution to the German war effort was indeed substantial.

17. The *Guides to German Records Microfilmed at Alexandria, Va., No. 40, Records of German Field Commands, Army Groups, Part I*, prefaces its records of various Army groups with a summary of their deployment. The summaries as to the whereabouts of Army Groups A, B, and C are located on pages 1, 11, and 16 respectively. In preparation for the Russian campaign, Army Group C was redesignated Army Group North; Army Group B renamed Army Group Center; and Army Group A became Army Group

South on April 1, 1941. See also the outstanding official history, Gordon Harrison, *Cross-Channel Attack (U.S. Army in World War II. European Theater of Operations)* (Washington: US Government Printing Office, 1950), 130–131.

18. The 211th, 215th, 216th, and 223rd Infantry Divisions remained behind. Oberbefehlshaber West, Heeresgruppenkommando A, Abt. T, Ia Nr. 540/41 g.Kdos., "Gliederung der Heeresgruppe A, Abt. T, Stand vom 16.4.1941, "National Archives Microcopy T-311 (Records of German Field Commands, Army Groups) (hereafter cited as T-311), Roll 13, Frames 7012655-7012658; Heeresgruppenkommando D, Ia Nr. 12/41 g.Kdos., "Gliederung der Heeresgruppe A, Abt. T, Stand vom 9.5.1941," T-311/13/7012692–7012694.

19. The three additional divisions—the 208th, 222nd, and 227th—were given to the Fifteenth Army, which was responsible for guarding the Channel coast. GenStdH, Op. Abt. III Prüf.-Nr. 10918 "Schematische Kriegsgliederung vom 21.12.1940," as cited in KTB/OKW, I, 1127–1130; and GenStdH, Op. 2 Abt. III, Prüf.-Nr. 16272, "Schematische Kriegsgliederung vom 27.6.1941 abends," as cited in KTB/OKW, I, 1135-1138.

20. Naval High Command, Chief, Naval Staff B. Nr. 1, Skl. I op 262/41 g.Kdos.Chefs., Directive No. 1 for Operation 'Barbarossa,'" 6 Mar. 1941, as contained in *Führer Directives and Other Top-Level Directives of the German Armed Forces, 1939–1945* (Washington: U.S. Naval Department, 1947), I, 149.

21. Oberbefehlshaber des Heeres, GenStdH, O. Qu 1/Op. Abt. IIa/ V Nr. 718/41 g. Kdos. Chefs., "Anweisung für die Vorbereitung der Unternehmens 'Haifisch,'" 24.4.1941, T-312/498/8092638–8092639; and Wheatley, *Operation Sea Lion*, 97-98. For a more detailed examination of "Haifisch" and "Harpune," see my article, "'Shark' and 'Harpoon': German Cover Operations against Great Britain in 1941," *Military Affairs*, XXXVIII (Feb. 1974), 1–4.

22. Oberbefehlshaber des Heeres, GenStdH, O Qu I Op/Abt. IIa/ V, 719/41 g.Kdos.Chefs., "Harpune," 23.4.1941, PG-32444.

23. Oberkommando der Wehrmacht, WFSt/Abt. L (I Op) Nr. 44277/41 g.K.Ch., "Richtlinien für die Feindtauschung," 12 März 1941, T-77/777/5503711–5503716.

24. Oberbefehlshaber West, Ia Nr. 146/41 g. Kdos.Ch., "Einheitliche Befehlsführung bei Abwehrkampfhandlungen im Küstengebiet im Westen," 3.4.1941, National Archives Microcopy T-78 (Records of Headquarters, German Army High Command) (hereafter cited as T-78), Roll 317, Frame 6270989.

25. 82. Infanterie Division, Kommandeur der Truppen des Heeres, Abt. Ia Nr. 1365/41 geh., "2.Befehle für die Ausbildung für die Zeit Mai-Juni 1941," 1.5.1941, T-312/498/8092273; and AOK 15, Abt. T, IaF Nr. 2252/41 g. Kdos., "Uebungsverband," 24 Juni 1941, T-312/498/8092215.

26. (Heeresgruppe D), Ia, geh.Kdos., "Besprechungs-Notiz," 20.5.1941, T-311/13/7012744.

27. Sir Winston Churchill, *The Grand Alliance* (Boston: Houghton Mifflin, 1950), 298–311; Sir Anthony Eden, *The Reckoning* (Boston: Houghton Mifflin, 1950), 305–312; Ivan Maisky, *Memoirs of a Soviet Ambassador: The War, 1939–43*, trans. Andrew Rothstein (New York: Scribner's, 1967), 155–156; and James R.M. Butler, *Grand Strategy, Vol. II, September 1939–June 1941* (*History of the Second World War: United Kingdom Military Series*) (London: HMSO, 1957), 541–544.

28. Oberkommando des Heeres, GenStdH, Op. Abt., IIa Nr. 1284/41 g.Kdos., 'Harpune," 22.6.1941, T-312/1560/000233; and Sammelmappe "Barbarossa": Militärgeschichtliches Forschungsamt, Freiburg/Br., Signatur III W59/2, as cited in Hillgruber, *Hitlers Strategie*, 450.

29. Donald Detwiler in his *Hitler, Franco und Gibraltar; Die Frage des spanischen Eintritts in den Zweiten Weltkrieg* (Wiesbaden: Franz Steiner, 1962) argues that German-Spanish negotiations during the last half of 1940 were critical, and that after this time

Spanish entrance into the war on the side of the Axis was improbable.

30. The discussion of "Felix" is drawn from Hubatsch, ed., *Hitlers Weisungen*, 67–78; Hillgruber, *Hitlers Strategie*, 325–331; and Charles B. Burdick, *Germany's Military Strategy and Spain in World War II* (Syracuse: Syracuse University Press, 1968), 63–105.

31. Armed Forces High Command, WFSt/Abt. L (I) Nr. 44011/41 g.k.Chefs., 10 Jan 1941 as contained in *Führer Directives*, I, 131.

32. Weinberg, "German Colonial Plans," in Besson and Gärtringen, eds., *Geschichte und Gegenwartsbewusstsein*, 479–483.

33. Herbert Feis, *The Spanish Story: Franco and the Nations at War* (New York: Knopf, 1948), 129ff.

34. Hubatsch, ed., *Hitlers Weisungen*, 132.

35. KTB/OKW, I (30 Apr. 1941), 380.

36. The following discussion is based on Oberbefehlshaber West, Abt. T, Ia Nr. 15/41 geh. Kdos. Ch., "Isabella," 10.5.1941, T-312/24/7531026–7531031; and Burdick's detailed account in *Germany's Military Strategy*, 133–154.

37. Oberbefehlshaber West, Ia Nr. 121/41 g. Kdos.Chefs., "'Isabella' Gliederung Ob. West," 23.5.1941, T-312/24/7531013-7531015; and Oberbefehlshaber West, g.Kdos., "Gliederung Ob West, Stand vom 10.6.1941 (Karte)," T-311/13/7012775–7012781.

38. KTB/OKW, I (6 Juni 1941), 413.

39. Hubatsch (ed.), *Hitlers Weisungen*, 79-81.

40. Heeresgruppenkommando D, g.Kdos., "Gliederung im Bereich der H.Gru.D (Karte)" 7.1.1941, T-311/13/7012613–7012615.

41. KTB/OKW, I (3 Feb. 1941), 299-300. See Fig. 1.1, p. 23.

42. The sole division was the 215th Infantry Division. Heeresgruppenkommando D, Ia Nr. 41/41 g.Kdos.Ch., "Gliederung im Falle 'Attila,'" 3.2. 1941, T-311/13/7012506–7012507; and T-312/24/7531013–7531015.

43. Oberbefehlshaber West, Ia Nr. I10/41 g. Kdos.Chefs., "Isabella," 13.5.1941, T-312/24/7531018.

44. Oberbefehlshaber West, Ia Nr. HH30/41 geh.Kdos.Ch., "Besprechung mit O Qu I," 19.5.1941, T-311/13/7012737.

45. Der Oberbefehlshaber West, Ia Nr. 1400/40 geh., "Einheitliche Befehlsführung im Westen," 10.11.1940, T-78/317/6271062.

46. Genlt. Max Pemsel, "Preparations for Invasion," FMS, MS# B-234, 2. Four offensive batteries were eventually built: the Great Elector Battery, located near Cap Gris Nez with four guns of 28.0 cm. each; Todt Battery at Haringzelles, consisting of four 38.5 cm.guns; Friedrich August Battery, north of Boulogne at Trésorerie, with three 30.5 cm. guns; and during the last half of 1942, Lindemann Battery at Sangatte, with three 40.6 cm. guns.

47. Stjernfelt, *Alerte*, 26-27; Hans Speidel, *We Defended Normandy*, trans. Ian Colvin (London: Herbert Jenkins, 1951), 67; Basil Collier, *The Battle of the V-Weapons, 1944–45* (London: Hodder and Stoughton, 1964), 74; and Dipl. Ing. Xaver Dorsch, "Organization Todt—France," FMS, MS# B-670, 32-35.

48. Oberkommando des Heeres, GenStdH, Op. Abt. (IIa), Nr. 178/41 g.Kdos., "Einheitliche Befehlsführung bei Abwehrkampfhandlungen im Küstengebiet im Westen," 15 Feb. 1941, T-78/ 317/6271029.

49. T-78/317/6271062–6271064.

50. Oberkommando der Wehrmacht, WFSt/Abt. L (I Op), Nr. 44166/41 g.K. Chefs., "Einheitliche Befehlsführung bei Abwehrkampfhandlungen im Küstengebiet im Westen," 1 März 1941, as cited in KTB/OKW, I, 1005–1006.

51. Heeresgruppenkommando D, Ia Nr. 103–41 geh.Kdos.Ch., "Notizen zu der Besprechung H.Gru. D (Ia) bei H. Gru. A mit Mar. Gru. Kdo.West," 8.3.1941, T-311/13/7012579.

52. KTB/OKW, I, 1005–1006.

53. Oberbefehlshaber West, Ia Nr. 146/41 geh.Kdos.ch., "Einheitliche Befehlsführung bei Abwehrkampfhandlungen im Küstengebiet im Westen," 3.4.1941, T-78/317/6270980–6270986; and Oberkommando der Wehrmacht, WFSt/Abt. L (I Op/II Org), Nr. 627/41 g.Kdos., "Zusammenfassende

Richtlinien für die Kampfführung an den Küsten," 3 Mai 1941 T-78/317/6270945–6270949.

54. The following two paragraphs are based on T-311/13/7012572–7012581.

55. T-78/317/6270945.

56. T-312/24/7531014–7531015, and T-311/13/7012775–7012781.

57. "Schematische Kriegsgliederung vom 27.6.1941 abends," as cited in KTB/OKW, I, 1138; and "Schematische Kriegsgliederung vom 3.9.1941," as cited in KTB/OKW, I, 1143.

58. Oberkommando des Heeres, GenStdH, Op. Abt. (IIa), Nr. 38031/41 g.Kdos., "Stand vom 9.10.1941," T-78/317/6270905–6270906.

59. Oberkommando des Heeres, GenStdH, Op. Abt. (III), Nr. 1469/41 g.Kdos., "Küstenartillerie," 30 Aug. 1941, T-78/317/6270912. The three long-range batteries in the Pas de Calais area were not included on the list.

60. Warmbrunn, *The Dutch*, 27–34.

61. Viscount Chilston, "Belgium," in *Hitler's Europe*, ed., Toynbee and Toynbee, 479–480. The two departments were Nord and Pas de Calais. Luxembourg, Alsace, and Lorraine became part of the Reich administratively.

62. Summarized in Lucien Steinberg, ed., *Les autorités allemandes in France Occupée. Inventaire commente de la collection de documents conserves au C.D.J.C.* (Paris: Centre de Documentation Juive Contemporaine, 1966), 12–18.

63. The following discussion is drawn from a number of sources, including Generalmajor Manfred Mueller, "Military Commander France," FMS, MS# B-094, 2-5; Generalmajor Alfred Toppe, et al., "German Military Government," FMS, MS# P-033, 45–50; Generalleutnant Dr. Hans Speidel, "Military Commander France," FMS, MS# B-815, 1–5; Steinberg, ed., *Les autorités allemandes*, 18-31; Blumentritt, *Von Rundstedt*, 127; and the sections in Toynbee and Toynbee, eds., *Hitler's Europe*, written by Patricia

Harvey, Alfred Cobban, and Viscount Chilston, especially pages 183–233, 345–346, 407, and 479–480.

64. AOK 1, Ia, "Tagesmeldungen," 17.3.1941, T-313/19/7524387; and Armeeoberkommando 1, Ia Nr. 768/41 geh., "Tagesmeldungen," 26.3.1941, T-312/19/7524397.

65. FMS, MS# B-815, 1; and Steinberg, ed. *Les autorités allemande,* 28-31.

66. Hans Umbreit, however, in his *Der Militärbefehlshaber in Frankreich 1940–1944* (Boppard/Rhein: Harald Boldt, 1968) gives convincing evidence that in spite of the circumscribed conditions, the German military administrators in France did attempt to serve the interests of both countries.

Chapter 2

1. Oberkommando des Heeres, GenStdH, Op. Abt. IIa, "Notiz über Verlegung einer Divisions aus dem Bereich des Oberbefehlshaber West nach dem Osten," 14.8.1941, T-78/310/6261941; Oberbefehlshaber West, Ia Nr. 319/41 geh.Kdos.Ch., "Umgliederung weitere Abgaben nach dem Osten und Aufgaben in Westen," 18.12.1941, T-78/310/6261850-6261851; and AOK 1, "Tätigkeitsbericht für Nov. 1941," T-312/20/7525601.

2. Oberkommando des Heeres, GenStdH, Op. Abt. IIa, geh.Kdos., "Notiz," 22.12.1941, T-78/StdH, Op. Abt. IIa, Nr. 420025/42 g.Kdos., "Abgabe von Personaleinheiten," 12.1.1942, T-312/502/8097502; and "Die Gliederung des deutschen Heeres," 22.4.1942, as cited in KTB/OKW, II, 1365.

3. GenStdH, Op. Abt. III, Prüf.-Nr. 16284, "Schematische Kriegsgliederung vom 3.9.1941," as cited in KTB/OKW, I, 1143.

4. Charles B. MacDonald, *The Siegfried Line Campaign (U.S. Army in World War II. European Theater of Operations)* (Washington: OCMH, 1963), 30–31.

5. "Küstenverteidigung," 14. Dez. 1941, as cited in KTB/OKW, I, 1262-1264. An English translation is located in *Führer Directives*, I, 234-236.

6. Generalmajor Horst von Buttlar-Brandenfels, "OB West: Command Relationships. Commentary on MS# B-308," FMS# B-672, as continued in "Ob West, A Study in Command, "FMS, MS# T-121, 22–24, 107. See also Harrison, *Cross-Channel Attack*, 137–142.

7. The following discussion is based on Hubatsch, ed., *Hitlers Weisungen*, 176–181. An English translation is in Harrison, *Cross-Channel Attack*, 459–463, and Hugh R. Trevor-Roper, ed., *Hitler's War Directives, 1939–1945* (London: Sidgwick and Jackson, 1964), 111-116.

8. See the retrospective writing of Blumentritt, *Von Rundstedt*, 125–129; and the important recollections of the number two man in the operations staff at OKW headquarters, Walter Warlimont, *Im Hauptquartier der deutschen Wehrmacht, 1939–1945* (Frankfurt/Main: Bernard & Graefe, 1962), 247.

9. Commander-in-Chief Navy, Skl. Qu A II 771/42 g.Kdos., "Command Organization on the Coast," 27. March 1942, as contained in *Führer Directives*, II, 15.

10. Oberbefehlshaber West, Ia Nr. 2550/42 g.Kdos., "Gefechtsbericht über Feindlandung bei und beiderseits Dieppe am 19.8.1942," 3.9.1942, T-312/504/8099465.

11. Oberkommando des Heeres, GenStdH, Op. Abt. (II), 19 Feb. 1942, T-78/310/6262029.

12. Generalleutnant Bodo Zimmermann, "OB West, Command Relationships (1943-45)," FMS MS# B-308, as contained in FMS, MS# T-121, 16–19.

13. Oberbefehlshaber West, Ia Nr. 1002/42 g.Kdos., "Küstenverteidigung," 28.4.1942, T-312/502/8096973.

14. Der Oberbefehlshaber West, Ia Nr. 1001/42 g.Kdos., "Grundlegender Befehl der Oberbefehlshaber West Nr. 1," 28.4.1942, T-78/317/6270704–6270709.

15. Der Oberbefehlshaber West, Ia Nr. 1208/42 geh.Kdos., "Grundlegender Befehl des Oberbefehlshaber West Nr. 3," 10.5.1942, T-311/15/7016156–7016158.

16. Oberbefehlshaber West, Ia Nr. 1234/42 g.Kdos., "Grundlegender Befehl des Oberbefehlshaber West Nr. 4," 13.5.1942, T-311/15/7016151.

17. Oberbefehlshaber West, Ia Nr. 1662/42 g.Kdos., "Grundlegender Befehl des Oberbefehlshaber West Nr. 8," 19.6.1942, T-311/15/7106131; Oberbefehlshaber West, Gen.d.Trspw.West, Ia Nr. 1201/43 g.Kdos., "Grundlegender Befehl des Oberbefehlshaber West Nr. 5," 6.3.1943, T-78/317/6270716; and Oberbefehlshaber West, Ia Nr. 2067/42 g.Kdos., "Grundlegender Befehl des Oberbefehlshaber West Nr. 13," 21.7.1942, T-311/15/7016076.

18. Oberbefehlshaber West, Ia Nr. 1138/42 g.Kdos., (Fernschreiben), 5.5.1942, T-78/310/6272112; and Oberbefehlshaber West, Ia Nr. 741/42 g.Kdos.Ch., "Abschnittsgliederung in der Küstenverteidigung," 11.5.1942, T-312/25/7531459.

19. Commanding the Army Task Force was General of the Infantry Hans Felber, who later served in the Balkans and on the western front after the invasion. An *Armeegruppe* was positioned in the chain of command between an *Armee* and a *Heeresgruppe*, though in this instance it corresponded more closely to an army.

20. *Ob West* also proposed at this time that the Armed Forces in the Netherlands be redesignated an army, such as Twentieth Army, again as a deception measure. The Army High Command turned down the request. Oberbefehlshaber West, Ia Nr. 1463/42 g.Kdos., "Umbennung des W.B. Ndl.," 30.5.1942, T-78/310/6262159; and Oberkommando des Heeres, GenStdH/Org. Abt. (II) Nr. 2694/42 g.Kdos. "Umbennung des W.B. Ndl.," 9 Juni 1942, T-78/310/6262160.

21. Oberbefehlshaber West, Ia Nr. 84/42 g.K. Chefs., "Kriegsgliederung Ob West (Karte)," 21.5.1942, T-78/310/6262131.

22. The Führer and Supreme Commander of the Armed Forces, WFSt 551213/42 g.Kdos.Ch. (Telegram), 9 July 1942, as contained in *Führer Directives*, II, 35.

23. "Kriegsgliederung Ob West," 21.5.1942, T-78/310/6262131; and "Die Gliederung des deutschen Heeres," 12.8.1942, as cited in KTB/OKW, II, 1383.

24. Oberbefehlshaber West, Abteilung Ib Nr. 700/42 g.Kdos., "MAA, HKA, und Stell. Battr. Küste (ohne zugeteilte Flak)," 6 Juli 1942, T-78/309/6260997.

25. Generalleutnant Karl Sievers, "16th Luftwaffe Field Division (Invasion Possibilities in Holland)," FMS, MS# B-011, 1.
26. Warmbrunn, *The Dutch*, 53; and Supreme Headquarters Allied Expeditionary Force, GBI/OI-F 385.2-1 (Secret), "Battery Texts Covering the Hook-Hague Fortress Area," 20 Apr 1945, Records of United States Theaters of War, World War II, Records Group 331: Records of Supreme Headquarters Allied Expeditionary Force (hereafter cited as RG-331, SHAEF Records), U.S. National Archives.

27. Albert Benary, *Die Berliner Bären-Division; Geschichte der 257th Infanterie-Division 1939–1945* (Bad Nauheim: H.H. Podzun, 1955), 107–110. The German troops considered Brittany to be the "end of the world" with its bleak shoreline and its unfriendly, primitive inhabitants. On the other hand, it was still a welcome change after fourteen months on the eastern front, and many of the soldiers ate lobster for the first time.

28. The discussion of the Channel Islands is drawn from Generalleutnant Rudolph Graf von Schmettow, "319th Infantry Division (1941–1945)," FMS, MS# B-833, 10–20; Generalleutnant Rudolph Schmetzer, "Atlantic Wall-Invasion Sector (Jun 1942–Jan 1944)," FMS, MS# B-668, 10; and the Führer and Supreme Commander of the Armed Forces, OKW/WFSt/ Abt. L (I Op) Nr. 441760/41 g.Kdos.Ch., "Consolidation and Defense of the English Channel Islands," 20 Oct. 1941, as contained in *Führer Directives*, I, 224. See also Alan and Mary Wood,

Islands in Danger; The Story of the German Occupation of the Channel Islands, 1940–1945 (London: Evans Bros., 1955); and Ralph A. Durand, *Guernsey Under German Rule* (London: Guernsey Society, 1946).

29. "Consolidation and Defense," 20 Oct. 1941, as contained in *Führer Directives*, I, 224.

30. "Umgliederung, weitere Abgaben nach Osten," 18.12.1941, T-312/24/9530980; and Oberkommando der Wehrmacht, OKW/WFSt Op (H) 1893/43 g.K. (Fernschreiben), 19 Apr. 1943, T-78/317/6271513.

31. FMS, MS# B-833, 57. After the Normandy invasion the German forces planted potatoes and other vegetables on the islands during the summer of 1944. When supplies from the mainland were cut off after August, the soldiers lived off the vegetables and some milk products and fish. In December they received Christmas packets from the Red Cross, but by this time all their provisions were running low. To conserve their energy, the troops no longer engaged in construction or training exercises, doing only the most necessary work. They did get a few supplies from incoming aircraft and attempted several raids on the French mainland for the same purpose. The number of sick and wounded continued to mount, however, until the armistice, at which time the garrison capitulated. See also Morison, *The Invasion*, 303-309.

32. AOK 1, Ia Nr. 622/42 g.Kdos., "Gliederung der 1. Armee," 25.5.1942, T-312/22/7527295–7527298; AOK 1, Ia Nr. 1528/42 g.Kdos., "Gliederung der 1. Armee," 20.9.1942, T-312/24/6529897; and (AOK 1), Ia Nr. 0081/42 g.Kdos.Ch., "Feindbeurteilung nach dem Stande von Mitte Juli 1942," 20.7.1942, T-312/25/7531774–7531777.

33. Oberbefehlshaber West, Ia Nr. 296/41 g. Kdos.Ch., "Geplanter Einsatz von Kdo.-Behörden und grossen Verbänden in den Fällen von 'Isabella,' 'Attila,' 'Küstenverteidigung Bretagne,' und

'Küstenverteidigung AOK 15,'" 23.10.1941, T-312/24/7530970-7530974.

34. Oberbefehlshaber West, Ia Nr. 182/42 g. Kdos.Ch., "Zuführung grosser Verbände in den verschiedenen 'Fällen,'" 25.8.1942, T-78/310/6262226. The troop movements were designated as follows:

> Netherlands—Troop Movements 1A and 1B;
> Channel coast—Troop Movements 1A, 2B, and 3A;
> Brittany—Troop Movement 3B;
> Gironde River—Troop Movement 4.

35. For examples of specific planning, see Armeeoberkommando 1, Ia Nr. 976/42 g.Kdos., "Zuführung von Verbänden beim Angriff gegen die besetzte Küste," 12.7.1942, T-312/25/7531756–7531767. For a general discussion, see FMS, MS# B-308.

36. Oberbefehlshaber West, Ia Nr. 1441/42 geh.Kdos., "Grundlegender Befehl des Oberbefehlshaber West Nr. 7," 15.6.1942, T-78/317/6270726–6270727.

37. (Oberkommando des Heeres), Operationsabteilung (V) Nr. 50103/42 g.Kdos., "Ausbau der Küstenverteidigung im West," 20 Juni 1942, T-78/317/6271601–6271602.

38. Oberbefehlshaber West, Ia/General der Pioniere, Pi. 1 Nr. 526/42 g.Kdos., "Grundlegender Befehl Nr. 12," 8.7.1942, T-78/317/6270730.

39. T-78/317/6270720.

40. O.T. Einsatzgruppe West, "Monatliche Betonleistungen seit Beginn der Bauarbeiten," n.d., T-311/25/1030171.

41. T-78/309/6260997, and T-78/317/6270912.

42. The following paragraph is based on Armeeoberkommando 15, A.Pi.Fü./Stoart/A.N.F./Ia Nr. 512/42 g.Kdos., "Ausbau der Küstenbefestigung," 1.2.1942, T-312/502/8097483–8097486; Armeeoberkommando 7, Ia Nr. 770/42 g.Kdos., Anlage 6, "Festungsmässiger Ausbau 327. Div.," 16 Mai 1942, T-312/1549/000252-000256; and Hans-Heinrich Lebram, "Kritische

Analyse der Artillerie des Atlantikwalles," *Marine-Rundschau*, LII (1955), 36.

43. The following paragraph is drawn from *Illustrated Records of German Army Equipment 1939–1945* (5 vols. in 6 parts; London: The War Office, 1948), II, Part 1, Appendix E; and Part 2, Appendixes A and C; and Seacoast Artillery Evaluation Board United States Forces, European Theater (Restricted), *German Seacoast Defenses, European Theater*, 7 vols., 20 Dec. 1945, II–III, as contained in Records of the War Department General and Special Staffs, Record Group 165: Files of the Assistant Chief of Staff for Intelligence (G-2) (hereafter cited as RG-165, G-2 files), Washington National Records Center.

44. WFst/Op. (H) (g.Kdos.), "Meldungen des W.Bfh. Norwegen und Ob. West über Küstenartillerie," 19.10.1942, T-77/1424/000605.

45. "Die Gliederung der deutschen Heeres," 22.4.1942, as cited in KTB/OKW, II, 1365; and "Die Gliederung des deutschen Heeres," 12.8.1942, as cited in KTB/OKW, II 1383.

46. See, among others, Der Oberbefehlshaber West, Ia Nr. 352/43 g.Kdos.Ch., "Beurteilung der Lage Ob. West am 25.10.1943," 28.10.1943, T-311/27/7032458–7032466.

47. Der Oberbefehlshaber West, Ia Nr. 235/42 g.Kdos.Ch., "Die Lage im Bereich des Oberbefehlshaber West," 14.10.1942, T-311/27/7032366-7032374.

48. AOK 15, Ia Nr. 1037/42 geh. (Fernschreiben), 28.2.1942, T-312/502/8097478; and Armeeoberkommando 15, Ia Nr. 1099/42 geheim, "Eng. Fallschirmunternehmen in der Nacht 27.-28.2.42," 3.3.1942, T-312/502/8097991–8097993. Both sides sustained light losses.

49. The following summary is taken from Capt. Robert E.D. Ryder, *The Attack on St. Nazaire; 28th March 1942* (London: John Murray, 1947). Also helpful were Cecil E.L. Phillips, *The Greatest Raid of All* (Boston: Little, Brown, 1960); H.E. Horan, "Operation Chariot: The Raid on St. Nazaire, 27th–28th March 1942," *Jour-*

nal of the Royal United Services Institution, CVII (1961), 561–566; and Sir Stephen W. Roskill, *The War at Sea, 1939-1945: Vol. II: The Period of Balance (History of the Second World War: United Kingdom Military Series)* (London: HMSO, 1956), 168–173.

50. The *Campbeltown* was one of the fifty obsolete United States destroyers transferred to Britain in the bases-for-destroyers deal. It had been called the *Buchanan* in the U.S. Navy, but was more commonly referred to as "Old Buck."

51. Phillips counts only 611 taking part, with 169 dead or unaccounted for (p. 261). Roskill says 621 British were involved with 144 killed (pp. 170–173).

52. Oberbefehlshaber West, Ia Nr. 671/42 g. Kdos., "Englisches Unternehmen gegen Kriegshafen and U-Boot Stützpunkt St. Nazaire in der Nacht 27/28.3.42," 5.4.1942, T-312/502/8097925.

53. Armeeoberkommando 15, Ia Nr. 1563/42 g. Kdos., "Führerbefehl von 23.3.1942," 24.3.1942, T-312/502/8097457–8097458.

54. Seekriegsleitung, 1. Abt. 6318/42 g.Kdos. "Schutz der U-Boot-Stützpunkte an Atlantik-Küste gegen überraschende Feindangriffe," 21. März 1942, T-78/317/6271296.

55. Generaloberst Alfred Jodl, "Tagebuch," 13.4.1942, T-84/268/000569.

56. T-312/502/8097925.

57. Armeeberkommando 15, Ia Nr. 2254/42 geheim, "Landungsunternehmen der Engländer in der Nacht vom 21/22.4 südl. Boulogne," 29.4.1942, T-312/502/8097879–8097885.

58. Armeeoberkommando 15, Ia Nr. 3211/42 geheim. "Engl. Landungsunternehmen in der Nacht vom 3/4.6. 1942, T-312/502/8097818–8097836.

59. J.M.A. Gwyer and James R. M. Butler, *Grand Strategy, Vol. III. June 1941–August 1942 (History of the Second World War: United Kingdom Military Series)* (London: HMSO, 1964), 645–646.

60. The only armored formations listed under *Ob West* in the Army High Command's order of battle on April 12 were the 24th

Panzer Division and the 100th Panzer Brigade (KTB/OKW, II, 1365). By August 12 the number had risen to eight and included the 6th, 7th, and 10th Panzer Divisions; SS Divisions "Das Reich" and "Leibstandarte Adolf Hitler"; Panzer Brigade "Hermann Göring"; and still the 100th Panzer Brigade (KTB/OKW, II, 1383).

61. Marine Verb. Offiz. zum OKW, B-Nr. 2054/42 geh., "Günstigste Landungszeiten im Raum Ostende-Brest," 13 März 1942, T-78/317/6271298; and Der Oberbefehlshaber der Armee 15, Ia Nr. 5150/42 geheim, "Armeebefehl," 3.9.1942, T-312/502/8097634.

62. Naval High Command, B-Nr. 1, Skl I Op. 8329/42 geh.Kdos., "Coastal Defenses," 11 Apr. 1942, as contained in *Führer Directives*, II, 21; T-78/317/6271192; and Der Chef des Oberkommandos der Wehrmacht, WFSt/Op. Nr. 55663/42 g.Kdos.Ch., 16.4.1942, T-78/317/6271206.

63. The Führer and Supreme Commander of the Armed Forces, WFSt/Op. Nr. 551213/42 g.Kdos.ch. (Telegram), 9 Jul. 1942, as contained in *Führer Directives*, II, 34.

64. General der Pioniere und Festungen bei ObdH, L III, g.Kdos., "Aktennotiz über Führerbesprechung am 2.8.1942 (21.30–23.30) im Führerhauptquartier," 3.8.1942, T-78/317/6271595.

65. 303. I.D., Ia Nr. 1098-42 geh., 17.8.1942, as contained in Supreme Headquarters Allied Expeditionary Force, SHAEF 116G/4/INT (Confidential), "German Report on the Dieppe Raid," 26 Feb. 1944, RG-331, SHAEF Records. This folder also contains a captured German document dealing with the Cotentin Raid.

66. Little can be added to the masterful research and description in Col. Charles P. Stacey's *Six Years of War*, 326–406, and his subsequent findings published in *The Victory Campaign*, from which this summary is taken. Portions of Stacey's evidence dealing with the German side of the operation are corroborated in

Generalkommando LXXXI A.K., Ia Nr. 1118/42 geh., "Engl. Angriff auf Dieppe am 19.8.1942," 29.8.1942, T-312/504/8099329–8099366. Eric McGuire in *Dieppe, August 19* (London: Jonathan Cape, 1963), feels that the Dieppe Raid was not worth the cost and effort.

67. "Gefechtsbericht über Feindlandung," 9.1942, T-312/504/8099470–8099471.

68. Stacey, *Six Years of War*, 390–391.

69. Armeeberkommando 1, Ia Nr. 1743/42 g. Kdos., "Englisches Störmunternehmen gegen Sark," 16.10.1942, T-312/23/7529771–7529772.

70. AOK 1, Abt. Ic/Ia Nr. 2356/42 g.Kdos., 21.12.1942, T-312/24/7530837.

71. T-78/317/6271594–6271596.

72. General der Pioniere und Festungen beim ObdH, L III, g.Kdos., "Besprechung beim Führer über den Atlantik-Wall am 13 Aug. 1942 (21.40-0.50 Uhr)," 14.8.1942, T-78/317/6271090–6271098.

73. T-78/317/6270743.

74. (ObdH), Op. Abt. IIa, "Grundsätze des 'ständigen Ausbaues' beim Bau des Atlantik-Walles (Vortrag des Gen. Lt. Schmetzer, Inspekteur für die Landesbefestigung West am 30.9.42, in der Pi-Schule Karlshorst)," 3.10.1942, T-78/317/6271578.

75. (Oberkommando des Heeres), Op. Abt. IIa, "Führerrede zum Ausbau des Atlantik-Walles am 29.9," 3.10.1942, T-312/23/7429710.

Chapter 3

1. Sir Frederick E. Morgan, *Overture to Overlord* (Garden City, NY: Doubleday, 1940), 83–84.

2. T-78/317/6271199–6271200.

3. Hubatsch, ed., *Hitlers Weisungen*, 189-191.

4. Oberbefehlshaber West, Ia Nr. 127/42 g. Kdos.ch., "Grund-legende Weisung für 'Anton' Nr. 1," 15.7.1942, T-312/25/7531391–7531394.

5. Oberbefehlshaber West, Ia Nr. 245/42 geh. Kdos.Ch., "Anton I," 27.10.1940, T-312/25/7531411–7531412, 7531417–7531419.

6. General der Artillerie Walter Warlimont, "Norway; North Africa; French Resistance; German-U.S. Relations; Dieppe; Sitzkrieg," FMS, MS# ETHINT-2, 3; and Generalfeldmarschall Wilhelm Keitel, "German Attitudes Toward the U.S. (1939–43)," FMS, MS# A-912, 2.

7. Armeeoberkommando 1, Ia Nr. 0187/42 g. Kdos.Ch., "Befehl zur Besetzung der grenznahen Stockierungslager im unbetzten Gebiet (Fall 'Anton')," 7.11.1942, T-312/24/7531254.

8. KTB/OKW, II, 916 (7 Nov. 1942).

9. Eberhard Jaeckel, *Frankreich in Hitlers Europa* (Stuttgart: Deutsche Verlags-Anstalt), 240–244. It is doubtful if the attempts by Pierre Laval, Vichy's collaborationist prime minister, on November 9 and 10 to dissuade Hitler from occupying the area had any effect. For a thorough discussion of the French Armistice Army, see Paxton, *Parades and Politics at Vichy*.

10. (AOK 1), "Kriegstagebuch," 10.11.1942, T-312/24/7530871.

11. Armeeoberkommando 1, Ia Nr. 4496/42 geh. "Operation-sbefehl Nr. 2," 11.11.1942, T-312/24/7530613–7530616.

12. KTB/OKW, II, 940–941 (11 Nov. 1942).

13. Jäckel, *Frankreich*, 250. Pétain himself responded by reading von Rundstedt a strongly worded protest condemning Germany's action. For a judicious summary and assessment of the conflicting evidence that surrounds the Vichy government's ambivalent position at this time, see Richard Griffiths, *Marshal Pétain* (London and New York: Constable, 1970), 307–314.

14. Armeeoberkommando 1, Ia Nr. 4521/42 geh. "Operations Befehl Nr. 3," 12.11.1942, T-312/24/7530644–7530645; and KTB/OKW, II, 947-948 (12 Nov. 1942).

15. Ibid., 940–941 (11 Nov. 1942); and Blumentritt, *Von Rundstedt,* 139.

16. KTB/OKW, II, 947-948 (12 Nov. 1942); and Armeeoberkommando 1, Ia Nr. 4522/42 geh., "Operations Befehl Nr. 4," 13.11.1942, T-312/24/7530667–7530668.

17. Paxton, *Parades and Politics,* 374; and KTB/OKW, II, 1031–1032 (27 Nov. 1942).

18. The following discussion of the Toulon portion of "Lila" is based on ibid.; Paxton, *Parades and Politics,* 383–390; and Paul Auphan and Jacques Mordal, *The French Navy in World War II,* trans. A.C.J. Sabalot (Annapolis: U.S. Naval Institute, 1969), 255–267.

19. The Italians did manage to raise some thirty vessels, however, and used several of them during 1943. See Marc Antonio Bragadin, *The Italian Navy in World War II,* trans. Gale Hoffman (Annapolis: U.S. Naval Institute, 1957), 232.

20. Armeeberkommando 1, Ia Nr. 5252/42 geh. "Armeebefehl für Befehlsübergabe an Armeegruppe Felber," 14.12.1942, T-312/24/7530802.

21. Armeeoberkommando 1, Ia Nr. 4575/42 geh. "Einsatz von Zollgrenzschutz an der französisch-spanischen Grenze des neu besetzten Gebietes," 17.11.1942, T-312/24/7530723.

22. KTB/OKW, II, 1165 (18 Dez. 1942).

23. "Kriegsgliederung 1.1.1943," as cited in KTB/OKW, III, 8; "Kriegsgliederung 9.4.1943, as cited in KTB/OKW, III, 261; and Armeegruppe Felber, Ia Nr. 049/43 g.Kdos., 24.4.1943, T-312/977/9168470–9168471.

24. "Kriegsgliederung 7.7.1943," as cited in KTB/OKW, III, 735.

25. Generalmajor Wilhelm Ullersperger, "Nineteenth Army—Fortress Engineers (1943–Aug 1944)," FMS, MS# B-449, 13–14.

26. Armeegruppe Felber, Ia Nr. 4251/43 g.K. "Bericht über Überprüfung der Verteidigungsfähigkeit der Mittelmeerküste vom 13 Juli–21 Juli 1943," 21.7.1943, T-312/978/9170035–9170057. See also KTB/OKW, III, 751 (5 Juli 1943).

27. Armeegruppe Felber, "Kriegstagebuch," 19.7.1943, T-312/977/91677801-9167802; and General der Infanterie Erich Petersen, "Southern France (Jul 1943–Sep 1944)," FMS, MS# 980, 3–4.

28. Der Chef des Generalstabes der Heeres-gruppe D, Ia Nr. 288/43 g.Kdos.Ch., "Beurteilung der Lage," 6.7.1943, T-312/977/9168453–9168454.

29. See, for example, his book, *Germany's Military Strategy and Spain in World War II*, and his article, "Plannungen für das Einrücken deutschen Kräfte in Spanien in den Jahren 1942–1943. Die Unternehmen 'Ilona' und 'Gisela,'" *Wehrwissenschaftliche Rundschau*, XIII (Mar. 1963), 164–178.

30. "Isabella" is discussed thoroughly in Burdick, *Germany's Military Strategy*, 131–154.

31. Hubatsch, ed., *Hitlers Weisungen*, 179–181.

32. Burdick, *Germany's Military Strategy*, 164.

33. Our discussion of "Gisela" is taken from ibid., 171–180.

34. Ibid., 185–187.

35. Armeeoberkommando 1, Ia Nr. 014/44 g. Kdos.Ch., "2. Fall aa," 3.Feb.1944, T-312/28/7535029-7535033.

36. Marinegruppenkommando West, B.-Nr. g.K. 6000 A I Chefs., "Gisela Neu," 26 Mar. 1944, PG-37635; and Marinegruppen-kommando West, B-Nr. Quartiermeisterstab Gkdos 578/44 Chefs., Qu/S "Gisela Neu," 4.4.1944, PG-37635.

37. German units participating in "Gisela-Neu" were to receive the codeword "Friedrichsruh" if Spanish officials agreed to coop-erate. The codeword "Griefswald," on the other hand, meant that no Spanish help was to be expected.

38. Albert N. Garland and Howard M. Smyth, *Sicily and the Surren-der of Italy (United States Army in World War II. Mediterranean The-ater of Operations)* (Washington: Office of the Chief of Military History, 1965), 469–474.

39. (AOK 19), "Kriegstagebuch," 1.8.1943, T-312/977/9167828–9167834.

40. Ibid., 29.8.1943, T-312/977/9167902. German occupation of the southern coast of France in the Fourth Italian Army sector during the "Alarich" period was known as Operation "Siegfried." The seizure of the Mont Cenis pass between France and Italy was called "Kopenhagen" (Garland and Smyth, *Sicily and the Surrender*, 284).

41 (AOK 19), "Kriegstagebuch," 8.9.1943, T-312/977/9167928-9167936.

42. AOK 19, Ia Nr. 6132/43 g.Kdos. (Fernschreiben), 9.9.1943, T-312/978/9169202; and Armeeoberkommando 19, Ia Nr. 6043/43 g.Kdos. (Fernschreiben), 9.9.1943, T-312/978/9169197. The three German divisions engaged along the coast were the 356th Division in the Toulon area, the 715th Infantry Division near St. Raphael and Cannes, and Panzer Grenadier Division "Feldherrnhalle" at Nice and the border region.

43. T-312/977/9167930-9167933.

44. AOK 19, Ia Nr. 7073/43 g.Kdos. (Fernschreiben), 9.9.1943, T-312/978/9169193. The German unit, Kampfgruppe Münch, was detached from the 715th Infantry Division.

45. AOK 19, Ia Nr. 6179/43 g.Kdos. (Fernschreiben), 9.9.1943, T-312/978/9169190; and AOK 19, "Kriegstagebuch," 10.9.1943, T-312/977/9167948.

46. AOK 19, Ia Nr. 6743/43 g.Kdos., (Fernschreiben), 11.9.1943, T-312/978/9169176. The German troops disarmed 1,250 Italians without incident, although some Italian troops did flee into nearby woods leaving behind their weapons.

47. AOK 19, Ia Nr. 6227/43 g.Kdos., (Fernschreiben), 12.9.1943, T-312/978/9169168.

48. (AOK 19), "Kriegstagebuch," 30.9.1943, T-312/977/9168000; Armeeoberkommando 19, Abt. O Qu Ia Nr. 6857/43 geh., "Behandlung der Soldaten der ital. Wehrmacht und Miliz," 30.9.1943, T-312/978/9168997; and (AOK 19), "Tatigkeitsbericht der Abteilung IIa/b des AOK 19 für die Zeit vom 1.7.-31.12.1943, n.d., T-312/979/9170877–9170888. Besides the

more than 10,000 Italians shipped to the Reich, the Germans distributed 20,012 to the four Armies in the West, 5,000 to Organization Todt, 3,900 to the Luftwaffe, and 1,920 to the Military Commander in France.

49. Armeeoberkommando 19, Ia Nr. 6253/43g. Kdos., "Sicherung der Eisenbahstrecken durch R.A.D. Abteilungen," 23.9.1943, T-312/978/9169162; and AOK 19, Ia Nr. 6820/43 g.Kdos., "Besichtigungsreise zur Überprüfung der Verteidigungsfähigheit von den Italienen übernommenen Abschnittes der franz. Mittelmeerküste," 28.9.1943, T-312/978/9170089–9170104.

50. Armeeoberkommando 19, Ia Nr. 8002/42 g. Kdos., "Zusammenfassung der Veränderungen im Bereich der 19. Armee," T-312/978/9169475-9169476; and AOK 19, Ia Nr. 914/43 g.Kdos.Ch., (Fernschreiben), 31.12.1943, T-312/977/9168133.

51. T-311/27/7032467. Included in the total figure were thirty-six infantry, twelve panzer, and five panzer grenadier divisions. Portions of von Rundstedt's important and detailed report to the Armed Forces High Command are summarized in Lionel F. Ellis, *Victory in the West. Vol. I. The Battle of Normandy (History of the Second World War: United Kingdom Military Series* (London: HMSO, 1962), 54–55; and Harrison, *Cross-Channel Attack*, 140–142.

52. T-311/27/7032465–7032466.

53. See the perceptive comments in Harrison, *Cross-Channel Attack* 145–146.

54. The following paragraph is taken from "Beurteilung der Lage Ob. West," 28.10.1943, T-311/27/7032458; Armeeoberkommando 1, Ia Nr. 2338/43 g.Kdos., "Kriegsgliederungsmässige Eingliederung von Ost-Btlen. in bödenständige Div.," 9.10.1943, T-312/27/7533775; and Generalmajor Ralph von Heygendorff, General der Kavallerie Ernst Köstring, and Dr. Hans-Günther Seraphim, "Eastern Nationals as Volunteers in the German Army," FMS, MS# C-043, 20–37. See also Alexander Dallin, *German Rule in Russia, 1941–1945; A Study in*

Occupation Policies (New York: St. Martin's, 1957), 539–540, 551–552, and 582–583.

55. George H. Stein, *The Waffen SS; Hitler's Elite Guard at War, 1939–1945* (Ithaca: Cornell University Press, 1966), 189–195.

56. Armeeoberkommando 1, Ia Nr. 4420/43 geh. "Armeebefehl Nr. 38," 13.9.1943, T-312/26/7533510.

57. Der Oberbefehlshaber der 1.Armee, Ia Nr. 1690/43 g.Kdos., "Bewertung der Divisionen im Bereich der 1 Armee," 29.7.1943, T-312/26/7533421–7533427; and Harrison, *Cross-Channel Attack*, 145.

58. Oberbefehlshaber West, Ia Nr. 2065/43 g.Kdos., "Befehl für Aufstellung und Organization der Festungsstamm-Abteilungen im Bereich Ob.West," 22.4.1943, T-312/507/8103464–8103466.

59. Oberbefehlshaber West, Ia/O Qu West 12623/42 g.Kdos., "Grundlegender Befehl des Oberbefehlshaber West Nr. 19," 1.12.1942, T-78/317/6270769–6270770.

60. The following composite picture of a defense area is based on Hoheres Kommando z.b.V. XXXVII, Ia/Stopi Nr. 80/42 g.Kdos., 23.3.1942, National Archives Microcopy T-314 (Records of German Field Commands: Corps) (hereafter cited as T-314), Roll 895, Frames 000398–000401; Kommand. Adm. in Frankreich, B-Nr. gKdos. 9486/42, "Übersicht über die von der Netzsperrgruppe-West im Bereich Marinebefehlshaber Kanalkueste ausgelegten Sperren,' n.d., PG-37679; Seekriegsleitung, B-Nr. 1. Skl. I Op 16934/42 gKdos., "Gegnerlandungen im Westraum," 11. Juli 1942, PG-32480; Seekriegsleitung, Skl. Qu A I 1633/42 gKdsos.Chefs., 21 Aug.1942, ibid.; and Seacoast Artillery Evaluation Board, *German Sea Coast Defenses*, I, 2–4; II, 39; as contained in RG-165, G-2 Files.

61. Ibid., II, 38–39; III, Incl. 4, 1–2; as contained in RG-165, G-2 Files.

62. Oberbefehlshaber West, Ia Nr. 1659/42 g.Kdos., "Lagebeurteilung durch Ob. West," 29.3.1943, T-78/311/6263121; and

Oberbefehlshaber West, Ia Nr. 3324/43 geh.Kdos., "Lagebeurtei-lung durch Ob. West," 30.6.1943, T-78/311/6263160.

63. Diplomingenieur Xaver Dorsch, "Organization Todt—Opera-tions in West," FMS, MS# B-671, 11-16. Dorsch, an important Organization Todt official in the West, estimated that only 15,600 of the 260,000 laborers were Germans.

64. (OKW/WFSt), Generaloberst Alfred Jodl, "Die strategische Lage am Anfang der 5. Kriegsjahre; Vortag des chefs der Wehrmachtführungsstabes von der Reichs- und Gauleitern in München am 7.11.1943," 11 Nov. 1943, T-77/1433/000486.

65. Stoart AOK 15, Nr. 376/43 g.Kdos., "Stand vom 8.8.43," T-312/510/8107225; and Oberkommando der Heeres, Gen StdH Op. Abt. (IIa), Nr. 38031/41 g.Kdos., "Stand vom 9.10.1941," T-78/317/6270905–6270906. Commander-in-Chief West's total inventory in mid-1941 was 1,215 artillery pieces.

66. FMS, MS# B-871, 12.

67. This paragraph is drawn from Armeeoberkommando 1, Ia Nr. 2340/43 g.Kdos., "Fragebogen über die Verteidigungsfähigkeit der 1 Armee nach dem Stand vom 1.10.1943," 9.10.1943, T-312/27/7533779.

Chapter 4

1. The following paragraph is based on Admiral Theodor Krancke, "Marine Gruppen-Kommando West (1943–14 June 1944), FMS# B-169, 1–3.

2. Ibid., 6-7; Vizeadmiral Friedrich Frisius "Marine Gruppen-Kommando West," FMS, MS# B-341, 8; Blumentritt, *Von Rundstedt*, 122-126; and Stjernfelt, *Alerte*, 30–31, 51.

3. The Chief of Staff of the Armed Forces High Command, WFSt/Op. Nr. 004688/42 g.Kdos., "Problem of Utilization and Command of the Coastal Artillery," 25 Dec. 1942, as contained in *Führer Directives*, II, 55; and Armeeoberkommando 1, Ia/Stoart

Nr. 100/43 g.Kdos., "Taktische Gliederung der Artillerie im Abschnitt der 1. Armee," 30.11.1943, T-312/27/7534118.

4. T-312/504/8099327; and Stjernfelt, *Alerte*, 68–69.

5. Naval High Command (Telegram), 11 Apr. 1942, as contained in *Führer Directives*, II, 21; FMS, MS# B-341, 4; and Friedrich Ruge, *Sea Warfare 1939–1945: A German Viewpoint*, Trans. M.G. Saunders (London: Cassell, 1957), 258–262.

6. Marine Gruppenkdo. West, "Gliederung der Marine im Westen, Stand 12.1942," n.d., T-312/1566/000059; and Sir Stephen Roskill, *The War at Sea, 1939–1945; Vol. III, The Offensive (History of the Second World War: United Kingdom Military Series)* (London: HMSO, 1960), Pt. 2, 16.

7. Der Oberbefehlshaber West, Der Oberquartiermeister West, Qu 1 Br. B-Nr. 0700/44 g.Kdos., "Versorgunglagebericht Januar 1944," 12.2.1944, T-311/14/7014595. See also General der Panzertruppen Leo Freiherr Geyr von Schweppenburg, "Marine Gruppenkommando West (Critique of MS# B-169)," FMS, MS# B-342, 2–5.

8. Der Oberbefehlshaber der 15. Armee, Ia Nr. 0176/43 g.Kdos.Ch., 26.10.1943, T-312/514/8112924.

9. General der Flieger Alfred Buelowius, "II Air Force Corps (Jan-28 Jun 1944), "FMS, MS# B-620, 3–4; General der Flakartillerie Eugen Weissmann, "Flak in Coastal and Air Defense; The Atlantic Wall," FMS, MS# D-179, 13; and Luftflottenkommando 3, Führer. Abt/Ia Nr. 4173/42 g.Kdos., "Befehl des Luftflottenkommandos 3 für die Kampfführung in der Küstenverteidigung," 3.5.1942, T-312/502/8096944–8096950.

10. Asher Lee, *The German Air Force*, 35, 44.

11. Ellis, *Victory in the West*, I, 567.

12. The most used antiaircraft weapon was the 20 mm. gun, which could fire at 280 rounds per minute and had a ceiling of 9,200 feet. But the Germans also possessed higher caliber flak guns, including the deadly 88s, which had a maximum vertical range

of 34,750 feet (*Illustrated Records*, II, Pt. 2, Appendix A). This paragraph is based on General der Flakartillerie Wolfgang Pickert, "III Flak Corps (May–14 Sep 1944)," FMS, MS# B-597, 4–6; Generalleutnant Werner Prellberg, "Employment of Flak in an Army Defense Zone," FMS, MS# D-050; and Ellis, *Victory in the West* I, 58.

13. FMS, MS# B-169, 20; Oberst Rudolph Kogard, "Brest—343rd Infantry Division (May–18 Sept 1944)," FMS, MS# B-427, 5; and Oberkommando der Wehrmacht, WFSt/Gen.d.Pi. u. Fest./ Abt. L(IIa), Atl. Kü. Nr. 729/42 g.Kdos., "Fortsetzung des Ausbaues des Atlantikwalles im Bereich Ob West bis 31.12.1943," 7 Mai 1943, T-78/317/6271638.

14. FMS, MS# B-234, 11; FMS, MS# B-670, 29–31; T-78/317/ 6271578; and Helmut Heiber, ed., *Hitlers Lagebesprechungen; Die Protokollfragmente seiner militärischen Konferenzen, 1942–1945* (Stuttgart: Deutsche Verlags-Anstalt, 1962), 538.

15. Generalmajor Horst von Buttlar-Brandenfels, "OB West: Command Relationships. Commentary on MS# B-308," FMS, MS# B-672, 6. Von Buttlar was Chief of Army Operations on the Armed Forces Operations Staff (OKW/WFSt).

16. Generalleutnant Dr. Hans Speidel, "Rommel's Views (1 Apr–May 1944)," FMS, MS# B-720, 10–11.

17. T-312/514/8112925; Armeeoberkommando 1, Ia Nr. 451/43 g.Kdos., "Besprechung über Atlantik Ausbau," 6.1.1943, T-312/ 26/7532260; FMS, MS# B-234, 8–9; and FMS, MS# B-668, 12.

18. T-311/27/7032426–7032428.

19. T-311/27/7032465.

20. T-311/27/7032424–7032475.

21. The comparison between 1942 and 1943 of German combat units in the West is taken from T-311/27/7032465–7032466.

22. Der Oberbefehlshaber der Heeresgruppe D, Ia Nr. 6228/43 g.Kdos., 28.10.1943, T-311/27/7032418.

23. Der Chef des Generalstabes der Heeresgruppe D und des Oberbefehlshabers West, Ia Nr. 550/43 g.Kdos.Ch., 28.10.1943, T-311/27/7032420.

24. The relatively short Basic Order No. 32 is much less critical of the weaknesses in Germany's western defenses than the comprehensive report of *Ob West* that we have been discussing. The Basic Order can be found in Der Oberbefehlshaber West, Ia Nr. 6260/43 g.Kdos., "Grundlegender Befehl des Oberbefehlshaber West Nr. 32," 28.10.1943, T-311/15/7016267–7016273.

25. Hubatsch, ed., *Hitlers Weisungen*, 233–237.

26. Heiber, ed., *Hitlers Lagebesprechungen*, 450–452, and Harrison, *Cross-Channel Attack*, 231.

Chapter 5

1. Der Oberbefehlshaber West, Ia Nr. 673/43 g.Kdos.Ch., "Vorbereitung für den Kampf," 18.11.1943, T-78/317/6271440–6271444.

2. T-311/21/7024111–7024114; and Der Chef der Generalstabes, Armeeoberkommando 1, Ia Nr. 239/43 g.Kdos.Ch., "Aktennotiz über die Besprechung beim Chef des Generalstabes Ob West am 11.12.1943," T-312/27/7533954.

3. The Naval Staff, B-Nr. 1/Skl. I Op 340/43 g.K. Chefs., 13 Nov. 1943, as contained in *Führer Directives*, II, 106.

4. Der Oberbefehlshaber West, Ia Nr. 818/43 g.Kdos.Ch. (Letter from von Rundstedt to Hans von Salmuth, Fifteenth Army), 27.12.1943, T-312/514/8112911. Portions of this chapter are "Reprinted from MILITARY AFFAIRS, Dec., 1975, with permission. Copyright 1975 by the American Military Institute. No additional copies may be made without the express permission of the author and of the editor of MILITARY AFFAIRS."

5. OKW/WFSt/Op. 662642/43 g.Kdos.Ch. (Telegram to the Naval Staff), 6 Nov. 1943, as contained in *Führer Directives*, II, 105.

6. Vizeadmiral Friedrich Ruge, "Rommel and the Atlantic Wall (Dec 1943–Jul 1944," FMS, MS# A-982, 3–4. Admiral Ruge at this time was the Naval Liaison Officer on Rommel's staff. He was a close confidant of the field marshal. After World War II, Ruge for a time headed the West German Navy.

7. Harrison, *Cross-Channel Attack*, 246–247.

8. OKW/WFSt/Op (n)/West Nr. 663174/43 g.Kdos. Ch. (Telegram), 1 Jan. 1944, as contained in *Führer Directives*, II, 118.

9. Der Chef des Generalstabes der Heeresgruppe D des Oberbefehlshaber West, Ia Nr. 43/44 g.Kdos.Ch. (Letter from Blumentritt to Jodl), n.d., T-311/27/7032403–7032404.

10. See, for example, Blumentritt, *Von Rundstedt*, 200–213; Ellis, *Victory in the West*, I, 118; Ronald Lewin, *Rommel as Military Commander* (Princeton: Van Nostrand, 1968), 211–218; Hans Speidel, *We Defended Normandy*, passim; Stacey, *The Victory Campaign*, 58; Stjernfelt, *Alerte*, 168–180; Chester Wilmot, *The Struggle for Europe* (New York: Harper, 1952), 190–193; and Leo Geyr von Schweppenburg, "Reflections on the Invasion," *Military Review*, LXI (Feb. 1961), 2–11, and (Mar. 1961), 12–21. The controversy has also been discussed in a number of Foreign Military Studies interviews, including Oberst i.G. Anton Staubwasser, "Army Group B—Intelligence Estimate (1 Jun 1944)," MS# B-675, 2-3, 13; and MS# B-308, 49–51. The most perceptive analysis remains Harrison, *Cross-Channel Attack*, 151–156, 246–258.

11. T-311/27/7032368 and T-311/27/7032438.

12. Oberbefehlsaber West, Ia Nr. 1788/42 geh.Kdos., "Grundlegender Befehl des Oberbefehlshaber West Nr. 10," 2.7.1942, T-311/15/7026117–7026118.

13. Oberbefehlshaber West, Ia Nr. 997/43 g. Kdos., "Grundlegender Befehl des Oberbefehlshaber West Nr. 21," 26.2.1943, T-78/317/6270792–6270793.

14. T-311/27/7032437–7032438.

15. Oberkommando der Heeresgruppe B, Ia Nr. 138/43 g.Kdos.Ch., "Bericht zur Verteidigungsbereitschaft in Artois," 31.12.1943,

T-311/27/7032494–7032495; AOK 15, "Besprechung mit Feldmarschall Rommel an 20.12.1943," T-312/509/7106019; Generalmajor Rudolf von Gersdorff, "Critique of the Defense against Invasion," FMS, MS# A-895, 4–5; and Erwin Rommel, *The Rommel Papers*, ed. Basil H. Liddell Hart, trans. Paul Finlay (New York: Harcourt, Brace, 1953), 454–455.

16. Ibid.

17. MS# B-720, 12.

18. T-311/27/7032494, and FMS, MS# B-597, 9.

19. The following two paragraphs are taken from Rommel, *The Rommel Papers*, 469; Geyr von Schweppenburg, "Reflections," 2; and especially Panzer-Gruppen-Kommando-West, Der Chef des Generalstabes, Ia Nr. 17/44 g.Kdos.Ch., "Gedenkliche Beschäftigung mit der Frage des Einsatzes der operativen Reserven," 30.1.1944, T-311/27/7032392-7032394. The author has concluded in this instance that the views of Geyr's Chief of Staff, Generalmajor Edler von Dawans, reflect those of his commander.

20. Ibid., and Rommel, *The Rommel Papers*, 469.

21. Oberbefehlshaber West, Ia Nr. 1656/44 g.Kdos., "Grundlegender Befehl des Oberbefehlshaber West Nr. 37," 24.2.1944, T-311/15/7016379–7016381.

22. (AOK 15), "Besprechungspunkte Feldm. Rommel mit AOK 15," 17.1.1944, T-312/515/8113777; and Geyr von Schweppenburg, "Reflections on the Invasion," 9.

23. (AOK 15), "Besuch von Gen. Oberst Guderian beim AOK am 7.2.1944," T-312/515/8113762; and Heinz Guderian, *Panzer Leader*, trans. Constantine Fitzgibbon (New York: Ballantine, 1957), 261–266.

24. Rommel, *The Rommel Papers*, 469; and KTB/OKW, IV, 277, 300.

25. Der Oberbefehlshaber West, Ia Nr. 2434/44 g.Kdos., (Directive from von Rundstedt to Rommel), 24.3.1944, T-311/23/7027172–7027174. Von Rundstedt had already intimated on

December 27 that he expected to utilize armored divisions near the coast as soon as he had more of them at his disposal. (Der Oberbefehlshaber West, Ia Nr.818/43 g.Kdos.Ch. [Letter from von Rundstedt to von Salmuth], 27.12.1943, T-312/514/0112912.)

26. T-311/23/7027174; and Armeeoberkommando 1, Ia Nr. 017/44 g.Kdos.Ch., "Vortragsnotiz anlässlich des Besuch des Generalfeldmarschalls Rommel," 9.2.1944, T-312/28/7535090-7535091.

27. T-311/15/7016385; (Ob West), g.Kdos., "Besprechungs-Notizen zur Besprechungs des Heeren Oberbefehlshabers West am 8.5.," 8.5.1944, T-311/24/7028384. Von Rundstedt had even said as early as November 18, 1943, that Rommel's group might be entrusted with leading the strategic counterattack (Oberbefehlshaber West, Ia Nr. 673/43 g.Kdos.Ch. ("Vorberei-tung für den Kampf," 18.11.1943, T-78/317/6271440–6271441).

28. Rommel, *The Rommel Papers*, 469; and Leo Geyr von Schweppenburg, "Invasion without Laurels: The Story of the Allied Invasion of Normandy, June 1944," *An Cosantoir* IX (Dec. 1949), 577.

29. Oberbefehlshaber West, Ia Nr. 2893/44 g. Kdos., 9.4.1944, T-311/23/7027607.

30. This paragraph is based on (Ob West), g. Kdos., 9.4.1944, T-311/23/7027607.

31. German officials divided the specific motorized units in the West as follows: The Panzer Lehr division, which was just returning to the West, and the 1st SS Panzer, 12th SS Panzer, and 17th Panzer Grenadier Divisions made up the strategic reserve; Army Group B was responsible for 2nd Panzer, 21st Panzer, and 116th Panzer Divisions; and Army Group G for 2nd SS Panzer, 9th Panzer, and 11th Panzer Divisions (Ob West, Ia Nr. 3565/44 g.Kdos., "Stand der Neuaufstellungen," 4.5.1944, T-311/24/7028278).

32. As cited in Stacey, *The Victory Campaign*, 58–59.

33. (Oberbefehlshaber West), g.Kdos., "Tagesmeldung," 2.5.1944, T-311/24/7028080–7028081.

34. (Oberbefehlshaber West), g.Kdos., "Tagesmeldung," 4.5.1944, T-311/24/7028086.

35. Hans Rothfels, *The German Opposition to Hitler*, trans. Lawrence Wilson (London: Wolff, 1961), 73–74; and Constantine Fitzgibbon, *20 July* (New York: Berkeley Publishing Co., 1956), 150–158. It was perhaps not accidental that only in the West did the conspirators achieve temporary success in the July 20, 1944, assassination attempt on Hitler's life.

36. T-311/24/7028384–7028385.

37. The following sketch of von Rundstedt is taken from among others, Heiber, ed., *Hitlers Lagebesprechungen*, 335; and General der Infanterie Günther Blumentritt, "OB West; Command Relationships, Commentary on MS# B-308," FMS, MS# B-344, 77–84. Chester Wilmot's contention in *The Struggle for Europe* that von Rundstedt had "lost his grip" (p. 190) is difficult to uphold in view of his subsequent command activity on the western front during late 1944 and early 1945. He may have lost some of his energy but not his grip.

38. Von Rundstedt was actually not quite as chivalrous as his supporters would lead us to believe. In a report issued by *Ob West* toward the end of 1942, he suggested that Russian prisoners be transported west to work on the Atlantic Wall. One of the advantages, he pointed out, in using Russian labor was that they were "simple spirits," and if they did not obey, they could simply be shot (T-311/27/7032372–7032373).

39. General Blumentritt, his energetic Chief of Staff, remarked after the war, for instance, that von Rundstedt "had a photographic memory for 1:1,000,000 maps" (Blumentritt, "Ob West," FMS, MS# B-344, 79).

40. Among the many evaluations of Rommel, see FMS, MS# A-982, 6–7; FMS, MS# B-308, 55–56; Blumentritt, *Von Rundstedt*,

204-207; Warlimont, *Im Hauptquartier*, 435–437; Speidel, *We Defended Normandy*, 54–57; Lewin, *Rommel*, passim; and Desmond Young, *Rommel, The Desert Fox* (New York: Harper and Row, 1951), passim.

41. Der Oberbefehlshaber West, Ia Nr. 3442/44 g.Kdos., "Grundlegender Befehl des Oberbefehlshaber West Nr. 38," 7.5.1944, T-311/24/7028351–7028352; FMS# B-308, 14–15; and Blumentritt, *Von Rundstedt*, 120.

42. FMS, MS# B-633, 52; and FMS, MS# B-344, 79–81.

43. T-311/24/7028346–7028347.

Chapter 6

1. T-311/15/7016385; and T-311/21/7024111–7024114.

2. OKW/WFSt/Op. Nr. 00606/44 g.Kdos. (Telegram), 19 Janv. 1944, as contained in *Führer Directives*, II, 119.

3. OKW/WFSt/Op. (H) West Nr. 001524/44 g. Kdos. (Telegram), 3 Mar. 1944, as contained in *Führer Directives*, II, 126; and KTB/ OKW, IV, 266, 277–278. The OKW excluded the Mediterranean ports of Toulon and Marseilles from being named fortresses since their defenses were considered incomplete (*Unvollkommen*).

4. In addition to the fourteen fortresses, the Germans also expended a great deal of energy building up the defenses at Den Helder in the Netherlands, Marseilles and Toulon, and the Scheldt River approaches to Antwerp. The following general discussion of the improvements undertaken at the major ports during 1944 is set forth in a series of detailed reports, including Festung Ijmuiden, Der Kommandant, Nr. 53/44 g.Kdos., "Befehl für die Verteidigung des Festung Ijmuiden," 19.2.1944, T-311/27/7033107–7033122; Der Festungskommandant, Abt. Ia Nr. 110/44 g.Kdos., "Kampfanweisung für die Festung Le Havre," 8.2.1944, T-311/28/7034057–7034087; Ob West, Ia Nr. 2177/44 g.Kdos., "Kampfanweisung St. Nazaire," 8.3.1944,

T-311/28/7033820–7033896; and Marinegruppenkommando West, B-Nr. Führunggsstab g.Kdos. 6170 Chefs., "Lageübersicht des Marinegruppenkommandos West," 2 Mai 1944, PG-32100.

5. Oberbefehlshaber West, Ia/Gen.d.Trans./Gen.d.Pi. (III) Nr. 1070/43 g.Kdos., "Auszug aus Einzelbefehl des Oberbefehlshaber West Nr. 37," 10.12.1943, T-311/26/7031701–7031704. The Cherbourg fortress commander even went so far as to request that he be given permission to destroy Cherbourg's quays and harbor area several weeks before the actual invasion took place. He felt that if the Allies knew the port had been demolished, they would put off their landing attempt, and the Germans would gain time in preparing their defenses. His request was denied (FMS, MS# B-845, 22–23).

6. T-311/24/7030171.

7. Ob West, ia Nr. 236/44 g.Kdos., "Lagebeurteilung durch Ob. West," 10.1.1944, T-311/22/7025370–7025371; Ob West, Ia Nr. 4366/44 g.Kdos., "Lagebeurteilung durch Ob. West vom 29.5. bis 4.6.1944," 5.6.1944, T-311/24/7029167–7029168; and Der Kommandierende Admiral der französischen Südküste, B-Nr. g.Kdos. 77/43 Chefs., "Lagebeurteilung der französischen Südküste Dezember 1943," 23.12.1943, T-312/977/9168172–9168175.

8. The following two paragraphs are based on Seacoast Artillery Evaluation Board, *German Seacoast Defenses*, II, Incl. 11, pp. 6–29, as contained in RG-165, G-2 files. These figures are, of course, subject to modification because the survey was conducted after the war. Nevertheless, most of these positions were undoubtedly occupied at the time of D-Day, when Germany's defensive posture in the West was at its peak.

9. Oberbefehlshaber West, Ia Nr. 6050/43 g. Kdos., "Grundlegender Befehl des Oberbefehlshaber West Nr. 31," 21.10.1943, T-311/15/7016279–7016282.

10. Armeeoberkommando 19, Ia Nr. 162/43 g. Kdos.Ch., "Erste Planung des Verlaufes eine 2. Stellung," 31.10.1943, T-312/977/

9168150; Hiltrop, Major i.G., "Notizen über die Besprechung am 8.11.1943, 11.30 Uhr bei Ob West," T-312/978/9169438–9169439; and Oberbefehlshaber West, Ia/Gen.d.Pi. (I) Nr. 372/44 g.Kdos., "Meldung über Ausbau der 2. Stellung," 24.2.1944, T-311/26/7032030. Armed Forces High Command toward the end of 1943 also considered building several secondary defense lines based on the river systems that form almost a natural barrier in the Netherlands, Belgium, and northern and northeastern France. *Ob West* sent out several inspection teams to reconnoiter positions along the Somme-Oise-Aisne-Marne-Saône river line in France and along the Ijssel and Meuse rivers and the Scheldt River and Albert Canal in the Low Countries, but nothing came of the inspection until after the D-Day invasion, when the Germans once again started thinking about setting up a defense line east and north of Paris (Erkundungsstab General der Inf. Fischer von Wietersthal, Gen.kdo. LXVII Res.Korps, Ia Nr. 9/43 g.Kdos.Ch., 9 Dez. 1943, T-311/27/7032685–7032686; Generalkommando LXVII Res. Korps, Erkundungsstab, General der Inf. Fischer von Wietersthal, Ia Nr. 2/44 g.Kdos.Ch., 23.1.1944, T-311/27/7032695; and Martin Blumenson, *Breakout and Pursuit (United States Army in World War II, European Theater of Operations)* (Washington: USGPO, 1962), 419, 678.

11. *Ob West* declared in a basic Order on February 24: "There can be no doubt as to the value I place on field-type construction. Many things are possible: large minefields, earthworks, flooding, hindrances of all kinds. For the inventive spirit there are no limits. [For example] the Commander of Army Group B has begun the erection of 'hindrances' in the water for use against enemy landing craft, and this program is to be propelled forward." (T-311/15/7016385).

12. Inspekteur der Landesbefestigung West, Der Chef des Stabes Nr. 1741/43 g.Kdos.Ch., "Überschwemmung der rechten flanke des Abschnittes Calais," 2.1.1944, T-311/27/7032526;

Oberbefehlshaber West, Ia Nr. 3900/44, "Bericht des Sonder-stabes Öhmichen" 17.5.1944, T-312/1568/000698; and KTB/ OKW, IV, 304–305.

13. T-312/515/8113777-8113778. See also the excerpt from the Army Group B War Diary in Rommel, *The Rommel Papers*, 457–458.

14. General der Pioniere, Oberkommando Heeresgruppe D, (II)/ Ia Nr. 971 g.Kdos., "Minenverlegung," 30.10.1943, T-311/26/ 7031739.

15. Stabs-Offz.d.Pion.b.Ob.West, Nr. 140/44 g.Kdos., "Minenmel-dung-Stand 30.5.44," 2.6.1944, T-311/28/7034017.

16. Harrison, *Cross-Channel Attack*, 264.

17. The following description of the various foreshore hindrances is taken from among others, ibid., 250–251; Ruge, *Sea Warfare*, 362; Morison, *The Invasion*, 101, 113–115; Stjernfelt, *Alerte*, 177–178; Rommel, *The Rommel Papers*, 458–459; Armeeober-kommando 1, Ia Nr. 461/44 g.Kdos., 10.2.1944, T-312/28/ 7535103; and Der Oberbefehlshaber der Heeresgruppe B, Ia Nr. 2050/44 geh., 22.5.1944, T-311/3/7002123–7002126.

18. Supreme Headquarters Allied Expeditionary Force, SHAEF/ 12NX/INT (Secret), "German Coastal Defenses in the West, Pamphlet No. VII: Underwater Obstacles," 7 Aug. 1944 2; RG-331, SHAEF Records.

19. T-311/23/7027959.

20. May 13 entry in the War Diary of Army Group B as cited in Rommel, *The Rommel Papers*, 458.

21. Morison, *The Invasion*, 46–47. The Germans did not use a new pressure mine, however, for fear the British would lay similar mines in the Baltic. The pressure mine was set off by water pressure from passing ships and was immune to all known sweeping devices.

22. Among the many descriptions of the anti-landing obstacles, see ibid., 89; and Rommel, *The Rommel Papers*, 470–471.

23. The following summary of the V-weapons is drawn from Joseph W. Angell, "CROSSBOW," in Wesley F. Craven and James L. Cate, eds., *Europe: Argument to V-E Day, January 1944 to May 1945 (The Army Air Force in World War II,* vol. III*)* (Chicago: Univ. of Chicago Press, 1951), 84–106, 325–329; Basil Collier, *The Battle of the V-Weapons,* passim; Hilary St. G. Saunders, *The Fight is Won: Royal Air Force 1939–1945;* Vol. III (London: HMSO, 1954), 147–169; Heiber, ed., *Hitlers Lagebesprechungen,* 403–404; and Oberst i.G. Eugen Walter, "V-Weapon Tactics (LXV Corps)," FMS, MS# B-689, 9–11.

24. According to a British flyer, the Germans made no effort to camouflage the ski sites and erected them in wooded areas where they were easily identifiable from the air. Had they set them instead in open fields, he pointed out, it would have been almost impossible to find them (Saunders, *The Fight is Won,* 150).

25. Angell, "CROSSBOW," in Craven and Cate, eds., *Europe,* III, 102.

26. Collier, *The Battle of the V-Weapons,* 47.

27. (Heeresgruppe B), Ib g.Kdos., "Vortragsnotiz," 3.6.1944, T-311/1/7000664.

28. Works on the Resistance are legion. The following is based on Henri Michel, *Les courants de pensée de la Résistance* (Paris: Presses Universitaires de France, 1962); Harrison, *Cross-Channel Attack,* 203–205, 224–225; Ellis, *Victory in the West,* I, 49-52, 121–122; Robert Aron, *France Reborn: The History of the Liberation, June 1944– May 1945,* trans. Humphrey Hare (New York: Scribner's, 1964), 144–145; Michael R.D. Foot, *SOE in France (History of the Second World War: United Kingdom Military Series)* (London; HMSO, 1966), 438–440; and KTB/OKW, IV, 261–262.

29. A Canadian officer has given an excellent example as to how French railway employees effected a work slowdown. The officer relates that he went to a roundhouse in Dieppe railroad yards immediately after that port city had been captured in Sep-

tember 1944 to see if an important supply line to a nearby town could be reestablished: "Six engineers were in the shed, all bearing placards stating their defects; the minimum repair period was stated to be three months. As the officer was expressing his disgust, the foreman came into the shed and took down the placard, saying, 'pour les Allies demain soir' (For the Allies tomorrow evening)" (Ellis, *Victory in the West*, I, 122).

30. Kontrollinspektion der DWStK, Kontrollabteilung, "Monatsbericht Nr. 11, Feb. 1944," 8 März 1944, T-77/848/5592002–5592013; and Kontrollinspektion der DWStK, Kontrollabteilung, "Monatsbericht Nr. 10 für Jan. 1944," 8 Feb. 1944, T-77/848/5591944.

31. Der Chef des Generalstabes Ob West Blumentritt, Ia Nr. 3640/44 g.Kdos. (Fernschreiben), 6.5.1944, T-311/24/7028328; KTB/OKW, IV, 306; and Harrison, *Cross-Channel Attack*, 228.

32. KTB/OKW, III, 1159 (26.10.1943).

33. Ibid., 1401 (26.12.1943).

34. Oberbefehlshaber West, Der Oberquartiermeister West Qu 1 Br. B Nr. 01800/44 g.Kdos., "Versorgungslagebericht März 1944," 8.4.1944, T-311/14/7014856-7014857; FMS, MS# B-720, 17; and Ellis, *Victory in the West*, I, 116–117.

35. The following two paragraphs are based on ibid., 120; and Harrison, *Cross-Channel Attack*, 471. The 2nd Parachute and 19th Panzer Divisions began moving into the area several days after June 6 (Ob West, Ia Nr. 4414/44 g.Kdos., 8.6.1944, T-311/25/7029373).

36. Wehrmachtführungsstab/Ic Nr. 06166/43 geh., "Kriegsgliederungen," 8.12.1943, T-78/534/000793; Harrison, *Cross-Channel Attack*, 238–241; and Blumenson, *Breakout and Pursuit*, 44–45.

37. KTB/OKW, IV, 308–309.

38. The summary of the 1944-type divisions is based on AOK 15, Ia Nr. 3115/44 g.Kdos., "Inf. Div. 44," n.d., T-312/516/

8115042; Oberst i.G. Rudolph Kogard, "Brest—343d Infantry Division (May–18 Sep 1944)," FMS, MS# B-427, 2–14; Harrison, *Cross-Channel Attack*, 238–239; and Ellis, *Victory in the West*, I, 554.

39. T-78/310/6262677–6262685; T-312/1566/000208; (AOK 7), g.Kdos., OKW/WFSt/Abt. L (I Op), 17.4.1944, T-77/775/5501176; and FMS, MS# B-427, 2–3.

40. Armeeoberkommando 15, Ia Qu/I Nr. 70/44 g.Kdos., "Bericht über der Versorgungslage der 15. Armee," 7.1.1944, T-312/517/8115892–8115896.

41. For a description of the airborne formations, see Oberst Frhr. Von der Heydte, "6th Parachute Regiment (1 May–20 Aug 1944)," FMS, MS# B-839; and Generalleutnant Gustav Wilke, "5th Parachute Division (6 Jun–24 Jul 1944)," FMS, MS# B-820. The Germans by June 1944 had deployed four Air Force Field divisions in the West.

42. The following paragraph is based on Stoart AOK 15 Nr. 490/44 g.Kdos., "Artl. Gliederung der 15. Armee," 1.5.1944, T-312/516/8115256–8115258; AOK 1, Ia/Stoart Nr. 289/44 g.Kdos., "Artilleriegliederung der 1. Armee," 1.3.1944, T-312/28/7535667–7535672; and Sonderstab Öhmichen, z. Zt. Armeeoberkommando 7, Ia/Stopak Nr. 67/44 g.Kdos., "Bericht über das Kommando des Sonderstabes zum AOK 7," 13.5.1944, T-312/1568/000707.

43. The three panzer divisions were the 9th and 10th SS Panzer Divisions and Panzer Lehr Division, and the infantry formation was the 349th Infantry Division (Warlimont, *Im Hauptquartier*, 439, 447; and KTB/OKW, IV, 273–275).

44. Harrison, *Cross-Channel Attack*, 235.

45. Der Chef des Generalstabes der 7. Armee, Ia Nr. 6117/43 g.Kdos., "Operative Vorbereitungen," 30.11.1943, T-312/1566/00388; Armeeoberkommando 1, Ia Nr. 2951/43 g. Kdos., 17.12.1943, T-312/27/7533948; Armeeoberkommando 15,

g.Kdos., "Beurteilung der Lage am 1.1.1944," T-312/514/
8113018; and Rommel, *The Rommel Papers*, 453.

46. T-311/27/7032427–7032428

47. Felix Gilbert, ed., *Hitler Directs His War; The Secret Records of His Daily Military Conferences* (New York: Oxford University Press, 1950) 75. The entire text of this military conference that took place on December 20, 1943, is located in Heiber, ed., *Hitlers Lagebesprechungen*, 435–456.

48. Ob West, Ia Nr. 19/44 g.Kdos., "Herauslösung aus dem Küstenfront and Versammlung hinter der Front A.O.K. 15 und recht Fluegel A.O.K. 7," 1.1.1944, T-311/22/7025227; Ob West, Ia Nr. 689/44 geh.Kdos., "Lagebeurteilung durch Ob. West," 24.1.1944, T-311/22/7025660; and General der Infanterie Günther Blumentritt, "OB West (6 Jun–24 Jul 1944)," FMS, MS# B-284, 5.

49. Adjutant des Chefs der Generalstabes der Heeres, Nr. 576/43 g.Kdos.Ch. (Fernschreiben), 23 Dez. 1943, T-78/310/6262659-6262660; and 1 Skl. Teil A (g.Kdos.Ch.), "Kriegstagebuch, Heft 53," 18.1.1944, PG-302073. If the Western Powers landed in northern Italy, for example, specified Wehrmacht units, including several formations from the western theater, were to converge on that area upon receipt of the codeword "Marder." The codeword for an attack on Denmark was "Hanna"; for Norway, "Falke"; and for the Balkans, "Gertrud" or "Forelle."

50. Ob West, Ia Nr. 1409/44 g.Kdos., "Lagebeurteilung durch Ob.West," 14.2.1944, T-311/22/7026103; Ob West, Ia Nr. 1609/44 g.Kdos., "Lagebeurteilung durch Ob. West," 21.2.1944, T-311/22/7026336; and OKW/WFSt/Op. Nr. 00566/44 g.Kdos. Ch., "Verstärkung der Küstenverteidigung und Reserve im Bereich des AOK 7, AOK 1, und AOK 19," 18.2.1944, T-78/317/6271383–6271384.

51. FMS, MS# A-895, 5–6.

52. Oberbefehlshaber West, Ic Nr. 1920/44 geh., "Feindlagebeurteilung vom 1.4.44," T-311/26/7030793.

53. Warlimont, Generalleutnant (Letter from Warlimont to Blumentritt), 8 März 1944, T-311/24/7032409.

54. Seekriegsleitung, B-Nr. 1. Skl.. I Op 16934/43 g.Kdos., "Gegnerlandungen im Westraum," 11 Juli 1942; Marinegruppenkommando West, B-Nr. Führungsstab g.Kdos. 5801 AI Chefs., "Lageübersicht des Marinegruppenkommandos West-Führungsstab-Rückblick Monate Dezember 1943 und Januar 1944," 8.2.1944, PG-32100; and 1. Skl., Teil A, g.Kdos.Ch., "Kriegstagebuch, Heft 56," 23.4.1944, PG-32076.

55. Generalleutnant Fritz Bayerlein, "Panzer Lehr Division, Mission (Jan–28 Jul 1944)," FMS MS# ETHINT-66, 6; and FMS, MS# B-720, 3.

56. Ia/Ob. West, "Notiz über Chefbesprechung bei Ob. West am 26.4.1944," T-311/23/7027959; Ob West, Ia Nr. 3332/44 g.Kdos., 26.4.1944, T-311/23/7027962; and KTB/OKW, IV, 302.

57. Der Oberbefehlshaber West, Ia Nr. 3428/44 g.Kdos., 29.4.1944, T-311/23/7028028–7028030.

58. Warlimont, *Im Hauptquartier*, 437–439; Liddell Hart, *History of the Second World War*, 548.

59. (Ob West), g.Kdos., "Tagesmeldung," 2.5.1944, T-311/24/7028080–7028081.

60. T-311/24/7028086.

61. T-311/24/7028324; FMS, MS# B-845, 23; FMS, MS# B-839, 5, 9; and Harrison, *Cross-Channel Attack*, 259–260.

62. T-311/24/7028102; and (Ob West), g.Kdos. 9.5.1944, T-311/24/7028105.

63. Ob West, Ia Nr. 3889/44 geh.Kdos., "Lagebeurteilung durch Ob.West für die Zeit vom 8. bis 14.5.44," 15.5.1944, T-311/24/7028533.

64. ObKdo.d.H.Gr.B, Ia Nr. 2700/44 g.Kdos., "Wochenmeldung 15-20.5," 21.5.1944, T-311/3/7022142; and Oberkommando der Heeresgruppe B, Ia Nr. 2880/44 g.kdos., "Wochenmeldung 21.-27.5," 29.5.1944, T-311/3/7002149-7002150.

65. Von Rundstedt had included in one of his Basic Orders on February 24, for instance, this statement: "I hope this will be the last 'Basic Order' before the beginning of the invasion" (T-311/15/7016386). The Allied commanders undoubtedly felt relieved, too, for they had already had to postpone the Normandy operation for a day. It was originally scheduled for June 5.

66. The remaining portion of this paragraph is based on AOK 15, Ia Nr. 5115/44 g.Kdos., "Lagebericht für die Zeit vom 21. bis 28.5.1944," T-312/515/8113671; (Ob West), g.Kdos., 28.5.1944, T-311/24/7028171; and T-311/3/7002149–7002150.

67. T-311/3/7002156; and T-311/24/7029166.

68. The following paragraph is based on Harrison, *Cross-Channel Attack*, 275–276; and Liddell Hart, *The German Generals Talk*, 242.

Chapter 7

1. The following two paragraphs are based on (Ob West), g.Kdos., "Besprechungs-Notizen zur Besprechung des Heeren Oberbefehlshabers West am 8.5.," T-311/24/7028385; T-311/24/7028776; T-311/24/7028952; T-311/24/7029166; Ellis, *Victory in the West*, I, 120; and Harrison, *Cross-Channel Attack*, 471.

2. Theodor Krancke, "Invasionsabwehrmassnahmen der Kriegsmarine im Kanalgebiet 1944, "*Marine-Rundschau*, LXVI (Juni 1969), 171–172; and Ellis, *Victory in the West*, I, 121.

3. Saunders, *The Fight is Won*, 112–113; and *United States Strategic Bombing Survey: Overall Report (European War)* (Washington: USGPO, 1945), 7.

4. Stacey, *The Victory Campaign*, 60. German intelligence consistently overestimated the number of Allied divisions in Great Britain, placing the figure at sixty-five or more (FMS, MS# B-675, 9–10).

5. Ellis, *Victory in the West*, I, 507.

6. David G. Rempel, "Check at the Rhine," in Craven and Cate, eds., *Europe*, III, 596.

7. The various accounts and descriptions of the Normandy campaign are too numerous to mention. The summary that follows is based primarily on KTB/OKW, IV, 311–335; Harrison's *Cross-Channel Attack*; and Ellis' *Victory in the West*, I.

8. An excellent detailed description of the Normandy defenses is contained in Stjernfelt, *Alerte*, passim.

9. Marcks, the son of a well-known German historian, had lost his leg on the Russian front earlier in the war. He was able to direct the defensive effort of the LXXXIV Corps only in its initial phases since he was killed in an Allied air attack on June 12.

10. Ellis, *Victory in the West*, I, 223.

11. Oberkommando der Heeresgruppe B, Ia Nr. 4043/44 g.Kdos., "Lagebeurteilung im Grossen 19.-26.6.1944," T-311/3/7002167; and Ob West, Ia Nr. 4593/44 geh. (Fernschreiben), 7.6.1944, T-311/25/7029356.

12. (AOK 15), g.Kdos., "Kriegstagebuch," 24.6.1944, T-312/514/8113203; and T-311/3/7002165.

13. Oberkommando der Heeresgruppe B, Ia Nr. 5360/44 g.Kdos., "Lagebeurteilung im Grossen vom 24.7.-30.7.44," 31.7.1944, T-311/3/7002214.

14. For a description of the "Mulberry" harbors, see Albert B. Stanford, *Force MULBERRY: The Planning and Installation of the Artificial Harbors off U.S. Normandy Beaches in World War II* (New York: Morrow, 1951).

15. The 12th SS Panzer was located around Lisieux, more than forty miles away, the Panzer Lehr Division, southwest of Chartres, more than ninety miles from the battle zone.

16. Ob West, Ia Nr. 4392/44 g.Kdos., "Fernsprüchen Gen. D. Artl. Warlimont mit Chef des Gen. St. Ob.West von 6.6.44, 14.30 Uhr," T-311/25/7029340.

17. Ob West, Ia Nr. 4590/44 geh, (Fernschreiben), 6.6.1944, T-311/25/7029341; AOK 7 (g. Kdos.), "Kriegstagebuch," 6.6.1944, T-312/1564/000283; and 1. Skl., Teil A (g.Kdos.Ch.), "Kriegstagebuch, Heft 57," 6.6.1944, PG-32078.

18. Panzergruppe West, Ia Nr. 2532/44 g. Kdos., "Verlaufe Eindruecke vom Westkampf," 13.6.1944, T-311/25/7029549.

19. Rommel, *The Rommel Papers*, 478–480. The new western theater commander, Field Marshal Günther von Kluge, was later recalled by Hitler on August 16. The disillusioned von Kluge committed suicide on the way back to Germany.

20. Pickhardt, Hauptmann, "Reisebericht an 8. und 9. Juni 1944," n.d., T-311/25/7029429-7029438; and Armeepionierführer beim A.O.K. 7, Nr. 1739/44 geh., "Erster Erfahrungsbericht," 30 Juni 1944, T-78/641/00086–00088. A navy report, Marinegruppenkommando West, B-Nr. Führungsstab g Kdos. 6460 AI Chefs., "Lageübersicht des Marinegruppenkommandos West Führungsstab—Rückblick Monat Juni 1944," 6 Juli 1944, PG-32100, is more optimistic at least with regard to the effectiveness of the naval artillery batteries.

21. Blumenson, *Breakout and Pursuit* 339–343.

22. Heiber, ed., *Hitlers Lagebesprechungen*, 593–594.

23. Four ports—Dunkirk, Lorient, St. Nazaire, and La Pallice-La Rochelle—actually held out until the end of the war (Jacques Mordal, (pseud.), *Die letzten Bastionen: Das Schicksal der deutschen Atlantikfestungen 1944/45* (Oldenbourg: Gerhard Stalling Verlag, 1966), 10, 20–21; Roland G. Ruppenthal, *Logistical Support of the Armies, Vol. II (United States Army in World War II. European Theater of Operations)* (Washington: OCMH, 1959), 46–48, 104–106; and Stacey, *The Victory Campaign*, 300–346.

24. T-312/977/9168212; Der Oberbefehlsaber der 1. Armee, Ia Nr. 056/44 g.Kdos.Ch., "Lage im Bereich der 1 Armee," 8.4.1944, T-312/28/7535241–7635245; and Der Oberbefehlshaber der 1. Armee, Ia Nr. 069/44 g.Kdos.Ch., 24.4.1944,

T-312/28/7535277. The chief Wehrmacht construction effort in southwestern France during early 1944 was generally confined to facilities at La Rochelle and at the mouth of the Gironde River.

25. T-311/22/7026195; and T-311/24/7029167.

26. Ibid., and Morison, *The Invasion*, 240. The tidal variations along the French Mediterranean coast were not extreme enough to warrant the extensive use of foreshore obstacles.

27. KTB/OKW, III, 1401 (26.12.1943).

28. Ellis, *Victory in the West*, I, 120, and Olaf Groehler, *Krieg im Westen* (Berlin: Deutscher Militaerverlag, 1968), 163–164.

29. (Ob West), g.Kdos., "Tagesmeldung," 5.4.1944, T-311/23/7027355; (Ob West), g.Kdos., "Tagesmeldung," 3.5.1944, T-311/24/7028084; and T-311/24/7028346–7028352. *Armeegruppe G* functioned like a *Heeresgruppe*, but it did not have as large a staff as a normal army group.

30. General Blaskowitz most recently had served for several years as the commander of the First Army in southwestern France. A highly regarded officer, the new head of Army Task Force G had incurred Hitler's disfavor for his criticism of the SS and army units for their treatment of the population in Poland after the German takeover in 1939.

31. Generaloberst Johannes Blaskowitz, "German Reaction to the Invasion of Southern France," FMS, MS# A-868, 1.

32. Oberst Fritz Schulz, "Nineteenth Army (15 Aug–15 Sep 1944)," FMS, MS# B-514, 4–8; FMS, MS# A-890, 4–5; and Jörg Staiger, *Rückzug durchs Rhônetal, Abwehr-und Verzögerungskampf der 19. Armee im Herbst 1944 (Die Wehrmacht im Kampf, Band 39)* (Neckargemünd: Kurt Vowinckel Verlag, 1965), 13–14.

33. Generalleutnant Heinz von Gyldenfeldt, "Army Group G (May–Jul 1944)," FMS, MS# B-440, 28.

34. Kontrollinspektion der DWStK, Kontrollabteilung Nr. 890/44 geh., "Monatsbericht Nr. 15, 1–30 Juni 1944," 7 Juli 1944, T-77/848/5592321–5592322.

35. Kontrollinspektion der DWStK, Kontrollabteilung Nr. 1126/ 44 geh., "Lagebericht Nr. 7, 3-10 Aug 1944," 11 Aug. 1944, T-77/848/5592414.

36. Oberkommando Armeegruppe G, Der Chef des Generalstabes, Ia Nr. 1496/44 g.Kdos., "Lagebeurteilung der Armeegruppe," 31.7.1944, T-311/140/7185770.

37. (Armeegruppe G), "Lagebeurteilung," 7.8.1944, T-311/140/ 7185871; FMS, MS# A-868, 2; and FMS, MS# B-440, 22-23.

38. Obkdo. Armeegruppe G, Ia Nr. 1800/44 g. Kdos. (Fernschreiben), 12.8.1944, T-311/140/7185931.

39. The rest of the paragraph is based on Oberst Horst Wilutzky, "Battles in Southern France" FMS, MS# A-882, 7; Morison, *The Invasion*, 239–240, 257–262; and Staiger, *Rückzug*, 13–14. See fig. 7.3, p. 137.

40. The chief objective of the commando teams was to capture several artillery batteries which dominated the approaches to the invasion beaches, but after taking them, the United States and French units found them to be dummy positions. The summary of the Provence invasion that follows is taken from Morison, *The Invasion*, 236–274; and the popularized account of Jacques Robichon, *The Second D-Day*, trans. Barbara Shuey (New York: Walker and Company, 1969).

41. Oberkommando Armeegruppe G, Ia Nr. 1926/44 g.Kdos., (Fernschreiben), 17.8.1944, T-311/140/7185993; Oberkommando Armeegruppe G, Ia Nr. 1933/44 g.kdos. Ch. (Fernschreiben), 18.8.1944, T-311/140/7185401; FMS, MS# A-882, 15–18; and FMS, MS# A-868, 2–4.

42. Blumenson, *Breakout and Pursuit*, 535, 697.

Chapter 8

1. Diplomingenieur Xaver Dorsch, "Organization Todt—Operations in the West," FMS, MS# B-671, 10.

2. The following two paragraphs are drawn from Harrison, *Cross-Channel Attack*, 176; Morison, *The Invasion*, 45; Stjernfelt, *Alerte*, 307–308; Aron, *France Reborn*, 4; Albert Norman, *Operation Overlord: Design and Reality* (Harrisburg, PA: Military Service Publishing Co., 1952), 210; and especially Liddell Hart, *History of the Second World War*, 543.

Bibliography

The sources for this book are primarily the captured and microfilmed German World War II records and the Foreign Military Studies prepared after the war by the historical section of the United States Forces in the European Theater.

The voluminous German documents captured toward the end of the war have been microfilmed by the National Archives as part of a continuing project instituted in 1955 by a group of scholars who became known as the Committee for the Study of War Documents of the American Historical Association. These records, which form the basis of numerous works dealing with contemporary history, are of crucial importance in our study of the Atlantic Wall concept. Since literally thousands of rolls of microfilm are in this collection, the *Guides to Records Microfilmed at Alexandria, VA* (68 vols. to date; Washington: National Archives, 1955ff), is an indispensable reference aid. The films are readily available from the National Archives in Washington.

It would be an almost impossible task to compile from these microfilmed German records an exhaustive list of the specific documents that pertain to the Atlantic Wall and to Western Europe in general during the wartime period. Nevertheless, it is possible to discuss the major "groups" of records within the collection which are of special significance and to point out other materials from this vast and rich source of information which are helpful in examining the German military's western defense complex.

One extremely valuable source within these major record groups are those at the upper command level and contained in the National Archives Microcopy T-77 series, Records of Headquarters, German Armed Forces High Command (*Oberkommando der Wehrmacht/OKW*). Especially pertinent for an overall view of the war are the files of the Armed Forces operations staff (*Wehrmachtführungsstab/WFSt*), Rolls 774–778, 786–788. Part of these materials have conveniently appeared in published form in several documentary collections, including *Führer Directives and Other Top-Level Directives of the German Armed Forces, 1939–1945* (2 vols.; Washington: Naval History Division, U.S. Office of Chief of Naval Operations, 1948), and the less complete Walther Hubatsch, ed., *Hitlers Weisungen für die Kriegsführung, 1939–1945* (Frankfurt/Main: Bernard & Gräfe, 1962) (Abridged English edition, Hugh R. Trevor-Roper, ed., *Hitler's War Directives 1939–1945* (London: Sidgwick and Jackson, 1964).

The various German army materials form an additional important source for the study of the Atlantic Wall. The highest level army records appear in the T-78 series, Records of Headquarters, German Army High Command (*Oberkommando des Heeres/OKH*). Within this series many significant documents relating to the western theater can be found in the operations branch (*Operationsabteilung*) materials (Rolls 309–319), and in the estimates prepared by one of the OKH intelligence sections, Foreign Armies West (*Abteilung Fremde Heere West*), Rolls 443–452. These estimates include German appraisals of United States and British forces, the French Armistice Army, developments in northern Africa and Spain, and so on, as the situation changed throughout the course of the war.

Another invaluable source are the records of the German Army commands deployed in the West. The highest echelon of command in the theater was the Army Group (*Heeresgruppe*), and the *Heeresgruppe* materials are located within the T-311 series, Records of German Field Commands: Army Groups. The pertinent records (Rolls 12–18) of the overall theater commander, Commander-in-Chief West (*Oberbefehlshaber West*), are, on the whole, of good quality, although some of the top secret files (*Chefsachen*) are missing. The records (Rolls 139–141) of Army Task Force G (*Armeegruppe G*, later *Heeresgruppe G*) though not formed until May 1944, are also excellent and included important top secret documents. The materials from Rommel's Army Group B, on the other hand, are fragmentary before June 6. On the period after the invasion they are much more complete.

Documentary records from the four German Armies that served in Western Europe during most of the pre-invasion period are for the most part of exceptional quality and consist of headquarters war diaries (*Kriegstagebucher*) and the various supporting documents (*Anlagen*). Following is a list of these armies and the relevant rolls which appear in the T-312 series, Records of German Field Commands: Armies:

First Army, Rolls 20–30;
Seventh Army, Rolls 1530–1571;
Fifteenth Army, Rolls 497–521;
Nineteenth Army, Rolls 976–979.

It is regrettable that the important pre-invasion records of Panzer Group West (*Panzergruppe West*), which was headed by General Geyr von Schweppenburg and attached to *Ob West*, have disappeared. The activities of this Panzer Group just after the D-Day landing are located in the T-313 series, Records of German Field Commands: Panzer Armies, under *Panzer-Armeeoberkommando 5*, Rolls 420–421.

Materials at the lower army command levels in the West are of assistance in answering specific questions that relate to particular areas and formations. Among the significant microfilm series, which are still appearing, are the T-314 series, Records of German Field Commands: Corps; and the T-354 series, Miscellaneous SS Records: Einwandererzentralstelle, Waffen-SS, and SS-Oberabschnitte, the latter series being especially important in assessing the role played by the SS panzer divisions that shuttled between East and West.

The extensive German naval documents form a category of their own. These records are part of a vast collection of materials which were catalogued in England after the war. Copies of these records, except for German U-boat documents, were housed for a number of years at the U.S. Naval History Division in Washington, but they are now available on microfilm as part of the National Archives collection under T-1022, Records of the German Navy, 1870–1945.

Naval records which are particularly pertinent for the study of the Atlantic Wall are, first of all, portions of the Naval High Command Operations Branch (*Oberkommando der Kriegsmarine, Seekriegsleitung*) documents. They include sections of the operations division war diary (British References Numbers PG-32041–PG-32071); situation and operational reports (PG-32100, PG-32164–PG-32166); orders dealing with cover operations "Shark" and "Harpoon" (PG-32444, PG-32636); and the German takeover of Toulon harbor in 1942 (PG-32462, PG-33409).

Additional valuable sources for an understanding of the coastal defense system and for a picture of the "Gisela" undertaking into Spain can be found among the materials of Navy Theater Command West (*Marine Gruppenkommando West*) and one of its subordinate commands, Navy Command Channel Coast (*Marinebefehlshaber Kanalküste*), especially numbers PG-37635–PG-37639, PG-37679–PG-37681, and PG-38550–PG-38551.

The German Air Force Records are sketchy, although materials in the National Archives T-405 series, German Air Force Records: Luftgaukommandos, Flak, Deutsche Luftwaffenmission in Rumanien,

Rolls 43–46, are of some help in understanding the Luftwaffe administrative apparatus in the western theater.

Also of some assistance in examining the German military occupation of Western Europe is the T-501 series, records of German Field Commands: Rear Areas, Occupied Territories, and Others. Especially germane are the files of Military Commander in Belgium and Northern France (*Militärbefehlshaber in Belgien und Nordfrankreich*), Rolls 96–116, and 355–356; and those of Military Commander in France (*Militärbefehlshaber in Frankreich*), Rolls 141–191. In addition, the T-501 series includes some records of the Commander of Army Troops in the Netherlands (*Kommandeur der Truppen des Heeres in den Niederlanden*), Rolls 197–201, which contain reports on the construction of the Atlantic Wall along with Dutch coast between 1941 and 1943.

Scattered among all of the microfilm cited above are documents that have appeared in published form as part of the Nuremberg Trials collection. This important group of documents includes the following published series:

> *Nazi Conspiracy and Aggression.* 8 vols. Plus 2 supplements. Washington: USGPO, 1946–1948 (Red Series).
>
> *Trial of Major War Criminals before the International Military Tribunal.* 42 vols. Nuremberg: International Military Tribunal, 1947–1949 (Blue Series).
>
> *Trials of the War Criminals before the Nuremberg Military Tribunals under Control Council Law No. 10.* 15 vols. Washington: USGPO, 1949 (Green Series).

The second basic unpublished primary source used in this analysis of Hitler's Atlantic Wall has been the Foreign Military Studies. The historical section of U.S. forces in the European Theater compiled these studies after the war from interviews and written questionnaires submitted to German military officers and administrative personnel. Many of these accounts were written from memory, and they contain a number of factual errors as well as apologetics, but all of them give details which are of immense value to the historian as can be seen from their skillful utilization in the United States World War II official histories.

An almost complete list of more than 1,000 studies, including materials dealing with the Russian and Mediterranean fronts, is published in *Guide to Foreign Military Studies 1945–54, Catalogue and Index* (Karlsruhe: Historical Division, Headquarters, United States Army Europe, 1954). All the documents, which were originally housed at the Office of the Chief of Military History in Washington, were microfilmed in 1972 and have become part of the National Archives collection. The various documents used from this collection are indicated in the textual footnotes.

Portions of two Allied documentary collections also provide additional technical data regarding Germany's western defenses in the absence of detailed Organization Todt materials. They are the Records of Supreme Commander Allied Expeditionary Force as contained in the Records of United States Theaters of War, World War II, Record Group 331, National Archives; and the Files of the Assistant Chief of Staff for Intelligence (G-2), as contained in the Records of the War Department General and Special Staffs, Records Group 165, Washington National Records Center, Suitland, Maryland. The G-2 Files includes the valuable reports of the Seacoast Artillery Evaluation Board United States Forces, European Theater, *German Seacoast Defenses, European Theater,* 7 vols., 20 Dec. 1945. This board was formed after the war and conducted a number of investigations of Germany's coastal artillery batteries from Norway to France's Atlantic coast.

Two published sources which deserve special mention are Percy E. Schramm, et al., eds., *Kriegstagebuch des Oberkommandos der Wehrmacht* (4 vols. in 7 parts; Frankfurt/Main; Bernard & Gräfe, 1961–1965); and Helmut Heiber, ed., *Hitlers Lagebesprechungen; Die Protokollfragmente seiner militarischen Konferenzen, 1942–1945* (Stuttgart: Deutsche Verlags-Anstalt, 1962), (abridged English edition, Felix Gilbert, ed., *Hitler*

Directs His War, The Secret Records of His Daily Military Conferences (New York: Oxford University Press, 1950). (*Hitler and His Generals. Military Conferences 1942-1945*, Helmut Heiber and David M. Glantz, eds. New York: Enigma Books, 2003. Complete English edition.) Two of Schramm's insightful essays into Hitler's enigmatic character, which appeared previously as part of the introductions to *Hitlers Lagebesprechungen* and the *Kriegstagebuch*, have been published together in *Hitler: The Man and the Military Leader*, trans. Donald S. Detwiler (Chicago: Quadrangle Books, 1971).

The remainder of the bibliography has been divided into other documentary materials; memoirs, autobiographies, and speeches; official histories; books; dissertations; and articles, pamphlets, and reports.

Other Documentary Materials

De Chambrun, Rene and Madame de Chambrun, eds., *France During the German Occupation 1940–1944 A Collection of 292 Statements on the Government of Marechal Pétain and Pierre Laval.* Trans. Philip W. Whitcomb. 3 vols. Stanford: Stanford University Press for the Hoover Institution on War, Revolution, and Peace, 1957.

Germany. Auswärtigen Amt. *Akten zur deutschen Auswärtigen Politik.* *Series E.* 3 vols. to date. Göttingen: Vandenhöck & Ruprecht, 1969ff. Series E, when complete, will cover December 1941 to 1945.

Supreme Headquarters Allied Expeditionary Force. *Reports by the Supreme Commander of the Combined Chiefs of Staff on the Operations in Europe of the Allied Expeditionary Force, 6 June 1944 to 8 May 1945.* Washington: USGPO, 1946.

United States. Department of State. *Documents on German Foreign Policy, 1918–1945. Series D.* 13 vols. Washington: USGPO, 1950–1966. Vols. XI-XIII cover the early war years up to Dec., 1941.

United States Navy. Office of Naval Intelligence. *Führer Conferences on Matters Dealing with the German Navy, 1939–1945.* 7 vols.; Washington: U.S. Navy Department, 1947.

Memoirs, Autobiographies, Speeches

Abetz, Otto. *Das offene Problem: Ein Rückblick auf zwei Jahrzehnte deutscher Frankreichpolitik.* Cologne: Greven, 1951.

Bryant, Sir Arthur. *Triumph in the West; A History of the War Years Based on the Diaries of Field Marshal Lord Alanbrooke, Chief of the Imperial General Staff.* Garden City, N.Y.: Doubleday, 1959.

— *The Turn of the Tide; A History of the War Years Based on the Diaries of Field-Marshal Lord Alanbrooke, Chief of the Imperial General Staff.* Garden City: Doubleday, 1957.

Butcher, Harry C. *My Three Years With Eisenhower.* New York: Simon and Schuster, 1957.

Churchill, Winston *The Second World War,* 6 vols. Boston: Houghton, Mifflin, 1948–1953.

De Gaulle, Charles. *Mémoires de guerre.* 3 vols. Paris: Plon, 1954–1959. (English edition, *The Complete War Memoirs.* trans. Jonathan Griffin and Richard Howard. New York: Simon and Schuster, 1964).

Dönitz, Karl. *Zehn Jahre und zwanzig Tage.* Bonn: Atheneum, 1958. (English edition, *Memoirs: Ten Years and Twenty Days.* Trans. R.H. Stevens. Cleveland: World Publishing Co., 1959).

Domarus, Max, ed., *Hitler, Reden und Proklamationen, 1932–1945.* 2 vols. Würzburg: Schmidt Verlagsdruckerei, 1962–1963.

Eisenhower, Dwight D., *Crusade in Europe.* Garden City: Doubleday, 1948.

Faber du Faur, Moriz. *Macht und Ohnmacht: Erinnerungen eines alten Offiziers.* Stuttgart: H.E. Günther, 1943. German military officer in Bordeaux, 1940–1942.

Freiden, Seymour, and William Richardson, eds. *The Fatal Decisions.* trans. Constantine Fitzgibbon. New York: W. Sloan Associates, 1956. German generals' apologia.

Görlitz, Walter, ed., *Generalfeldmarschall Keitel; Verbrecher oder Offizier? Erinnerungen, Briefe, Dokumente des Chefs OKW.* Göttingen:

Musterschmidt, 1961. (English edition, *Memoirs of Field Marshal Keitel*. Trans. David Irving. London: Kimber, 1965.)

Greiner, Helmut. *Die oberste Wehrmachtführung, 1939–1943*. Wiesbaden: Limes Verlag, 1951.

Halder, Franz. *The Halder Diaries*. 7 vols. Washington: Infantry Journal, 1950. (German edition; Hans-Adolf Jacobsen, ed.) *Generaloberst Halder. Kriegstagebuch; Tägliche Aufzeichnungen des Chefs des Generalstabes des Heeres, 1939–1942*, Stuttgart: W. Kohlhammer, 1962–1963.

von Manstein, Erich. *Verlorene Siege*. Bonn; Athenaeum, 1955 (English edition, *Lost Victories*, ed. and trans. Anthony G. Lowell. London: Methuen, 1958).

Morgan, Sir Frederick E. *Overture to Overlord*. Garden City: Doubleday, 1950. Head of COSSAC.

Picker, Henry, ed., *Hitlers Tischgesprache im Führerhauptquartier 1941-42*. Stuttgart: Seewald, 1963. (English edition, Hugh R. Trevor-Roper, ed., *Hitler's Secret Conversations, 1941–1944*. Trans. Norman Cameron and R.H. Stevens. New York: Farrar, Strauss, and Young, 1953.)

Räder, Erich. *Mein Leben: Von 1935 bis Spandau* 1955. Tübingen: F. Schlichtenmayer, 1956. (English edition, *My Life*. Vol. II. Trans. Henry W. Drexel. Annapolis: United States Naval Institute, 1960.)

Rommel, Erwin. *The Rommel Papers*. Ed. Basil H. Liddell Hart. Trans. Paul Finlay. New York: Harcourt, Brace, 1953.

Ruge, Friedrich. *Rommel und die Invasion: Erinnerungen*. Stuttgart: K.F. Koehler, 1959.

Speer, Albert. *Erinnerungen*. Frankfurt/Main: Ullstein, 1969. (English edition, *Inside the Third Reich*. Trans. Richard and Clara Winston. New York: Macmillan, 1970.)

Speidel, Hans. *Invasion 1944: Ein Beitrag zu Rommels und des Reiches Schicksal*. Tübingen: Rainir Wunderlich Verlag, 1950. (English edition, *We Defended Normandy*. Trans. Ian Colvin. London: Herbert Jenkins, 1951.)

Warlimont, Walter. *Im Hauptquartier der deutschen Wehrmacht, 1939–1945.* Frankfurt/Main: Bernard & Gräfe, 1962. (English edition, *Inside Hitler's Headquarters.* Trans. R.H. Barry. New York: Praeger, 1964.)

Westphal, Siegfried. *Heer in Fesseln; Aus den Papieren des Stabschefs von Rommel, Kesselring, und Rundstedt.* Bonn: Athenaeum, 1950. (Abr. English edition, *The German Army in the West.* London; Cassell, 1951.)

Official Histories

Blumenson, Martin. *Breakout and Pursuit.* (*United States Army in World War II. European Theater of Operations.*) Washington: OCMH, 1962.

Butler, James R.M. *Grand Strategy, Vol. II. September 1939–June 1941.* (*History of the Second World War: United Kingdom Military Series.*) London: HMSO, 1957.

Craven, Wesley F., and James L. Cate, eds. *Europe: Torch to Pointblank, August 1942 to December 1943.* (*The Army Air Force in World War II. Vol. II.*) Chicago: University of Chicago Press, 1949.

— and —, eds. *Europe: Argument to V-E Day, January 1944 to May 1945.* (*The Army Air Force in World War II. Vol. III.*) Chicago: University of Chicago Press, 1951.

Ehrman, John. *Grand Strategy, Vol. V. August 1943–September 1944.* (*History of the Second World War: United Kingdom Military Series.*) London: HMSO, 1956.

Garland, Albert N., and Howard M. Smyth. *Sicily and the Surrender of Italy.* (*United States Army in World War II. Mediterranean Theater of Operations.*) Washington: OCMH, 1965.

Gwyer, J.M.A., and J.R.M. Butler. *Grand Strategy, Vol. III. June 1941–August 1942.* (*History of the Second World War: United Kingdom Military Series.*) London: HMSO, 1964.

Harrison, Gordon. *Cross-Channel Attack.* (*United States Army in World War II. European Theater of Operations.*) Washington: OCMH, 1951.

Morison, Samuel Eliot. *The Invasion of France and Germany, 1944–1945.* (*History of United States Naval Operations in World War II. Vol. XI.*) Boston: Little, Brown, 1957.

Pogue, Forrest C. *The Supreme Command.* (*United States Army in World War II. European Theater of Operations.*) Washington: OCMH, 1954.

Roskill, Sir Stephen W. *The War at Sea, 1939–1945; Vol II: The Period of Balance.* (*History of the Second World War: United Kingdom Military Series.*) London: HMSO, 1960.

— *The War at Sea, 1939–1945; Vol. III. The Offensive.* (*History of the Second World War. United Kingdom Military Series.*) London: HMSO, 1960.

Ruppenthal, Roland G. *Logistical Support of the Armies. Vols. I and II.* (*United States Army in World War II. European Theater of Operations.*) Washington: OCMH, 1954–1958.

Saunders, Hilary St. G. *The Fight is Won. Royal Air Force 1939–1945;* Vol. III. London: HMSO, 1957.

Stacey, Charles P. *Six Years of War; The Army in Canada, Britain, and the Pacific.* (*Official History of the Canadian Army in the Second World War. Vol. I.*) Ottawa: Queen's Printer, 1957.

— *The Victory Campaign. The Operations in Northwest Europe, 1944–1945.* (*Official History of the Canadian Army in the Second World War. Vol. III.*) Ottawa: Queen's Printer, 1960.

Secondary Works: Books

Amouroux, Henri. *La vie des Français sous l'occupation (1940–1944).* Paris: Fayard, 1961.

Ansel, Walter. *Hitler Confronts England.* Durham: Duke, 1960.

Arnoult, Pierre, et al. *La France sous l'occupation.* Paris: Presses Universitaires de France, 1959. Reply to the documents collected by Rene and Madame de Chambrun.

Aron, Robert. *Histoire de la libération de la France (Juin 1944–Mai 1945).* Paris: Fayard, 1959. (English edition, *France Reborn: The History of the Liberation, June 1944–May 1945*. Trans. Humphrey Hare. New York: Scribner's, 1964.)

— *Histoire de Vichy, 1940–1941*. Paris: Fayard, 1954. (Abridged English edition, *The Vichy Regime, 1940–1944*. London: Putnam, 1958.)

Auphan, Paul, and Jacques Mordal. *The French Navy in World War II*. Trans. A.C.J. Sabalot. Annapolis: U.S. Naval Institute, 1959.

Bankwitz, Charles F. *Maxime Weygand and Civil-Military Relations in Modern France*. Cambridge: Harvard, 1967.

Baumbach, Werner. *Zu Spät? Aufsteig und Untergang der deutschen Luftwaffe*. Munich: Pflaum, 1949. (English edition, *Broken Swastika; The Defeat of the Luftwaffe*. Trans. Frederick Holt. London: R. Hale, 1960.)

Benary, Albert. *Die Berliner Bären-Division; Geschichte der 257. Infanterie Division 1939–1945*. Bad Nauheim: H.-H. Podzun, 1955.

Besson, Waldemar, and Freidrich Freiherr Hiller von Gärtringen, eds. *Geschichte und Gegenwartsbewusstsein, Historische Betrachtungen und Untersuchungen. Festschrift für Hans Rothfels zum 70. Geburtstag*. Göttingen: Vandenhöck & Ruprecht, 1963.

Blumentritt, Günther. *Von Rundstedt. The Soldier and the Man*. Trans. Cuthbert Reavely. London: Obhams, 1952. The author was von Rundstedt's Chief of Staff in the West.

Bölcke, Willi, ed. *Deutschlands Rüstung im Zweiten Weltkrieg. Hitlers Konferenzen mit Albert Speer 1942–1945*. Frankfurt/Main; Akademische Verlagsgesellschaft, 1969.

Bragadin, Marc Antonio. *The Italian Navy in World War II*. Trans. Gale Hoffman. Annapolis: U.S. Naval Institute, 1957.

Brehm, Werner. *Mein Kriegstagebuch 1939 bis 1945; Mit der 7. Panzer Division 5 Jahre im West und Ost*. Cassel: Selbstverlag, 1953.

Burdick, Charles B. *Germany's Military Strategy and Spain in World War II*. Syracuse: Syracuse University Press, 1968.

Carroll, Berenice A. *Design for Total War. Arms and Economics in the Third Reich*. The Hague: Mouton, 1968.

Collier, Basil. *The Battle of the V-Weapons, 1944–45.* London: Hodder and Stoughton, 1964.

Couture, Claude-Paul. *Operation "Jubilee": Dieppe, 19 août 1942.* Paris: France Empire, 1969.

Delandsherre, Paul, and Alphonse Ooms. *La Belgique sous les Nazis.* 4 vols. Brussels: L'édition Universelle, 1946. Day-by-day account of developments in Belgium from 1940 to 1944.

Detwiler, Donald S. *Hitler, Franco, und Gibraltar, Die Frage des spanischen Eintritts in der Zweiten Weltkrieg.* Wiesbaden: F. Steiner, 1962.

Dieckhoff, Gerhard. *3. Infanterie-Division, 3. Inf.-Div. (mot.), 3. Panzergrenadier-Division.* Bad Nauheim: H.-H. Podzun, 1961.

Durand, Paul. *La S.N.C.F. pendant la guerre. Sa résistance à l'occupant.* Paris: Presses Universitaires de France, 1968.

Durand, Ralph A. *Guernsey Under German Rule.* London: Guernsey Society, 1946.

Eisenhower Foundation. *D-Day: The Normandy Invasion in Retrospect.* Lawrence: University of Kansas Press, 1971.

Ellsberg, Edward. *The Far Shore—A Critical Reappraisal of D-Day.* New York: Dodd, Mead, 1960.

Feis, Herbert. *Churchill, Roosevelt, Stalin: The War They Waged and the Peace They Sought.* Princeton: Princeton University Press, 1957.

—— *The Spanish Story: Franco and the Nations at War.* New York: Knopf, 1948.

First United States Army. *Reports on Operations, 20 October 1943–1 August 1944.* 7 vols. Paris: First Army Headquarters, 1945.

Fleming, Peter. *Operation Sea Lion.* New York, Ace Books, 1957.

Galland, Adolf. *Die Ersten und die Letzten.* Darmstadt: Franz Schneekluth, 1953. (English edition, *The First and the Last, The German Fighter Forces in World War II.* Trans. Mervyn Savill. London: Methuen, 1955.)

Gambiez, Frenand. *Libération de la Corse.* Paris: Hachette, 1973.

Gamelin, Paul. *Le mur de l'Atlantique, Les blockhaus de l'illusoire.* Paris: Daniel, 1974. Misleading, but excellent photographs.

Gemzell, Carl-Axel. *Räder, Hitler und Skandinavien; Der Kampf für einem maritimen Operationsplan.* Lund: Gleerups, 1965.

Geschke, Günter. *Die deutsche Frankreichpolitik 1940 von Compiegne bis Montoire. (Wehrwissenschaftliche Rundschau Beiheft 12/13.)* Frankfurt/Main: E.S. Mittler, 1960.

Godefroy, Georges. *Le Havre sous l'occupation (1940–1944).* Le Havre: La Vigie, 1965.

Griffith, Richard. *Pétain: A Biography of Marshal Philippe Pétain of Vichy.* Garden City: Doubleday, 1972.

Gruchmann, Lothar. *Nationalsozialistische Grossraumordnung. Die konstruktion einer "deutscher Monroe-Doktrin." (Schriftenreihe der Vierteljahrsheft für Zeitgeschichte, Nr. 5)* Stuttgart: Deutsche Verlags-Anstalt, 1962.

Harnier, Wilhelm von. *Artillerie im Küstenkampf.* Munich: J.F. Lehmann, 1969. A German naval artillery expert during World War II.

Hayn, Friedrich. *Die Invasion: Von Cotentin bis Falaise. (Die Wehrmacht im Kampf, Bd. 2).* Heidelberg: Scharnhorst-Buchkameradschaft der Soldaten, 1954.

Hillgruber, Andreas. *Hitlers Strategie; Politik und Kriegsführung, 1940–1941.* Frankfurt/Main: Bernard & Gräfe, 1965.

Hinsley, Francis H. *Hitler's Strategy.* Cambridge: University Press, 1951.

Homze, Edward L. *Foreign Labor in Nazi Germany.* Princeton: Princeton University Press, 1967.

Illustrated Records of German Army Equipment 1939-1945. 5 vols. in 6 parts. London: The War Office, 1948.

Jäckel, Eberhard. *Frankreich in Hitlers Europa; Die deutsche Frankreichpolitik im zweiten Weltkrieg* Stuttgart: Deutsche Verlags-Anstalt, 1966.

Jacobsen, Hans-Adolf, and Jürgen Rohwer, eds. *Entscheidungsschlachten des zweiten Welt-krieges, 1939–1945.* Frankfurt/Main: Bernard & Gräfe, 1960. (English edition, *Decisive Battles of World War II.* New York: G.P. Putnam's, 1965.)

Jacquemyns, Guillaume. *La société belge sous l'occupation allemande.* 3 vols. Brussels: Nicholson et Watson, 1950.

Janssen, Gregor. *Das Ministerium Speer, Deutschlands Rüstung im Krieg.* Berlin: Ullstein, 1968.

Kammerer, Albert. *La passion de la flotte française De Mers-el-Kebir a Toulon.* Paris: Fayard, 1951.

Keiling, Wolf. *Das deutsche Heer, 1939–1945: Gliederung, Einsatz, Stellenbesetzung.* Bad Nauheim: H.-H. Podzun, 1955ff.

Klein, Burton H. *Germany's Economic Preparations for War.* Cambridge: Harvard, 1959.

Kurowski, Franz. *Die Panzer-Lehr Division, Die grösste deutsche Panzer-Division und ihre Aufgabe Die Invasion zerschlagen—die Ardennesschlacht entscheiden 1944.* Bad Nauheim: H.-H. Podzun, 1956.

Kwiet, Konrad. *Reichkommissariat Niederlande* Stuttgart: Deutsche Verlags-Anstalt, 1968.

Lee, Asher. *The German Air Force.* New York: Harper, 1946.

Lewin, Ronald. *Rommel as Military Commander.* Princeton: Van Nostrand, 1968.

Liddell Hart, Basil H. *The German Generals Talk.* New York: W. Morrow, 1948.

— *History of the Second World War.* London: Cassell, 1970.

Lohmann, Walther, and Hans H. Hildebrand. *Die deutsche Kriegsmarine 1939–1945; Gliederung, Einsatz, Stellenbesetzung.* Bad Nauheim: H-H. Podzun, 1956.

McGuire, Eric. *Dieppe, August 19.* London: Jonathan Cape, 1963.

Mellenthin, Friedrich Wilhelm von. *Panzer Battles, 1939–1945: A Study in the Employment of Armour in the Second World War.* Trans. H. Betzler. London: Cassell, 1956.

Michel, Henri. *Bibliographie critique de la Résistance.* Paris: Institut Pedagogique National, 1964.

— *Les courants de pensée de la Résistance.* Paris: Presses Universitaires de France, 1964.

— *La Seconde guerre Mondiale.* 2 vols. (*Peuples et Civilisations* XXI.) Paris: Presses Universitaires de France, 1968–1969.

Milward, Alan S. *The German Economy at War.* London: Athlone Press, 1965.

— *The New Order and the French Economy.* Oxford: Clarendon Press, 1970.

Mordal, Jacques (pseud.). *Les Canadiens à Dieppe.* Paris: Presses de la Cité, 1962.

— *Les Poches de l'Atlantique.* Paris: Presses de la Cité, 1965. (German edition, *Die letzten Bastionen: Das Schicksal der deutschen Atlantikfestungen 1944/45.* Oldenbourg: Gerhard Stallings, 1966.)

Müller-Hillebrand, Burkhart. *Das Heer, 1933–1945.* 3 vols. Darmstadt and Frankfurt/Main: E.S. Mittler, 1954–1969.

Munz, Alfred. *Die Auswirkungen der deutschen Besetzung auf Waehrung und Finanzen Frankreichs (Studien des Instituts fuer Besatzungsfragen in Tübingen zu den deutschen besetzungen im zweiten Weltkrieg. Nr. 9)* Tübingen: Instituts für Besatzungsfragen, 1957. One of a number of studies on the German occupation.

Norman, Albert. *Operation Overlord: Design and Reality.* Harrisburg, PA, Military Service Publishing Co., 1952. Based mainly on the files of Headquarters, Twelfth Army Group.

Paxton, Robert O. *Parades and Politics at Vichy: The French Officer Corps Under Marshal Pétain* Princeton: Princeton University Press, 1966.

— *Vichy France: Old Guard and New Order, 1940–1944.* New York: Knopf, 1972.

Phillips, Cecil E.L. *The Greatest Raid of All.* Boston: Little, Brown, 1960. St. Nazaire raid.

Rich, Norman. *Nazi War Aims.* 2 vols. New York: Norton, 1973–74.

Robichon, Jacques. *Le débarquement de Provence: 15 aout 1944.* Paris: Laffont, 1962. (English edition, *The Second D-Day.* Trans. Barbara Shuey. New York: Walker, 1969.) Popularized account.

Ruge, Friedrich. *Der Seekrieg, 1939–1945.* Stuttgart: Kohler, 1954. (English edition, *Sea Warfare, 1939–1945: A German Viewpoint.* trans. M.G. Saunders. London: Cassell, 1957.)

Ruppenthal, Roland G. *Utah Beach to Cherbourg*. (*American Forces in Action Series, No. 13.*) Washington: Historical Division, Department of the Army, 1948.

Ryan, Cornelius. *The Longest Day, June 6, 1944*. New York: Simon and Schuster, 1959.

Ryder, Robert E.D. *The Attack on St. Nazaire, 28th March 1942*. London: John Murray, 1947.

Schröder, Josef. *Italiens Kriegsaustritt 1943; Die deutschen Gegenmassnahmen im italienischen Raum. Fall "Alarich" und "Achse."* Göttingen: Musterschmidt, 1969.

Sherwood, Robert E. *Roosevelt and Hopkins: An Intimate History*. New York: Grosset and Dunlap, 1948. Republished by Enigma Books, 2002. Still one of the best accounts of Allied strategy in World War II.

Sinel, L.P. (comp.). *The German Occupation of Jersey. A Diary of Events from June 1940 to June 1945*. London: Transworld Publishers, 1959.

Snell, John L. *Illusion and Necessity; The Diplomacy of Global War, 1939–1945*. Boston: Houghton Mifflin, 1963.

Staiger, Jörg. *Rückzug durchs Rhônetal; Abwehrund Verzögerungskampf der 19. Armee im Herbst 1944*. (*Die Wehrmacht im Kampf, Bd. 39.*) Neckargemünd: K. Vowinckel, 1965.

Stanford, Albert B. *Force MULBERRY: The Planning and Installation of the Artificial Harbor off U.S. Normandy Beaches in World War II*. New York: Morrow, 1951. Mr. Stanford was one of the planners.

Stein, George H. *The Waffen-SS; Hitler's Elite Guard at War, 1939–1945*. Ithaca: Cornell University Press, 1966.

Steinberg, Lucien, ed. *Les autorités allemandes en France Occupée. Inventaire commenté de la Collection de documents conservés au C.D.J.C.* Paris: Centre de Documentation Juive Contemporaine, 1966.

Stjernfelt, Bertil. *Alerte sur le Mur de l'Atlantique*. Trans. Rolf Gauffin. Paris: Presses de la Cité, 1961. Stjernfelt was a Swedish artillery officer who inspected the Normandy defenses after the war.

Stöber, Hans-Jürgen. *Die Eiserne Faust, Bildband und Chronik der 17. SS-Panzergrenadier Division "Götz von Berlichungen."* Neckargemünd: K. Vowinckel, 1966.

Strawson, John. *Hitler as Military Commander.* London: B.T. Batford, 1971.

Taylor, Charles H. *Omaha Beachhead. (American Forces in Action Series, No. 7.)* Washington: Historical Division, Department of the Army, 1946.

Tessin, Georg. *Verbande und Truppen der deutschen Wehrmacht und Waffen SS, 1939–1945.* 8 vols. Frankfurt/Main: E.S. Mittler, 1965–1972.

Thomsen, Erich. *Deutsche Besatzungspolitik in Dänemark 1940–1945. (Studien zur modernen Geschichte, Bd. 4).* Düsseldorf: Bertelsmann Universitätsverlag, 1971.

Tippelskirch, Kurt von. *Geschichte des zweiten Weltkrieges.* Bonn: Athenaeum, 1959.

Toynbee, Arnold, and Veronica M. Toynbee, eds. *Survey of International Affairs, 1939–1946. Vol. IV. Hitler's Europe.* London: Oxford University Press for the Royal Institute of International Affairs, 1954.

— *Survey of International Affairs, 1939–1946. Vol. VIII. The War and the Neutrals.* London: Oxford University Press for R.I.I.A., 1956.

Umbreit, Hans. *Der Militärbefehlshaber in Frankreich, 1940–1944.* Boppard/Rhine: Boldt, 1968.

Warmbrunn, Werner. *The Dutch Under German Occupation, 1940–1944.* Stanford: Stanford University Press, 1963.

Warner, Geoffrey. *Pierre Laval and the Eclipse of France.* London: Eyre and Spottiswoode, 1968.

Weidinger, Otto. *Division "Das Reich." Band II: 1939–1943.* Osnabrück: Münin-Verlag, 1969

Weinberg, Gerhard L. *Germany and the Soviet Union, 1939–1941.* Leiden: Brill, 1954.

Wheatley, Ronald. *Operation Sea Lion. German Plans for the Invasion of England, 1939–1942.* Oxford: Clarendon Press, 1958.

Wilmot, Chester. *The Struggle for Europe.* New York: Harper, 1952.

Wood, Alan, and Mary Wood. *Islands in Danger: The Story of the German Occupation of the Channel Islands, 1940–1945.* London: Evans Bros., 1955.

Wright, Gordon. *The Ordeal of Total War, 1939–1945.* New York: Harper and Row, 1968.

Young, Desmond. *Rommel, The Desert Fox.* New York: Harper, 1951.

Ziegler, Janet. *World War II: Books in English, 1945–1965.* Stanford: Hoover Institution on War, Revolution, and Peace, 1970.

Ziemke, Earl F. *The German Northern Theater of Operations, 1940–1945. (Department of the Army Pamphlets 20–271).* Washington: Headquarters, Department of the Army, 1959.

Dissertations

Halstead, Charles R. "Spain, the Powers, and the Second World War." Doctoral Dissertation, University of Virginia, 1961.

Imhof, Helga-Maria. "Die Presse Frankreich zur Zeit der deutschen Besetzung, 1940–1944." Doctoral Dissertation, University of Vienna, 1950.

Articles, Pamphlets, and Reports

Assmann, Kurt. "Normandy, 1944," *Military Review,* XXXIV (Feb. 1955), 86–93.

Best, Werner. "Die deutsche Militärverwaltung im Frankreich," *Reich, Volksordnung, Lebensraum,* I (1941), 29–76.

Blumenson, Martin, and James B. Hodgson. "Hitler Versus His Generals in the West," *U.S. Naval Institute Proceedings,* LXXXII (Dec. 1956), 1281–1287.

Boudet, François. "Aspects économiques de l'occupation allemande en France," *Revue d'histoire de la deuxième guerre mondiale,* XIV (Avril 1964), 451–62.

De Boueard, Michel. "La répression allemande en France de 1940 a 1944," *Revue d'histoire de la deuxième guerre mondiale*, XIV (April 1964) 63–90.

Burdick, Charles B. "Plannungen für der Einrücken deutschen Kräfte in Spanien in den Jahren 1942–1943. Die Unternehmen 'Ilona' und 'Gisela,'" *Wehrwissenschaftliche Rundschau*, XIII (Mar. 1963), 164–178.

— "'Moro': The Resupply of German Submarines in Spain, 1939–1942," *Central European History*, III (Sept. 1970), 256–284.

Detwiler, Donald S. "Spain and the Axis During World War II," *Review of Politics*, XXXIII (Jan. 1971), 36–53.

Deutschland im Kampf. 1936–1944. German military magazine edited by A.I. Berndt of the Propaganda Ministry and Lt. Col. von Wedel of the Armed Forces High Command staff.

Devers, Jacob L. "Operation Dragoon: the Invasion of Southern France," *Military Affairs*, X (Summer 1946), 3–41. One of the American commanders.

DeWeerd, Harvey A. "The Reputation of Rommel," *Yale Review*, XXXVIII (1948/49), 67–81.

Geyr von Schweppenburg, Leo. "Reflections on the Invasion," *Military Review*, XLI (Feb. and Mar. 1961), 2–11 and 12–21. Commander of German Panzer Group West.

Gruchmann, Lothar. "Die 'verpassten strategischen Chancen' der Achsenmächte im Mittelmeerraum 1940 bis 1941," *Vierteljahrshefte für Zeitgeschichte*, XXVIII (Oct. 1970), 456–475.

Gundelach, Karl. "Drohende Gefahr West; Die deutsche Luftwaffe vor und während der Invasion 1944, *"Wehrwissenschaftliche Runschau*, IX (June 1959), 299–329.

Gunzenhäuser, Max. "Die bibliographie zur Geschichte des Zweiten Weltkrieges," *Jahresbibliographie, Bibliothek für Zeitgeschichte* XXXIII (1961), 511–566.

Harnier, Wilhelm von. "Küstenartillerie und Atlantikwall," *Marine-Rundschau*, LII (1955), 91–101.

Horan, H.E. "Operation 'Chariot': the Raid on St. Nazaire, 27th–28th March 1942," *Journal of the Royal United Services Institution,* CVII, (1961), 561–566.

Jacobsen, Hans-Adolf. "The Second World War as a Problem in Historical Research," *World Politics,* XVI (July 1964), 620–641.

Krancke, Theodor. "Invasionsabwehrmassnahmen der Kriegsmarine im Kanalgebiet 1944," *Marine Rundschau,* LXVI (June 1969), 170–187.

Lebram, Hans-Heinrich. "Kritische Analyse der Artillerie des Atlantikwalles," *Marine Rundschau,* LII (1955), 29–38.

Leighton, Richard M. "Operation Revisited: An Interpretation of American Strategy in the European War, 1942–1944," *American Historical Review,* LXVIII (July 1963), 919–937.

Loose, Gerhard. "The German High Command and the Invasion of France," *Military Affairs,* XI (Fall 1947), 159–164.

Neubronn, Alexander Freiherr von. "Als 'Deutscher General' bei Pétain," *Vierteljahrshefte für Zeitgeschichte,* IV (July 1956), 227–249.

Reeder, Eggert, and Walter Hailer. "Die Militärverwaltung in Belgien und Nordfrankreich," *Reich, Volksordnung, Lebensraum,* VI (1943), 7–53.

Röseler, Joachim. "Die deutschen Plaene für eine Landung im England (Operation Seelöwe) und die Luftschlacht um England (Battle of Britain) in der literatur," *Jahresbibliographie Bibliothek fuer Zeitgeschichte,* XXXIV (1962), 541–554.

Roskill, Sir Stephen W. "The Dieppe Raid and the Question of German Foreknowledge: A Study in Historical Responsibility," *Journal of the Royal United Services Institution,* CIX (1964) 27–31.

Ruge, Friedrich. "With Rommel Before Normandy," *United States Naval Institute Proceedings,* LXXX (June, 1954), 612–619.

Seraphim, Hans-Günther. "'Felix' and 'Isabella': Dokumente zu Hitlers Planungen betr. Spanien und Portugal aus den Jahren 1940/41," *Die Welt als Geschichte,* XV (1955), 45–86.

United States Army Corps of Engineers. Provisional Engineer Special Brigade Group. *Operation Report Neptune, Omaha Beach, 26*

Feb.–26 June 1944. Published by the First United States Army in 1944.

United States Strategic Bombing Survey. *The United States Strategic Bombing Survey: Overall Report (European War)*. Washington: USGPO, 1945.

Weber, J. "Torpedobatterien im Atlantikwall," *Marine Rundschau*, LIII (1956), 57–68.

Wilt, Alan F. "'Shark' and 'Harpoon'" German Cover Operations against Great Britain in 1941," *Military Affairs*, XXXVIII (Feb. 1974), 1–4.

Ziegler, Janet. "Bibliographies sur la Seconde Guerre Mondiale," *Revue d'histoire de la deuxième guerre mondiale*, XXI (Jan. 1971), 95–104. Survey of works appearing from 1966 through 1970.

Additional Selected Bibliography

When the first edition of *The Atlantic Wall: Hitler's Defenses in the West, 1941–1944* was published in 1975 I contended that by the time of the Normandy invasion the Germans had assembled a fairly formidable force behind a rather formidable defensive barrier. Although not impenetrable, it was certainly more than the mere propaganda bluff that a number of German generals asserted after the war. As with most defensive systems, the Wall constituted a combination of fortifications, firepower, and manpower, and it was a barrier that the Allies took very seriously in planning the assault.

Over the last few years, a number of historians and other writers have accepted my contention regarding the Wall's significance. The core of the book has therefore been kept unchanged and I have altered it only in so far as removing infelicities, making minor corrections, and adding factual data to improve the narrative. Nevertheless, it is still important to mention more recent writers' contributions, for they have deepened our appreciation of the context in which the Atlantic Wall concept took shape as well as the Allies' success in piercing it beginning on June 6.

Among the works that have focused primarily on building up the Wall, Rémy Desquesnes's *"Atlantikwall et Südwall" Les défenses allemandes sur le littoral français (1941–1944)*, 2 vols. (Ph.D. Université de Caen, 1987) is an extremely thorough, yet balanced account. Desquesnes has brought together a tremendous amount of information on almost every aspect of the Wall, and in his conclusion he asks a very important question: what would have been the result had there been no Atlantic Wall? His answer is that besides causing the Allies logistical problems after the assault, the placement of Germany's defenses dissuaded the Anglo-Americans from directly attacking the Pas de Calais area and further helped persuade them not to undertake a cross-Channel invasion until 1944. Two other excellent full-length accounts are Hans Wegmüller's *Die Abwehr des Invasion: Die Konzeption des Oberbefehlshabers West 1940–1944* (Freiburg: Rombach, 1979); and Dieter Ose's *Entscheidung im Westen: Der Oberbefehlshaber West und die Abwehr der alliierten Invasion* (Stuttgart: Deutsche Verlags-Anstalt, 1982). While Ose concentrates more on the post-June 6 phase than Wegmüller, both agree that Germany succeeded in holding back the Allies for seven weeks primarily because of the capabilities of its soldiers rather than because of the Wall itself. Among other books, a study which concentrates on the Wall's architectural significance is Colin Partridge's *Hitler's Atlantic Wall* (Guernsey, Channel Islands: DI Publications, 1976). Although there is no adequate work on Organization Todt's role in constructing the Wall, a portion of Franz W. Seidler's *Die Organisation Todt: Bauen für Statt und Wehrmacht, 1938–45* (Koblenz: Bernard & Gräfe, 1987) provides a start.

There are numerous biographies on Field Marshals Gerd von Rundstedt and Erwin Rommel, the two most important German commanders in the West. On von Rundstedt, the best treatment is Charles Messenger's *The Last Prussian: A Biography of Field Marshal Gerd von Rundstedt, 1875–1953* (Washington: Brassey's, 1991). Messenger shows that even though Rundstedt did not lead from the front, he truly had a strategic mind and was a capable theater commander. Regarding his role in the officers' plot against Hitler, Messenger convincingly argues that "there is no evidence that von Rundstedt ever showed the slightest willingness to support the plotters." A good shorter appraisal is Earl F. Ziemke, "Rundstedt," in Correlli Barnett, ed., *Hitler's Generals* (New York: Grove Weidenfeld, 1989).

On Rommel, there is no completely satisfactory work, but David Fraser in *Knight's Cross: A Life of Field Marshal Erwin Rommel* (New York: Harper Collins, 1993) correctly emphasizes the famous field commander's superior tactical abilities. The author also tries to assess Rommel's role in the July 20 assassination attempt in an even-handed manner. Fraser's problem is that, as a result of German generals who survived the war and of Rommel's family, so much myth has grown up about him that it is difficult to figure out the extent to which he was truly involved. For an historian who downplays Rommel's involvement, see Ralf Georg Reuth's short essay, "Erwin Rommel—Die Propagandaschöpfung" in Ronald Smelser and Enrico Syring, eds., *Die Militärelite des Dritten Reiches* (Frankfurt/Main: Ullstein, 1996).

Among the plethora of books on the Normandy invasion, four outstanding examples are Stephen E. Ambrose, *D-Day, June 6, 1944: The Climactic Battle of World War II* (New York: Simon & Schuster, 1994); Carlo D'Este, *Decision in Normandy* (London: Collins, 1983); Max Hastings, *Overlord: D-Day, June 6, 1944* (New York: Simon & Schuster, 1984); and John Keegan, *Six Armies in Normandy: From D-Day to the Liberation of Paris, June 6th–August 25th, 1944* (New York: Viking, 1982). Ambrose is especially effective in using soldiers' recollections to describe the campaign, and D'Este assesses in depth the myth that the campaign went according to plan, especially Britain's difficulties in quickly liberating Caen. Hastings' balanced account emphasizes not only Britain's difficulties, but also Germany's ability still to fight well after five years of war. Keegan's imaginative work highlights individual units from six armies—American, British, Canadian, German, French, and Polish—and then weaves them into the narrative as the basis to describe the operation.

Another book on Overlord that deserves mention is Robert Kershaw's profusely illustrated *D-Day: Piercing the Atlantic Wall* (Annapolis: Naval Institute Press, 1994). Kershaw concentrates on the first nine days of the attack, June 6–14, which he sees as decisive. Two outstanding collective works are Theodore Wilson, ed., *D-Day 1944* (Lawrence: University Press of Kansas, 1994); and Hans Umbreit, ed., *Invasion 1944: Im Auftrag des Militärgeschichtlichen Forschungsamtes* (Hamburg: Mittler, 1998).

Among more general accounts of the war, Volume 7 of Germany's official history *Das Deutsche Reich und der Zweite Weltkrieg: Das Deutsche Reich in der Defensive: Strategischer Luftkrieg in Europa, Krieg im Westen und in Ostasien 1943–1944/45* (Stuttgart: Deutsche Verlags-Anstalt, 2001), by Horst Boog, Gerhard Krebs, and Detlef Vogel, contains an excellent summary of the campaign. As has been the case for the entire series, an English translation under the general title of *Germany and the Second World War*, and published by Oxford, will soon follow. In the best single volume of the war, Gerhard L. Weinberg, *A World at Arms: A Global History of World War II* (New York: Cambridge, 1994), the author accepts my contention that the Allies realized breaching the Wall was not a sure thing.

In recent years, writers have devoted a good deal of attention to intelligence and deception measures. Regarding Normandy, Ralph Bennett, *Ultra in the West: The Normandy Campaign 1944–45* (New York: Scribner's 1979), and the relevant British official history, F.H. Hinsley, E.E. Thomas, C.A.G. Simkins, and C.F.G. Ransom, *British Intelligence in the Second World War*, Vol. 3, Pt 2, stand out. Also noteworthy are Roger Hesketh's *Fortitude: The D-Day Deception Campaign* (London: St. Ermin's Press, 1989), an exhaustive study of the Allies' deception operation against the Pas de Calais sector, and David Kahn's brilliant chapter, "The Ultimate Failure [Normandy]," in

Hitler's Spies: German Military Intelligence in World War II (New York: Macmillan, 1978).

A French series, "La Libération de la France," with the outstanding historian, Henri Michel, serving as general editor, appeared in the 1970s. Published by Hachette, books in the series generally follow a similar format: German occupation, French resistance, invasion, and aftermath. Pertinent works include Marcel Baudot, *La Libération de la Normandie* (Paris: Hachette, 1974); Marcel Baudot, *La Libération de la Bretagne* (Paris: Hachette, 1973); Etienne DeJanghe and Daniel Laurent, *Libération du Nord et du Pas de Calais* (Paris: Hachette, 1974); and Pierre Bécamps, *Libération de Bordeaux* (Paris: Hachette, 1974).

On the occupation of Belgium and of the Netherlands, see Etienne Verhoeyen, *La Belgique Occupée de l'An 40 à la Libération,* trans. by Serge Govaert (Brussels: DeBoeck-Wesmael, 1994), and Louis de Jong, *The Netherlands and Nazi Germany* (Cambridge: Harvard, 1990), a summary of the multivolume Dutch official history.

On the Provence, or French Riviera, campaign, the British and American official histories have now appeared. As one might expect, William G.F. Jackson in *The Mediterranean and the Middle East, Vol. VI: Victory in the Mediterranean, Part 2* (London: Her Majesty's Stationery Office, 1987), backs the British position, both before and after the invasion, that the southern France invasion was unnecessary. On the other hand, Jeffrey J. Clarke and Robert Ross Smith in *Riviera to the Rhine* (Washington: US Government Printing Office, 1993), accept the United States' assertion that the assault was necessary and that it definitely aided the Allies in carrying out subsequent operations in late 1944 and 1945. Arthur L. Funk's *Hidden Ally: The French Resistance and the Landings in Southern France, 1944* (Westport, CT: Greenwood, 1992) is particularly perceptive in assessing the role of France's resistance in the south, and Peter Leslie's *The Liberation of the Riviera: The Resistance to the Nazis in the South and the Story of Its Heroic Leader Ange-Marie Miniconi* (New York: Wyndham

Books, 1980) focuses on the role of one of the resistance's out-standing leaders. A volume in the "Libération" series is Pierre Guiral, *La Libération de Marseille et sa région* (Paris: Hachette, 1974). Alan F. Wilt's *The French Riviera Campaign of August 1944* (Carbondale: Southern Illinois University Press, 1981) is an accurate, convenient summary of the operation.

Books on aspects of the invasion and its aftermath are almost too numerous to mention, but among the perceptive studies see Adrian R. Lewis, *Omaha Beach: A Flawed Victory* (Chapel Hill: University of North Carolina Press, 2001); Michael D. Doubler, *Closing with the Enemy: How GIs Fought the War in Europe, 1944–1945* (Lawrence: University Press of Kansas); and Roman Johann Jarymowycz, *Tank Tactics: From Normandy to Lorraine* (Boulder: Lynn Rienner, 2001). Lewis contends that America's emphasis on aerial bombing rather than naval gunfire during Overlord's initial stages demonstrated a flaw in doctrine, and he further asserts that US tactical commanders were correct in preferring to land their amphibious forces under cover of darkness, since it would have lessened casualties. Doubler lauds US divisional and subordinate commanders for their flexibility in the fighting across France. As a consequence, the author goes a long way toward proving that by 1944 the Americans had learned how to fight and fight well. Jarymowycz shows what went right and what went wrong when Allied armored units engaged their German opponent in the summer and fall of 1944.

Among the many reference works on the Normandy campaign, two are especially noteworthy: David G. Chandler and James Lawton Collins, Jr., *The D-Day Encyclopedia* (New York: Simon & Schuster, 1994), and from a different perspective, Hans Sakkers, ed., *Normandie 6. Juni 1944, im Spiegel der deutschen Kriegstagebücher; Der Grossangriff auf dem Atlantikwall* (Osnäbrück: Biblioverlag, 1998).

As many are aware, Normandy's invasion coast has become a major tourist destination. The nearly forty museums, monuments, and cemeteries that dot the area cover almost every aspect of the

Overlord campaign, and they include separate museums for each of the five landing beaches, cemeteries for all of the combatants, and even an Atlantic Wall museum at Ouistreham in the British sector. An excellent general guide for the region's attractions is Georges Bernage, *The D-Day Landing Beaches: The Guide*, trans. by John Lee (Bayeux: Heimdal, 2001).

Index